# Forgiveness and Letting Go in Emotion-Focused Therapy

# Forgiveness and Letting Go in Emotion-Focused Therapy

LESLIE S. GREENBERG
CATALINA WOLDARSKY MENESES

AMERICAN PSYCHOLOGICAL ASSOCIATION
Washington, DC

Published by
American Psychological Association
750 First Street, NE
Washington, DC 20002
https://www.apa.org

Order Department
https://www.apa.org/pubs/books
order@apa.org

In the U.K., Europe, Africa, and the Middle East, copies may be ordered from Eurospan
https://www.eurospanbookstore.com/apa
info@eurospangroup.com

Typeset in Meridien and Ortodoxa.

Printer: Sheridan Books, Chelsea, MI
Cover Designer: Beth Schlenoff, Bethesda, MD

**Library of Congress Cataloging-in-Publication Data**
Names: Greenberg, Leslie S., author. | Meneses, Catalina Woldarsky, author.
Title: Forgiveness and letting go in emotion-focused therapy / by Leslie S. Greenberg and Catalina Woldarsky Meneses.
Description: Washington, D.C. : American Psychological Association, 2019. | Includes bibliographical references and index.
Identifiers: LCCN 2019001487 (print) | LCCN 2019021760 (ebook) | ISBN 9781433831195 (eBook) | ISBN 1433831198 (eBook) | ISBN 9781433830570 (hardback) | ISBN 1433830574 (hardcover)
Subjects: LCSH: Forgiveness. | Emotion-focused therapy. | Couples therapy. | BISAC: PSYCHOLOGY / Emotions. | PSYCHOLOGY / Clinical Psychology. | PSYCHOLOGY / Psychotherapy / Couples & Family.
Classification: LCC BF637.F67 (ebook) | LCC BF637.F67 G74 2019 (print) | DDC 155.9/2–dc23
LC record available at https://lccn.loc.gov/2019001487

http://dx.doi.org/10.1037/0000144-000

*Printed in the United States of America*

10 9 8 7 6 5 4 3 2 1

*This book would not have been written without the support of many individuals. In particular, I would like to acknowledge my mentors, colleagues, students, and clients who have contributed to the development of emotion-focused therapy as a distinctive treatment.*

—LESLIE S. GREENBERG

*For my mother, Adela Meneses, who teaches me to go through life with an open heart.*

—CATALINA WOLDARSKY MENESES

# CONTENTS

# Forgiveness and Letting Go in Emotion-Focused Therapy

# Introduction

Over the past 20 years, forgiveness has become an extremely popular topic for empirical studies and theoretical or clinical papers in the field of psychology. Social scientists, clinicians, and scholars in other fields (e.g., philosophy, theology, political science) have advanced many different definitions and meanings of forgiveness. Essentially, forgiveness can be classified into societal, therapeutic, and spiritual domains, each with different meanings (Shults & Sandage, 2003).

## MEANINGS OF FORGIVENESS

In the *societal* domain, justice and fairness are primary referents, and forgiveness occurs when injustices are forgiven. For example, Nelson Mandela forgave his White jailors for 27 years of brutal treatment while incarcerated, even inviting one to his presidential inauguration (Govier, 2002, p. 111). Luis Perez Aguirre, a Jesuit priest in Uruguay who was repeatedly imprisoned and tortured for his human rights work, later met his torturer on the street and forgave him, even offering him assistance (Walker, 2006; Weschler, 1998). In many communal societies, forgiveness is enacted through formal rituals and often occurs between family groups. For example, in some tribal contexts scripts about forgiveness and saving face can include restitution between families or clans, and the harmony of the group is often a highly valued motivation

http://dx.doi.org/10.1037/0000144-001
*Forgiveness and Letting Go in Emotion-Focused Therapy*, by L. S. Greenberg and C. Woldarsky Meneses

for forgiveness (Wangh, 2005). This is quite different from an individualistic emphasis on the personal benefits of forgiveness for the forgiver.

In the *therapeutic* domain, forgiveness relates to health and the healing of emotional wounds. Psychological definitions of forgiveness involve individuals attempting to forgive others to cope with the hurt and resentment of relational injuries. Here, people in therapy come to forgive others for painful emotional injuries (EIs), such as physical or sexual abuse, and for different forms of psychological maltreatment, neglect, and abandonment.

The *spiritual* domain refers to ultimate concerns and considers forgiveness to be spiritually transformative or good. Some notion of forgiveness can be found in most of the spiritual and religious traditions of the world. For many people, forgiveness is a sacred concept with meaningful referents in spiritual and religious texts, relationships with the Divine, and communal rituals.

These different understandings of forgiveness often overlap, but one thing is clear: Forgiveness has become a highly relevant social, personal, and spiritual topic.

## A NONAUTHORITARIAN APPROACH TO FORGIVENESS

This book presents a therapeutic approach to interpersonal forgiveness, in emotion-focused therapy (EFT), that addresses interpersonal EIs. EFT is an experiential approach to forgiveness and stands in contrast to other more psychoeducational, cognitive interventions available in the field (Enright & Fitzgibbons, 2015; Sells & Hargrave, 1998). We might term EFT a nonauthoritarian approach to working with the emotions in the process of forgiveness because the therapist withholds judgment about what clients should be feeling or should be aiming for as their therapy goal. Rather than prescribing a path and teaching a set of skills to achieve forgiveness, we describe the empirically derived emotional change processes that lead to emotional transformation and present examples of these processes in action. We also discuss how therapists and counselors can facilitate these processes. Our attention is on the emotional impact of the different types of EIs that occur in people's lives, and the ultimate goal of our approach is to promote emotional transformation—by letting go, forgiveness, or both processes combined, or by holding the other accountable for wrongs done. Thus, this book and its emphasis stand in contrast to other forgiveness interventions that have been developed that focus on achieving forgiveness as the sole goal. Forgiveness in EFT is seen as one possible, optional path to resolution of EI. Accepting other positive outcomes, such as letting go and moving on or holding the other accountable, opens the door for considering "healthy unforgiveness," which is currently downplayed in the field. As we highlight in the book, forgiveness may not always be the desired outcome; rather, what is important is the resolution of EIs by transforming the anger, sadness, fear, and shame associated with the injury.

The notion of EI that we have developed and used in this book comes from our recognition of both the pervasive degree of trauma in our society and the extremely potent effect of trauma on mental health. Many people with different kinds of diagnoses have been found to suffer from traumas. A *trauma* is essentially an EI or many interpersonal EIs such as betrayal, abandonment, maltreatment, and abuse. Forgiveness has come to be seen as one possible path to overcoming these types of injuries.

## THE ETHICS OF FORGIVENESS

Despite the variety of benefits that have been associated with forgiveness, many feminist critics and others have been wary of the ethics involved in the promotion of forgiveness. The spate of forgiveness promotion in the last decade has followed relatively quickly on the heels of several significant liberation movements, including civil rights and second wave feminism and the rise of queer politics. As Haaken (2002) noted, it may be no coincidence that, just when oppressed groups gain the strength to speak up and claim new rights, including the right to disengage from abusive relationships, the powerful (e.g., therapists and religious leaders) rediscover the virtues of forgiveness. There is some fear that in forgiving too widely, we waive our rights to a valuable form of moral and political protest. Others worry that the new ethics of forgiveness recapitulates a familiar and oppressive paradigm in which oppressed or violated groups and women, in particular, are taught the values of self-sacrifice and servility or concern for others at the expense of their own rights.

At the same time, there is an intuitive appeal of forgiveness based on a vision of morality that goes beyond formal duties and obligations to others and that imbues relationships as well as rights with value and significance. Forgiveness recognizes human imperfection and our capacity for change and improvement. When we forgive, we attempt to restore and revitalize moral relations between individuals in the aftermath of wrong rather than to sever them (Walker, 2006). This vision of repair, we feel, aligns well with feminist and other social justice orientations.

## OVERVIEW OF THE BOOK

This book is for practitioners of all types who work with people who have been emotionally injured. Specifically, it is for therapists and counselors who work directly in helping people resolve EIs. It is intended both for graduate students just starting out and experienced therapists and all practitioners in between, regardless of prior experience with EFT. Among other features, the book contains many details and examples of how to incorporate forgiveness into an empty-chair dialogue technique. The book also outlines the empirical support for the task-analytically derived models of the change processes involved in arriving at forgiveness.

Chapter 1 provides an entrance to the book by first illustrating just how common EIs, interpersonal offenses, and bad interpersonal feelings are in our lives. We then present definitions and make important distinctions between forgiveness and unforgiveness, forgiveness and pseudo forgiveness, and forgiveness and reconciliation. We next set out to provide answers to the questions "Why forgive?" and "Must people forgive?" We also discuss situations in which forgiveness and interventions that prescribe it are not recommended.

In Chapter 2 we explicate the EFT approach and its main principles and concepts. EFT theory related to EIs and forgiveness is then presented, and several examples are provided indicating what the therapy and the therapeutic stance should look like.

Chapter 3 provides a deepening of the previous chapter and a more explicit focus on EFT for the resolution of EIs in individual therapy, providing a framework for treatment. EFT for forgiveness is grounded in the empty-chair work intervention for the resolution of unfinished business, which is a hallmark of EFT. This intervention has been extensively researched across several clinical problems. We explain how the process works session-by-session, including details of the therapeutic tasks keyed to client change processes and the homework assignments that accompany and aid the interventions. We discuss two distinct forms of positive resolution of EI derived from research on actual therapy cases—that of holding the other accountable or that of understanding or forgiving the injurer. Please note that in Chapter 3 and throughout the book, all clinical examples are taken from our experience. Names and other details of cases have been disguised to protect individuals' privacy.

Chapter 4 presents research we conducted on the resolution of EIs in individual EFT. Two case illustrations are provided, and two paths of resolution of EI are presented: one through forgiveness and the other through letting go of the EI but not forgiving. We use transcripts to show specific steps of the client process and experience.

Chapter 5 is the first of the detailed sections on EFT for couples (EFT-C) dealing with EI. This chapter discusses the research on EFT-C and provides a concise description of EFT-C as well as its adaptation to the work on couple EI.

Chapter 6 discusses EIs and forgiveness in couple relationships from a theoretical perspective and also elaborates on the emotional processes in forgiveness and reconciliation. The phenomenology of forgiveness based on recent qualitative research with women who had overcome couple EI through forgiveness is also presented and provides further depth to the theoretical perspective presented in the chapter.

Chapter 7 describes the EFT-C forgiveness model derived from task analysis. The model and its components are elaborated, along with excerpts from real cases. We also discuss blocks on the path to forgiveness for couples.

Finally, Chapter 8 presents the case of a couple who successfully resolved their EI, with the injured partner forgiving her husband for his past affair. The case presents excerpts that illustrate the EFT-C forgiveness model. This case illustration acts to ground the theoretical and clinical aspects presented in the previous chapters.

We offer our concluding remarks to readers in the Afterword.

# 1

# Forgiveness

It is remarkable how many people struggle with carrying the burden of unresolved bad feelings toward others, often toward people in close relationships, such as parents, siblings, ex-spouses, or even current partners. Many people have their health and their lives ruined by the poison of bitterness, resentment, and unforgiveness. Having hateful feelings toward another person can be self-torture (Winch, 2014).

And yet, taking steps to forgive can be harder than living with negative feelings. In a way, forgiving takes courage. It is for those brave people who are willing to confront their pain, accept themselves as permanently changed, and make difficult choices.

Nearly everyone has been hurt by the actions or words of another. A mother might have criticized a daughter repeatedly; even now she might continue criticizing her adult child's parenting skills. Or perhaps a father was abusive. Perhaps a colleague sabotaged a project or stole credit for it from someone else, or a partner had an affair or shamed their spouse in public. These wounds can leave people with lasting feelings of anger or even vengeance. When people are hurt by someone they love and trust, they become angry or sad or feel hopeless. If people dwell on hurtful events or situations, feelings of resentment and hostile thoughts can take root. If people allow negative feelings to grow and fester, they might find themselves swallowed up by their bitterness or sense of injustice. This bitterness may begin to pervade their relationships. They become so wrapped up in the wrong that they cannot enjoy the present. They hold grudges and may become depressed or anxious.

http://dx.doi.org/10.1037/0000144-002
*Forgiveness and Letting Go in Emotion-Focused Therapy,* by L. S. Greenberg and C. Woldarsky Meneses

## THE IMPORTANCE OF ANGER

One of the great causes of grudges is unexpressed, assertive anger. As therapists, we have witnessed the tragic realities for both people in a relationship when anger is replaced by silence. That is when festering resentments begin, and important subjects are not dealt with. When it gets bad enough in a marriage, for instance, people may say they are just bored with each other. But boredom is often the sign of a silent grudge. The alternative is that we express what is bothering us, express the hurt and constructive anger, and make efforts to deal with these feelings, rather than distancing and burying them to fester unresolved.

When one is unjustly hurt by another, forgiveness involves overcoming resentment toward the injurer, not by denying one's right to the resentment but by offering the injurer unearned compassion, benevolence, or love. This is a process, one that begins with resentment and pain and ends with more positive feelings toward the other. For many scholars in this field (Enright, & Fitzgibbons, 2015; Webb, Hirsch, & Toussaint, 2015; Worthington, 2006), forgiveness involves giving up the feelings of indignation, resentment, and anger, as well as any actions to secure retributive justice. Does forgiveness then negate the necessity for anger? Because the injury was unfair and will continue to be unfair, the injured will naturally feel offended and will feel indignation and anger. We believe there is a positive, constructive purpose in the expression of anger and other painful feelings rather than these being seen as counterproductive and as contrary to forgiveness and trying to rise above them. They need to be given a voice. The experience and expression of indignation and anger play an important role in the early stages of the process of forgiveness (Enright & Fitzgibbons, 2015; Greenberg, Warwar, & Malcolm, 2008; Worthington, 2006).

For many people, views on forgiveness and anger are often deeply rooted in religious tradition and practice. Religious doctrine often preaches against the experience or expression of anger, especially in relation to forgiving and healing. Offense or anger is often viewed as an experience to be worked through and overcome as quickly as possible. Many authors who mention anger in relation to forgiveness cast anger in a negative light, with an exclusive focus on its destructive, inhibitory effects. Anger is grouped with such negative traits as hostility, vengeance, and rumination and is portrayed as preventing forgiving (Baskin & Enright, 2004; Miller, Worthington, & McDaniel, 2008; Wade & Worthington, 2005). Anger, then, is viewed as a barrier to forgiving, not as a part of the forgiveness process.

However, we believe that in the face of deep, personal hurt, strong emotions such as anger and sadness are endemic to the forgiveness process (Greenberg, Warwar, & Malcolm, 2010). Victims of injury have a right to feelings of indignation and anger, and we recognize that this emotion can play a role in the early stages of forgiveness by helping the injured person identify and understand the wrongs done and clarify the nature of his or her injury.

Anger also can motivate clients to take action, to right wrongs, to stand up and face problems, and to fight for their rights and enhance their self-esteem. Facilitating forgiveness requires an acknowledgment of the legitimacy of emotions such as resentment and hatred toward the offender.

## EXPERIENCING INTENSE EMOTIONS

In addition to acknowledging anger, an important difficulty in resolving emotional injury (EI) is the blocked pain, sadness, loss, hurt, and grief that people find so intolerable. In our clinical practice, we have observed that people are often haunted by the unexpressed intense sadness of a major loss caused by the injury. Clients can experience incredible relief when they begin to name what is or had been missed and to acknowledge what has been lost. This helps them accept the losses and move on to satisfy their unmet needs. Allowing themselves to experience their sadness also helps people articulate cherished beliefs that have been shattered and open themselves to the creation of new meaning, changing their narrative of what occurred. Forgiveness, then, should not bypass a process that includes grieving, mourning, or lament. It also is important to understand that sadness due to loss or injury is frequently covered by anger, although sometimes it is the reverse, when sadness covers anger; ultimately both have to be acknowledged and processed.

For example, Joyce,[1] a 34-year-old, married woman, had a father who was an alcoholic. He was not a violent man, but he would come home and pass out on the floor, and she would often have to look after him and put him to bed because her mother worked late night shifts. Joyce always felt ashamed of him and could never forgive him for being an inadequate father, parent, and reliable adult. She had a brother who needed a lot of care for some disabilities, and her mother was overwhelmed. Joyce became a caretaker to her brother and became overextended in her married life. In therapy, she addressed her unresolved feelings toward her father. The therapist guided her to imagine him in an empty chair in front of her and to express her feelings, the anger and the sadness and the shame. She brought up painful memories of feeling alone, frightened, and responsible, and she grieved the loss of a secure childhood. She expressed her anger first as blame but then constructively asserted what she had needed until she got to a sense that she had deserved to have a childhood free from the responsibility of an alcoholic father and of being the family caretaker and that she had deserved to get support and comfort.

After expressing her feelings and needs and having them validated by the therapist, Joyce began to see her father in a new way. She was able to see him as being highly concerned for the pain he had caused her, and she was touched by his imagined remorse and apology. After being able to see him as

[1] All clinical examples are taken from the authors' own experience. Names and other details of cases have been disguised to protect individuals' privacy.

having compassion for the pain he caused her, she found herself feeling more loving and generous toward him and forgave him for failing her as a father and parent.

We have found that in individual therapy, this type of process—one of accessing and expressing to the imagined other in an empty chair the painful feelings of loss and a sense of having deserved to have had the need met, followed by assertive anger and grief—leads to view of the injurer as compassionate toward the pain caused and leads to forgiveness. This is the process developed in emotion-focused therapy that has been found to be most helpful in facilitating the resolution of EIs and letting go and forgiveness.

## THERAPEUTIC APPROACHES TO FORGIVENESS

Several therapeutic approaches to promote forgiveness have been developed (e.g., Enright, 2001; Luskin, 2007; Worthington, 2001). Enright's (2001) treatment model emphasizes forgiveness as a decision. It contains four phases (Enright & Fitzgibbons, 2000): uncovering (negative feelings about the offense), decision (to pursue forgiveness for a specific instance), work (toward understanding the offending person), and discovery (of unanticipated positive outcomes and empathy for the offending person). Worthington's (2001) REACH forgiveness model, however, focuses more on emotional forgiveness. In this model, participants recall (R) the hurt they experienced and the emotions associated with it; then they empathize (E) with their offender, take the other's perspective, and consider factors that may have contributed to their offender's action. Participants then explore the idea that forgiveness can be seen as an altruistic (A) gift to the offender and make a commitment (C) to forgive. Last, participants seek to hold (H) onto or maintain their forgiveness through times of uncertainty or a return of anger and bitterness.

This book focuses on our emotion-focused therapy (EFT) approach with individuals and couples to overcome EIs and arrive at a place of forgiveness by processing painful emotions. This approach is based on forgiveness as a process of emotional change. In individual therapy, a key aspect is the promotion of empty-chair dialogues to process the client's unresolved emotions. A somewhat different process is helpful in couples therapy, where one's injuring partner is present. Here, additional interpersonal processes, such as the expression of shame and remorse by the injurer and the expression of previously unexpressed emotion by the injured, are important in leading to forgiveness. It also is important to note that in EFT we are not teaching people to forgive, nor do we see forgiveness as the only or even necessarily the best resolution to EIs, but we see forgiveness as one of the therapeutic processes that can be helpful. We therefore address when forgiveness may not be helpful, recognizing that forgiveness is not required for all people all the time and that people can accept or let go and move on without forgiving. We now first address what forgiveness is.

## WHAT IS FORGIVENESS?

Forgiveness can sometimes seem highly mystifying. We all know what it is until we are asked to give an account of it. A review of the literature shows that one of the challenges to investigating forgiveness is a definitional one: Forgiveness is defined differently by different researchers, and this, in turn, fuels the debate about whether it is a unitary or multifaceted phenomenon or a predominantly affective or cognitive one. A number of articles have been published examining the challenge of defining forgiveness (Elder, 1998; Enright & Coyle, 1998; Enright & Fitzgibbons, 2015; Pingleton, 1989; Sells & Hargrave, 1998; Worthington, 1998a, 1998b), highlighting the diversity of conceptualizations of forgiveness and related constructs. Indeed, a number of researchers interpret the lack of consensus in definition to be one of the most pernicious problems in the field (Elder, 1998; Enright & Coyle, 1998; Enright, Gassin, & Wu, 1992; McCullough, Pargament, & Thoresen, 2000).

Forgiveness has been described as deliberately giving up resentment toward an offender while developing beneficence and compassion toward him or her (Freedman & Enright, 1996). In this definition developing beneficence and compassion are added to a central aspect of forgiveness, which is "giving up resentment." The *Concise Oxford English Dictionary*, however, conflates *forgiveness*, which is defined as "to cease to feel angry or resentful towards (an offender)," with *pardon*, by which an offending act is pardoned without exacting a penalty (Forgiveness, 2011, p. 558). As we later illuminate, forgiveness is not pardoning someone. Forgiveness does not mean that you deny the other person's responsibility for hurting you, and it does not minimize or justify the wrong. You can forgive the person without excusing the act. Forgiveness differs from the legal concept of pardoning; from condoning, which involves justifying the offense; from excusing, implying that the transgression was committed because of extenuating circumstances or was in some way deserved; from forgetting, meaning the memory has faded or left consciousness; and from denial, which implies an unwillingness or inability to perceive the injuries one has incurred (McCullough & Witvliet, 2002).

Efforts have been made to derive a minimalist definition of forgiveness that does not overlap with related concepts such as excusing, pardoning, or condoning avoidable hurtfulness. Although this is done to bring clarity to the task of understanding definitional differences in the literature, DeCourville, Belicki, and Green (2008) pointed out that laypeople in the community do not necessarily make systematic or careful distinctions between forgiveness and phenomena that are associated with forgiveness. Everett Worthington Jr. (2006) proposed that definitions of forgiveness necessarily vary according to whether a valued relationship existed before a hurtful event. In his view, the focus of the definition is on the decisional, emotional, or interpersonal aspects of forgiveness. Although there is no definite consensus in the field on the conceptualization of forgiveness, most psychological investigators agree that forgiveness involves emotional, cognitive, and behavioral components.

Philosophical treatments of forgiveness too have acknowledged the multifaceted nature of forgiveness. They describe forgiveness as having both emotional and performance dimensions (Newberry, 2004; Norlock, 2008; Pettigrove, 2004), with such aspects as overcoming resentment, restoring moral relations, and putting the wrong in the past, none of which are necessarily crucial to any particular case of forgiveness.

In psychotherapy, one has to determine what forgiveness means to both the forgiver and the forgiven, in each case, by paying attention to how the concept is used by those in the situation. Forgiveness might mean letting go of resentment and feeling compassionate to the offender, or it may mean a change in view of the other and giving up a desire for revenge. Or it may mean accepting an apology and behaving in a nonpunishing way. In our view, an important element of forgiveness in psychotherapy is the "letting go," giving up, or cessation of painful emotions connected with memories of a hurtful act. In instances of betrayals and EIs the victim always feels some anger and resentment; the offender feels guilt and, possibly, fears consequences. Forgiveness, in the sense used here, means for both people to cease feeling any of these emotions. Thus, as their respective painful emotions are resolved, both offended and offenders can experience forgiveness similarly. Second, with the cessation of bad feelings, the victims feel some positive emotion toward the offenders. They often feel compassion for the offenders and wish them well; in Buddhist terminology, they send out loving kindness to the offender, which in this perspective is seen as the key to transcending the wound (Menahem & Love, 2013). The offenders feel relief, remorse, gratitude, and other positive feelings toward the victims. So, the second aspect of forgiveness that seems crucial is that new feelings are felt toward the other. Forgiveness, in our clinical conceptualization, thus has a lot to do with emotion.

Some theorists have viewed forgiveness as a decision or a choice to let go of resentment and thoughts of revenge (Enright, 2001). In our view, however, forgiveness, rather than being a decision, is the development of a feeling that involves, among other things, feelings of unburdening and peace and of love and generosity, as well as empathy and compassion for the one who hurt you. This has to be arrived at by processing the painful emotions accompanying violations and losses rather than by a decision to forgive. The process of forgiving and the qualities of forgiveness lie much more in the affective than the cognitive domain, so emotional forgiveness is not the same as decisional forgiveness (cf. Worthington & Scherer, 2004; Worthington, Witvliet, Pietrini, & Miller, 2007). Forgiving involves the emotional process of resolving the sadness and anger associated with feeling wronged and feeling different toward the injurer, more than the commitment to forgive or to change one's evaluation of the truth, value, or moral nature of the wrong. Neither is forgiveness a single action that you begin and complete in a short time. It usually involves a long journey in which one slowly moves toward forgiveness. The first step is letting go of a desire for revenge and only later letting go of feelings of hurt and anger. We may be able to not wish the person any harm, to not hope for the person's downfall, and to not feel the need for revenge but still feel upset, hurt, or angry. The second step occurs when one stops feeling hurt and angry. At this second stage, one might not be ready to relate to the person as one did before but can move on and let go to the point where one no longer carries feelings of hurt, anger, and resentment on any level.

It also is important to understand that forgiveness is a time-based process, often involving two steps forward and one step back—today I might feel forgiving, and tomorrow not so much. Also, the process of coming to forgiveness involves many steps. Different models describe forgiveness as a process with different components and a different number of stages and sequence, but significant similarities exist between models. Typically, models of forgiveness divide the process into four stages: (a) acknowledgment of the offense, (b) desire to forgive, (c) cognitive and emotional processing, and (d) behavioral action (McCullough & Worthington, 1994a, 1994b).

For some time in the literature, forgiveness has been incorrectly conflated with letting go of anger and hurt. This view is not fully adequate, because it fails to acknowledge that one can let go but not forgive. Forgiveness has to be conceived of as more than just accepting what happened or ceasing to be angry or being free from negative emotion. Most theorists (Enright, 2001; Worthington, 1998a, 1998b) now see forgiveness as including—in addition to a letting go and coming to terms with an offense—some benevolent orientation toward the offender, which serves the healing of the injured person and also, potentially, their relationship. Thus, at the core of forgiveness for psychotherapists is the notion of changing how one feels by letting go of negative feelings and generating positive feelings.

Forgiveness appears connected, though is not reducible, to the acceptance of an apology, renewed compassion for and trust in the wrongdoer, and a commitment to moving on. Forgiveness can "release" wrongdoers from the most damaging reminders of the wrong, either by initiating reciprocal goodwill or by tacitly giving wrongdoers permission to "reframe" their self-conceptions so that the wrong does not loom so large. Even if forgiveness does not ease the wrongdoer's guilt, guilty people may experience relief at not having their crimes "held against" them by others, and this relief seems to be one of the major benefits of forgiveness for the transgressor.

To summarize, the following are the important characteristics of interpersonal forgiveness:

- It is an internal process, not requiring anyone else.

It involves

- renouncing hostility against the offender,
- giving up the wish or hope that the past will change,
- feeling charitable or compassionate concern for the offender,

- accepting the offender's apology and contrition, and
- allowing for a remission of whatever punishment the forgiver controls.

Forgiveness may also lead to

- reconciling through an offer to "start over" or renew the relationship;
- giving up the desire for revenge or punishment, as well as resentment and negative evaluations;
- giving out undeserved compassion and generosity;
- sending out loving kindness to the other;
- accepting the unfairness of what happened and giving up the wish that other person's behavior made sense;
- giving up the sense of entitlement to hold a grudge or demand an apology;
- reaching a place of no longer wishing that the other person would suffer for their hurtfulness and truly wanting what is best for them; and
- identifying (and when appropriate, sharing) responsibility for harm done.

Finally,

- forgiveness is a process.

Forgivingness is multifaceted, and each feature can be understood and evaluated separately from the others. There are, for example, cases in which the remission of punishment is appropriate but not, however, the renewal of a relationship, or cases in which the victim is able to accept an apology sincerely but does not yet experience compassion. Although "forgiveness at its best," which involves all aspects of forgiving, is ideal, imperfect forgiving, which involves only some of the aspects of forgiveness, may be good enough. In addition, cases that have one or two features are not necessarily less forgiving, or even less admirable, than those that have three or four or all features. Some features are possible in many or most cases of forgiveness, whereas others are not. Nonideal forgiveness, then, is not inadequate forgiveness. In multifaceted views, some elements of forgiveness also may not be appropriate—the renewal of a meaningful relationship, for instance, may be contraindicated with someone who is repeatedly abusive.

Forgiveness involves feeling at peace with the injury, accepting what happened instead of continuing to fight against the unfairness of it, and letting go of the desire to retaliate. Forgiveness also involves giving something, sending out positive feelings of compassion, and feeling with and possibly even for the other person rather than feeling against the other. Taken together, these actions enable the forgiver to release the offender from the responsibility for "fixing" the effects of the injury. In addition, forgiveness opens the possibility, if desired and appropriate, of restoring the relationship through the process of reconciliation.

In addition to this, it is important to note that forgiveness is not

- acquiescing—allowing harmful actions to continue;
- condoning—not recognizing any harm or unfairness;
- forgetting—people rarely forget; rather, they reframe memories;
- denying, or excusing, what happened;
- reconciling—possible but not essential;
- overlooking the consequences or giving up on justice;
- granting amnesty or pardon; or
- merely resigning oneself to what cannot be changed.

In forgiving someone who has committed a transgression, the forgiver's responses toward the other changes by becoming affectively, cognitively, and behaviorally less negative and more positive.

## UNFORGIVENESS

In psychological research unforgiveness has been found to not be the opposite of forgiveness (Worthington, 2006). In other words, one can decrease one's unforgiveness without increasing forgiveness. *Unforgiveness* is defined by Merriam-Webster's dictionary as alternately being unwilling or unable to forgive or having or making no allowance for error or weakness (Unforgiveness, n.d.). Another more biblically influenced definition of unforgiveness is not having the compassion to forgive. Decreasing unforgiveness, then, involves letting go of bad feelings, especially anger, but not increasing positive feelings and is generally seen as not as desirable as forgiveness. However, it is highly likely that in the period directly after an injury people will feel hurt and angry and will not feel immediately forgiving. They will feel unforgiving. Often, in therapy it is helpful to ask people, in a dialogue with the imagined offending other, to express what they do not forgive the other for or that they do not forgive the other for the wrongs done. This helps access people's unresolved anger and helps them clarify their motivation to forgive or not.

According to Worthington (2006), unforgiveness is a type of stress reaction that arises when a transgression is appraised as a threat. There is empirical research showing that unforgiveness produces patterns of sympathetic and parasympathetic activity that are similar to stress reactions (for a review, see Worthington & Sotoohi, 2010), as well as similar hormonal patterns (including cortisol release patterns; Berry & Worthington, 2001; Tabak & McCullough, 2011).

It is useful in working with unforgiveness to distinguish between acute unforgiveness and chronic unforgiveness. *Acute* unforgiveness occurs immediately after a hurtful event. It is normal and reasonable to experience one or more of the following markers of acute unforgiveness:

- distressing feelings of shock, disbelief, emotional pain, self-respecting anger, and grief;
- the feeling of being stung by the unfairness or injustice of what happened;
- the belief that the injurer has incurred a debt and owes an apology or should make amends;
- the desire for the injurer to suffer for what he or she did; and
- the desire for the injurer to know what it was like to be hurt that way.

If acute unforgiveness goes on too long, it may become an unhealthy *chronic* unforgiveness and may manifest itself as

- bitter resentment, corrosive anger, debilitating sadness, and/or unwarranted shame;
- rumination that disrupts sleep and robs one of a sense of overall well-being and contentment;
- the devaluation of the other as "all bad," an intentional perpetrator who is without worth as a human;
- the overvaluing of oneself as "all good," a pure victim who is without choice or recourse; and
- an inability to move on with one's life.

Forgiveness creates the possibility of renewing positive feelings, thoughts, and actions toward the other, and out of this renewal comes the possibility of reconciliation. *Reconciliation* can be seen as involving a commitment to the restoration of love and trustworthiness by both parties so that their relationship may be transformed.

Forgiveness also involves a number of elements that result in the construction of a new narrative of self and other, which entails a shift in one's understanding of, and relationship to, the other person, oneself, and the world. With forgiveness, the implications of the original situation are cast in a new light (Rowe et al., 1989). The experience of violation and its impact on the forgiving person's life are different at the end of the process than at the beginning. Often, the forgiving person can see the offender in a more complex way, possessing both strengths and weaknesses, and is enabled to see him- or herself as having been made stronger, possibly better, by the struggle to forgive. Mansfield, Pasupathi, and McLean (2015) found that female participants' transgression narratives that featured growth-promoting connections were significantly correlated with higher forgiveness and self-compassion scores.

Our emphasis, however, is on promoting the emotional processes that underlie narrative change because we are concerned that reframing a transgression as an opportunity for resiliency may bypass negative feelings that have to be processed to heal from a transgression fully. Rowe and colleagues (1989) were among the first researchers to note that forgiveness has a positive impact on both the injured and the offending parties.

## WHY FORGIVE?

Why should one forgive? What do forgiving people have to show for their efforts once they have made the arduous journey in pursuit of forgiveness? Ultimately, forgiveness is for the forgiver, in that letting go of hurt and anger relieves the injured person's distress and promotes moving on and growth. The benefits of forgiveness, thus, are first and foremost for the forgiver.

## RESEARCH ON FORGIVENESS

In one of the most important meta-analyses of forgiveness treatments, Wade, Hoyt, Kidwell, and Worthington (2014) found that forgiveness treatments produced significantly greater forgiveness than alternative treatments or no treatment. Also, forgiveness treatments resulted in greater changes in depression, anxiety, and hope than in no-treatment conditions. The severity of the offense, however, was found to significantly affect how successful the treatment was in promoting forgiveness. Akhtar and Barlow's (2018) recent meta-analysis echoed these findings and also revealed that forgiveness interventions were effective in promoting positive affect and enhancing both state and trait forgiveness. From these results, it appears that using theoretically grounded forgiveness interventions helps clients deal with past injuries and achieve resolution in the form of forgiveness. Previous meta-analyses also indicated that interventions of this nature can effectively promote forgiveness (Baskin & Enright, 2004; Wade & Worthington, 2005).

In an early example of a set of studies of a forgiveness treatment, Suzanne Freedman and Robert Enright (1996) first investigated the effectiveness of an intervention program for incest survivors in which forgiveness was the end goal of treatment. The significant change from pre- to posttreatment demonstrated that forgiveness could be successfully promoted and that it was associated with increases in self-esteem and hope, as well as decreases in depression and anxiety. Catherine Coyle and Robert Enright (1997) replicated the Freedman and Enright study by investigating the psychological benefits of promoting forgiveness among a set of 10 men who identified themselves as having been hurt by a partner's choice to terminate a pregnancy. Analysis of a set of outcome measures demonstrated significant positive change from pre- to posttreatment in terms of increased forgiveness and decreased anxiety, anger, and grief.

The interpersonal injuries that bring clients to therapy involve betrayals of trust that range from harsh parental criticism and unkindness, neglect, abandonment, and marital affairs to physical or sexual abuse. Although these interpersonal events sometimes involve physical injury, they are best understood as EIs. People often come to therapy when their efforts to make sense of such experiences have been unsuccessful. The question then becomes, How do therapists help clients attain closure on such experiences?

Greenberg, Warwar, and Malcolm (2008) compared the effectiveness of EFT involving Gestalt empty-chair dialogue in the treatment of individuals who were emotionally injured by a significant other with a psychoeducation group designed to deal with these injuries. This study examined aspects of the emotional process of forgiveness in resolving interpersonal injuries and investigated the relationship between letting go of distressing feelings and forgiveness. A total of 46 clients assessed as having unresolved, interpersonal EIs were randomly assigned to an individual therapy treatment of EFT or a psychoeducation group. Results indicated that clients in EFT using empty-chair dialogue showed significantly more improvement than the psychoeducation treatment on all measures of forgiveness and letting go, as well as global symptoms and key target complaints and that the empty-chair dialogue treatment promoted higher emotional arousal than did the group psychoeducation condition.

In a study comparing decisional and emotional forgiveness, Lichtenfeld, Buechner, Maier, and Fernández-Capo (2015) found empirical support for "emotional forgiveness" versus decisional forgiveness. They found when people go through an emotional process to let go of anger and extend undeserving compassion, they forget traits relevant to the transgressor, whereas this was not the case for decisional forgiveness. This highlighted a link between unforgiveness and rumination.

Early on we found that forgiveness was one of the processes that helped distressed couples in emotion-focused couples therapy improve marital satisfaction (Greenberg & Johnson, 1988), and so forgiveness began to be studied more systematically in EFT for couples (Greenberg, Warwar, & Malcolm, 2010; Makinen & Johnson, 2006). In these studies, forgiveness was found to be related to improved marital satisfaction and trust, as well as improvement in psychological symptoms and target complaint measures. Forgiveness has been found by other investigators to increase the probability of a reduction in conflicts among married couples (e.g., Fincham, Beach, & Davila, 2004) and increments in relationship quality and overall marital satisfaction (e.g., Olson, Marshall, Goddard, & Schramm, 2015). Consistent with these observations, studies focusing on ex–prisoner of wars' families have found that couple forgiveness may result in higher qualities of marital relationship (Solomon, Dekel, & Zerach, 2009) and marital satisfaction (e.g., Dekel, 2010). Worthington and Sandage (2016) argued that a number of aspects of couples therapy can encourage forgiveness. They claimed that conflict and interactions promoting intimacy, attachment and differentiation, emotion processing and emotion regulation, and the development of hope and humility all help promote forgiveness.

## FORGIVENESS AND HEALTH

There is a growing body of evidence that a personality inclination to forgive is associated with physical and mental health benefits (Krause & Hayward, 2013; Randall & Bishop, 2013; Toussaint, Owen, & Cheadle, 2012; Webb, Phillips, Bumgarner, & Conway-Williams, 2013), and many counselors and therapists promote forgiveness as a positive response to interpersonal hurtfulness (e.g., Akhtar, 2002; Berecz, 2001; Enright & Fitzgibbons, 2000; Fitzgibbons, 1986; Karen, 2001). Forgiveness has been shown to have indirect links with physical, relational, mental, and spiritual health (Harris and Thoresen, 2005; Lawler et al., 2005; Toussaint, Marschall, & Williams, 2012; Toussaint & Webb, 2005; Weinberg, Gil, & Gilbar,2014), whereas unforgiveness can be distressing and may leave people ruminating about their injuries and feeling hostile toward those who injured them (Witvliet, Ludwig, & Vander Laan, 2001). Recent reviews of literature on forgiveness and health have argued that emotion-focused forgiveness promotes health (Worthington 2006; Worthington & Scherer, 2004) through reducing unforgiveness rather than creating positive emotional experiences (Harris & Thoresen, 2005).

In general, forgiveness has been found to be effective at reducing clients' anger, hostility, anxiety, and depression while increasing their sense of hope and self-esteem. It has been associated with decreased hostility, heart rate, galvanic skin response, mean arterial pressure (blood pressure in the arteries), and corrugator electromyograph response (eyebrow muscle tension), as well as with reductions in depressive symptoms (Zauszniewski et al., 2002), neuroticism and rumination, distorted thinking, and conflict (Vaillant, 2000).

Forgiveness has also been associated with increases in gratification with life (Vaillant, 2000) and perceived competence and social support (Thoresen, Harris, & Luskin, 2000) and a positive impact on mental and physical health (Lawler-Row et al., 2008; Lawler-Row, Hyatt-Edwards, Wuensch, & Karremans, 2011). In their review of studies that measured symptoms of depression and anxiety or overall mental health and well-being, Toussaint and Webb (2005) reported that they consistently found a relationship between measures of positive mental health and forgiveness. They suggested that it may be the rumination and negative emotions characteristic of sustained unforgiveness that give rise to significant mental health problems and, because forgiveness is understood to bring relief from rumination and involves the letting go of distressing negative feelings, interventions that facilitate forgiveness could have a bearing on improvements in mental health and well-being.

Similarly, Thoresen and his colleagues (2000; Harris & Thoresen, 2005, 2006) cited the well-established association between positive emotional states and greater immune competence, healthier heart rate, and lower blood pressure when they proposed a role for forgiveness in preventing physical illness. They highlighted the association between chronic anger and hostility and increased health risks (particularly of the cardiovascular type because sustained, reactive anger keeps the physiological system in a state of hyperarousal) and noted that forgiveness has its most noticeable effect in either neutralizing sustained negative emotion or in changing it to positive feelings.

## MUST PEOPLE FORGIVE?

Forgiving is a strong element of the Judeo-Christian religious tradition. But forgiving need not be related to religious conviction alone; for some, it is a matter of ethics. Ethicists, however, disagree about whether forgiveness should be regarded as a moral duty or as a gift to be bestowed. Some philosophers have even argued against the benefits of forgiveness. Kant (1931/1963), for example, believed that forgiveness was unethical because it subverted justice and argued that wrongdoing should be compensated for by action, whereas Hegel (1821/1965) opposed forgiveness because it denied the offender the "right" to be punished.

In certain situations, forgiveness may not be the most helpful or moral solution. Although the capacity to forgive is an important aspect of an examined life, the enshrining of universal forgiveness as a panacea, as a requirement of health, or as the only moral choice is too rigid and simplistic a view and can be harmful. Although we tend to think of forgiveness as the best, healthiest way to resolve an intimate injury and of learning to forgive as one of life's great lessons, sometimes the opposite is true. Learning not to forgive, after a life in which forgiveness has been compulsive, imposed, or unconsidered, is an impressive achievement. A religious imperative to forgive can make people feel guilty if they do not or cannot forgive. People may be told that if they do not forgive they are being vengeful. In this view, vengeance involves holding onto rage and bitterness and letting a sense of victimization rule one's life and that this is why one should forgive. Choosing not to forgive, however, can differ from holding onto a grudge in that it can involve profound self-examination, just like forgiveness—only with a different conclusion.

Unfortunately, some practitioners now idealize forgiving and demonize not forgiving. Failure to forgive, they say, may doom clients to being victims for the rest of their lives, whereas some warn that not forgiving leads to a recycling of evil. Yet in some situations, some highly admirable, emotionally developed people have not forgiven or believe that not forgiving is ethical (Weisenthal, 1969; Wiesel, 1982). Not forgiving should be conceived of as a viable option in certain situations for some people. Not forgiving is not an avoidance of forgiveness or a retreat into holding a grudge, but a legitimate action in itself, with its own progression, motivation, and justification. There are many circumstances in which it is the proper and most emotionally authentic course of action.

Healthy unforgivers may see asserting fundamental rights and opposing injustice as more important than forgiving. For example, a client who had been severely damaged and medically traumatized by the health system did not see forgiveness as an appropriate option. Doctors had acted uncaringly and unethically had hidden information to prevent liability. She experienced great pain, and in therapy, she expressed her outrage at what had happened and received validation and support for her sense of outrage and for her powerlessness. Her path to resolution did not involve forgiveness but holding the system accountable and engaging in legal and public action to prevent further harm to others.

In other examples, some unforgivers accept the painful reality that they cannot experience the positive internal connection with a betrayer—usually a parent—that forgiving would require. Some clients having faced conflicts between feelings, religious principles, and ethics or social responsibilities reject forgiveness as a desirable option. One client whose parents had looked the other way when her brother sexually abused her held them accountable for wrongs done. As this client put it, "Not forgiving them validated that what they did, which was to deny the truth and pressure me to sacrifice myself, was wrong. For me not to forgive my brother at my parents' behest for abusing me is my self-affirmation." These parents never acknowledged what her brother did to her and confused her by saying it was all out of love. As a child, she had no recourse. Not forgiving is a recourse that abused children can create only as independent adults as a way to free themselves from years of being coerced to agree that hate or simple inaction is really love. Forgiveness should not be exercised indiscriminately.

Under the pressure of promoting family harmony, parents who deny abuse in the family and their negligence may try to force the victimized child to be "mature" and "rise above it." The more intact, obedient siblings continue to make the same demands of themselves. Their willingness to accept bad treatment, to feel they deserve it, or to define it out of existence then extends beyond their families and damages their later lives. Sometimes the need to forgive abusive parents is a last-ditch effort to get their love. That kind of forgiveness can be a mistake because it discourages the healthy anger and indignation that may be needed for a more enduring solution. Even those in less extreme circumstances tend to absorb parental values as an unexamined template for their own responses, making it difficult for them to distinguish what they truly feel from what has been imposed on them.

In some instances, it is better to make the moral choice to distinguish between extreme circumstances, in which it is better to sever a relationship, rather than forgive, and other, more commonplace injuries where forgiveness or reconciliation is a healthy choice. Refusing to forgive or have further contact with an unrepentant, abusive relative can be therapeutic. Before people take a stand and assert boundaries, they may be depressed and accede to others' needs and be confused about their rights and about what is real.

Although forgiving promotes mental health and alleviates depression, doing the opposite can express a person's very right to live.

Responsible unforgivers are not antiforgiveness. By recognizing the distinction between actions worthy and unworthy of tolerance and upholding a moral point of view, therapists can provide the foundation of a solid sense of self. Proponents of universal forgiveness refuse to recognize that moral unforgivers exist. They find it inconceivable that unforgiving victims of injustice could be outraged but not obsessed by their injuries, that they could even sympathize or retain conditional connections with those they refuse to forgive.

People who struggle with EIs must reengage with the experience, actively choosing to think and feel what was once unbearable. But facing the pain, mourning the loss, and developing understanding need not lead to forgiveness. Indeed, it is a major accomplishment for some people to temper their hatred, come to accept, let go of their bad feelings, and tolerate their indifference. As a person matures, fear and hatred can evolve into indifference, without bitterness. People can accept responsibility for their part in the injury without self-blame and end the blaming of others. Taking responsibility and a self-reliant attitude is the opposite of vengefulness and can alleviate the influence of past violation.

One client who let go and held her mother accountable said,

> When I realized that I didn't love her because she didn't love me, I understood that I could still love. I haven't forgiven her, but I'm not angry anymore. She had some nice qualities, like her energy, but in the most important way, she was never really my mother.

Refusing to forgive a rejecting mother or other betrayer expresses a person's right to his or her feelings. Recognizing that one is under no obligation to profess love that one does not feel can be a hard-won therapeutic change.

Forgiving without reconciling is acceptable; why can reconciling without forgiving also not be possible? In marriages, injuries sometimes are resolved not by forgiving but by mutually bracketing the injury and getting on with one's life. Intimate betrayals can be resolved in ways other than forgiveness. The follow-up data on the couples in our study that did not forgive revealed that some separated 3 months following the end of therapy and were contemplating divorce, whereas some reconciled despite never forgiving the past EI. In addition, a number of couples in the larger sample did not forgive but did improve their marital satisfaction (Greenberg et al., 2008). Clearly, more research is needed to outline how couples resolve EIs besides forgiveness. We hypothesize that some couples may resolve their past injuries by both accepting that an unforgivable injury took place in the relationship, creating a shared narrative that captures this, deciding to not focus on it further ("putting it in the vault"), and committing to moving forward with their relationship.

The pressure to forgive everything and everybody is responsible for the phenomenon of *false forgiveness*. Forgiving is hard work. It takes time and involves pain; it is not just a simple declaration or automatic, reflexive action. False forgiveness is going through the motions without anything changing on the inside. It is lip service, and it actually interferes with authentic resolution and estranges people from their real feelings. Forgiveness should be a capacity to be exercised when the situation warrants it, not a compulsion to be applied indiscriminately. And no one—including a parent, a mental health professional, or a member of the clergy—can dictate how a betrayal should be resolved. Therapists should help their patients come to terms with the past in whatever way is right for the individual. Often, people need permission not to forgive. Pushing an agenda of automatic absolution leads many to secret despair. The perspective we wish to share in this book is that therapy should teach people to choose for themselves.

Forgiveness, possibly because of its religious roots, also can be an emotionally loaded concept, and culturally it can mean different things to different people. For example, collectivist cultures tend to focus on how we behave toward one another and, for the sake of social harmony, encourage individuals within the culture to suppress feelings that, if expressed, would cause the other person to lose face socially. In different cultural contexts, forgiveness may, or may not, be a healthy choice. It is important in therapy to be aware of individual and cultural differences because the therapeutic alliance can be negatively impacted if the therapist incorrectly assumes that therapist and client share the same understanding of what forgiveness is and whether it is a desirable outcome of therapy.

Recently, Nussbaum (2016), a legally situated philosopher, in a book titled *Anger and Forgiveness*, argued that forgiveness might not be an optimal concept because it often implies hierarchy and power. In her work she described what some people might intuitively feel about forgiveness: It is a hierarchical concept in which the wretched seeking forgiveness are expected to go down on their knees and beg for forgiveness and then engage in some form of penance, and only then are they able to be granted forgiveness from a higher power, spiritual or secular.

Nussbaum (2016) suggested as an alternative that love and generosity are far better concepts. She argued first that forgiveness is often thought of as helping overcome anger but that most instances of anger for which forgiveness is presumed to be a cure involve what she called "payback" or restoring status. She saw the concept that forgiving someone who has wronged you will resolve the anger aroused by the injury as problematic and argued against the culture of apology and forgiveness that has arisen over the past decades. She challenged the often-held view that the road to forgiveness involves moving through confrontation, confession, and apology and working through of emotion and that this frees the wronged person of anger. Rather, she viewed confession as involving abasement and that the requiring of an apology and the making of amends is unloving and quite often vindictive in its own way. She argued that the rights of anger of the injured are based ultimately on a notion of payback to restore balance but that anger in no way helps people restore any balance, nor is it an assertion of self-respect.

Rather than promoting the value of forgiveness for resolving injuries, she argued for unconditional love and generosity (Nussbaum, 2016). She demonstrated this using the biblical parable of the prodigal son. She highlighted how the father on the return of the younger son, who had squandered all that was given him, rather than feeling angry and requiring apology and penance as the path to possible forgiveness (as the angry older son expected of him), celebrates the return of his lost son with love and generosity. Here, forgiveness is made unnecessary because of love and generosity. We agree with Nussbaum (2016) that some clients could see forgiveness as involving payback and lead to resentment, and we feel that her framework may be helpful in situations in which forgiveness is not desired by the client or for clients who have a negative view of forgiveness seeing it as hierarchical and vindictive in the way Nussbaum described it.

The following are some of the situations in which forgiveness is not indicated:

- when the person does not want to forgive;
- when it is immediately after a hurtful event;
- when the hurt person is in a relationship with the injurer and the maltreatment is ongoing;
- when the hurt person is being pressured to forgive; and
- when the hurt person is taking too much responsibility for what happened.

A refusal to forgive validates an experience that has been denied or remains unacknowledged by the injurer. Thus, therapists, although understanding the importance of forgiveness also have to understand that forgiveness is not always the best or only solution and remember that clients have legitimately idiosyncratic understandings of forgiveness. The task in therapy is to work within the client's understanding and even refrain from using the word *forgiveness* altogether if it has negative connotations for the client, as shown in the following example.

Arthur and Beth married young and started a family while Arthur was finishing his education and getting established in his profession. Despite efforts to talk about it, Beth had not been able to convey to Arthur how desperately lonely and abandoned she often felt. In time, Beth confided in one of their mutual male friends, and eventually, their friendship became both sexually and emotionally intimate. Once Beth revealed the affair, Arthur and Beth worked through the immediate crisis and agreed to stay together because they were committed to the well-being of their children. The hurtfulness of that period in their lives eventually became a dull ache, and many years passed in what they described as an emotionally detached but functional marriage. It was not until Beth's father died unexpectedly that they discovered that they had forged a fragile peace. When Beth turned to him in grief, Arthur was troubled to find himself reliving the distressing memories and painful feelings of the time immediately after he learned about Beth's affair. Beth, in turn, was shocked by the intensity and freshness of his anger and was overwhelmed by his unwillingness to come close. To salvage the marriage, they had both made so many compromises for, they decided to participate in a treatment to resolve EIs.

As much as he wanted relief from the pain of reliving unwanted, relentless memories of the humiliation he experienced when he discovered that his best friend was his wife's lover, Arthur was adamant that forgiveness was out of the question. In exploring this insistence, it became clear that Arthur equated forgiveness with forgetting what had happened. Not only was he helpless to forget what happened but he also believed it would be morally wrong to forget. If forgiveness required forgetting, he would not forgive. Accepting his reasons for refusing to forgive and agreeing that forgetting was neither desirable nor necessary, therapy moved forward without reference to forgiveness until the seventh session, when Arthur was asked to write a letter to Beth. In having had the freedom not to forgive he wrote that he forgave her and subsequently expressed great surprise that he felt forgiving and was able to forgive when he had never believed in the importance or correctness of forgiveness. This process exemplifies a nonauthoritarian approach to working with forgiveness in therapy.

## RETRIBUTIVE VERSUS RESTORATIVE JUSTICE

It is important to note that forgiveness without justice can often lead to lingering resentment on the part of the victim. When people try to forgive major transgressions without first exacting justice, the result can be harmful not only to people's sense of self-worth but also to the relationship as a whole. Forgiveness that comes too quickly fails to communicate the seriousness of the transgression to the offender and does not keep the problematic behavior from recurring in the future. The ability to truly forgive also depends on the form of justice. There are two forms of justice—retributive and restorative—based on different ideas about the purpose of punishment (Shapland, 2016; Witvliet et al., 2008).

Many people feel that when a wrong has been committed, it somehow creates an imbalance in the world—criminals are sent to prison to "pay their debt" to society. This sort of "balance theory" of crime and punishment can carry into personal relationships. At a party, Michael was drinking a lot, and he said some unflattering things about his partner, Maria, in front of some friends. It was all meant to be playful banter, but still, she felt hurt by his comments. Later, she saw him with a younger woman. When she scolded him, he said he was just having fun and making small talk. She gave him the cold shoulder during the ride home and went to sleep in another room without saying goodnight. Michael was in the doghouse, and there he remained until Maria felt balance had been restored and justice had been served.

After all this, though, it was still not clear to both whether she had forgiven him. Michael could salvage the situation by making a sincere apology; if it is accepted, it lays the groundwork for true forgiveness to take place. Michael, however, may now feel his own sense of injustice, in that from his perspective, the punishment does not fit the crime. Such a small mistake should not lead to such dire consequences. Even if he offers an apology, it may be filled with resentment rather than remorse. This is why *retributive* justice is an unfruitful approach to mending a relationship after a transgression. Although the victim may feel that the score has been evened, nothing has been done to ensure the same problem will not happen again in the future.

A better approach is to seek *restorative* justice. Here the purpose of punishment is to communicate the victim's pain to the transgressor to find a way to avoid the transgression in the future so that the relationship can be restored. Instead of giving the cold shoulder, the injured party has to express disappointment at the hurt. Maria could explain, "I'm just too upset to share my bed with you tonight because I feel humiliated and abandoned, so I'm sleeping in the other room." Michael would now explicitly understand the severity of the transgression and the reason for his punishment and feel compassion for the pain he caused. Now he would sincerely want to relive Maria's suffering. Restorative justice requires open communication between the victim and the transgressor. However, this can certainly be hard when tempers are flaring, and therapy often helps.

Retributive justice may restore a sense of balance, but it leaves behind a lingering resentment in both parties. The transgressor may apologize, although probably not sincerely, and the victim may forgive but probably not completely. A sincere apology takes steps to prevent the transgression from recurring and accepts punishment not as a price to be paid but rather as an act of atonement. In this case, Michael would be showing Maria his commitment to their marriage. As a result, Maria would feel safe wholeheartedly forgiving Michael and letting go of any lingering resentment. Having overcome a difficult situation together, both would feel stronger in their relationship than they did before.

Finally, it has been our experience that clients are particularly likely to contextualize resolving their difficulties in terms of forgiveness when one or more of the following are true:

- The client has a deep commitment to a faith tradition that considers forgiveness to be a virtue or behavior to strive for and is intrinsically motivated to work toward forgiveness for spiritual as well as relational reasons but is having difficulty tolerating and working through the intense emotions and vulnerability involved in opening him- or herself to the possibility of forgiveness. In this case, it would be appropriate to see the emotion work as the main task of the therapy and forgiveness as the "measure" of the success of the therapy (i.e., the outcome goal).

- The client is part of a culture or community that has a high view of forgiveness and is being pressured by others to forgive, although she or he is torn between the teachings of faith tradition and other competing motivations. For example, an adult survivor of childhood parental abuse may fundamentally want to distance him- or herself from the abusive parent if they have been unwilling or unable to acknowledge their abusive behavior or have acknowledged the hurtfulness in some token form without expressing heartfelt regret or remorse for the harm they have done to the client. If the client's faith community is pressuring her or him to forgive and reconcile, but she or he is unsettled about the wisdom of doing so, the client will be torn between what she or he wants and what the community is urging her or him to do. In this case, one of the main tasks of therapy will be to assist the client in evoking and exploring her or his emotional responses to the hurtful event to find a way to a satisfactory resolution on which the client can stand firm. Because the task (of resolving what is importantly unfinished about the childhood abuse experiences) will reveal the goal (of forgiveness or some other satisfying form of resolution), the process work is much the same in both cases. The difference is that the therapist knows that letting go may be a sufficient resolution and she or he, therefore, does not have to add her or his voice to those who are pushing the client to forgive. One does not have to forgive to overcome abuse.
- The client wishes to remain in a relationship with the hurtful other, and that person is pressuring the client to forgive. This can be true even when there is no faith-based motivation involved. When this happens, helping the client to engage in a process of attending to emotions and tending to needs relative to the EI and helping the client assert the right to do this are therapeutic tasks that would take precedence over setting an outcome goal. Again, letting go of the pain and suffering associated with the EI may be sufficient to achieve resolution, and helping the client see that it is his or her right to choose how to respond to the hurtfulness empowers the client to make that choice and relinquish the role of victim that has been thrust on him or her by the other person's hurtfulness and then underscored by the insistence that he or she ought to forgive.

## CONCLUSION

Notwithstanding the need to recognize that forgiveness is not the desired process for the resolution of all conflict and that pressure to forgive can be countertherapeutic and lead to a type of "blaming of the victim," the value of forgiveness in therapy has been recognized in a growing body of theory and research (Akhtar, 2002; Gordon & Baucom, 1998, 1999; Worthington, 1998a, 1998b). Clients sometimes indicate that they want (or think they ought) to forgive the hurtful other but have been unable to do so. When this is true, clients may present their difficulties in forgiving as the core issue that has brought them to therapy. Therapists have to draw on their clinical experience and knowledge of the specific clients and their situations in formulating whether the presenting problem is primarily about forgiveness or whether the deeper issue is that the clients' concerns about forgiveness are part of what is keeping them from exploring other equally adaptive ways of resolving the hurtful experience. The process of helping clients work on self-strengthening, self-assertion, and letting go of maladaptive emotions held in reference to the hurtful other are also discussed as alternatives to forgiveness for some clients (e.g., survivors of childhood abuse or domestic violence).

In addition to those who explicitly state that their desire to forgive (or their difficulty with forgiveness) is one of the reasons they have come to therapy, there will also be clients who do not formulate their distress and difficulties in terms of chronic unforgiveness or set forgiveness as a goal of therapy. Instead, they may express a longing to be free of the rumination, resentment, and other distressing effects of not being able to let go of the memories and pain of what happened. Given that the therapeutic process of letting go of unresolved hurt, emotional pain, and anger is embedded within the forgiveness process, we need neither urge nor preclude the possibility of forgiveness when clients do not set it as the desired outcome of their therapy. Some clients will let go of the unresolved emotions associated with the injury and find that sufficiently beneficial to consider the therapy successful; others will persist beyond letting go until they have forgiven the hurtful others before they consider the process complete. Still others will let go and then have the experience of discovering that, for them, forgiveness "naturally" or "automatically" flows out of the experience of letting go.

In addition, therapists must be cognizant of their beliefs about the value of forgiveness (which may or may not be faith based) and make sure that those beliefs do not become unhelpful biases in interacting with clients. The risk otherwise is that therapists may unwittingly interfere with the therapeutic process rather than work in concert with it to facilitate healing. Therapists' beliefs and values can interfere with healing in several ways. If therapists have never thought about forgiveness as a potentially beneficial outcome of therapy, they might simply overlook it and focus on some other task, thereby unintentionally denying the client that option as a potential outcome. If therapists hold a priori convictions that forgiveness is always a desirable resolution for interpersonal hurtfulness, they run the risk of being too directive, forceful, and/or simplistic in their efforts to get clients to set, and work toward, forgiveness as the goal of therapy. Similarly, if therapists come to work convinced that some groups of clients should never forgive (e.g., those who were sexually abused as children or victims of past domestic violence), they may be too directive, forceful, and/or simplistic in their efforts to dissuade them from forgiving.

# 2

# Emotion-Focused Therapy

Emotion-focused therapy (EFT) is an integrative approach to psychotherapy that is designed to foster clients' emotional processing skills and emotional competence. EFT helps people better use, transform, and regulate their affect and thereby enhances their well-being (Greenberg, 2002; Greenberg & Paivio, 1997; Greenberg, Rice, & Elliott, 1993; Greenberg & Watson, 2006). EFT has been shown to be effective in the treatment of depression, trauma, anxiety disorders, eating disorders, interpersonal injuries, and couple's distress. A number of major therapeutic tasks (Greenberg, Rice, & Elliott, 1993), each dealing with a specific affective–cognitive problem, such as problematic reactions, self-criticisms, self-interruption of emotional experience, and unfinished business, form the core of the EFT approach to intervention in individual therapy. What is notable about the empirical basis of EFT is that each step of successful client change processes in these tasks has been identified and verified through a series of process studies (Greenberg, 1986, 2006; Rice & Greenberg, 1984). We found that one of the tasks, empty-chair dialogue for the resolution of unfinished business, was of particular relevance to working on emotional injuries (EIs) and forgiveness.

In couples therapy, in which the main focus is on the partners' revealing their underlying attachment- and identity-oriented vulnerable feelings to each other, we found that what most promoted forgiveness was helping the injurer take responsibility for the harm done and express shame or distress for the pain caused (Woldarsky Meneses & Greenberg, 2011, 2014). Later in this book, we describe EFT methods of working with the resolution of EIs in both individual and couples therapy, explain the process of forgiving as we have seen it take place in therapy, and discuss how to facilitate it in therapy.

---

http://dx.doi.org/10.1037/0000144-003
*Forgiveness and Letting Go in Emotion-Focused Therapy*, by L. S. Greenberg and C. Woldarsky Meneses

Next, we present the argument for the importance of working with emotion and the basic principles of EFT.

## EMOTION IN EMOTION-FOCUSED THERAPY

Until recently, the prevalent commonsense view of emotion, endorsed by much of early cognitive behavior therapy, was that emotions were disruptive to functioning, were due to misinterpretation, and were to be controlled, tempered, bypassed, or avoided (Beck, 1976). Control of emotion, however, is not always wise or adaptive, and overregulation of emotion, or its avoidance, does not ensure health or happiness. From a psychodynamic viewpoint, emotions were sometimes seen as discharge phenomena and secondary to motivation. Both of these major traditions also often saw emotions as something to be gotten rid of by catharsis, understanding, cognitive restructuring, or regulation. A large volume of research has now been collected, however, on the debilitating physiological effects of not expressing and making sense of deeply felt emotions (Traue & Pennebaker, 1993). It appears that inhibiting the expression of emotion can lead to impaired immune system function and poorer health on a variety of indices. In addition, there is increasing evidence of the importance of emotion knowledge and emotional intelligence in enhancing social competence and healthy development (Mayer & Salovey, 1997). EFT thus emphasizes the central role of emotions in adaptive functioning in psychotherapy and change.

## EMOTIONS AS AN ADAPTIVE RESOURCE

At the most basic level of human functioning, emotion is seen as an adaptive form of information processing and action readiness that orients people to their environment and promotes their well-being and is the basis of social connectedness. Emotions provide a meaning system that informs people of the significance of events to their well-being, and they organize people for rapid adaptive action (Frijda, 1986; Izard, 1991; Oatley & Jenkins, 1992; Tomkins, 1963). From birth on, emotion is also a primary signaling system that communicates intentions and regulates interaction (Sroufe, 1996). Emotion regulates self and other and gives life much of its meaning. Emotion is foundational in the construction of the self and is a key determinant of self-organization. The lives of human beings are viewed as profoundly shaped and organized by emotional experiences. Our assumption (fully articulated in Beck, 1976; Frijda, 1986; Greenberg, 2015; Greenberg, Rice, & Elliott, 1993; Izard, 1991; Oatley & Jenkins, 1992; Sroufe, 1996; Tomkins, 1963; Traue & Pennebaker, 1993) is that emotion is a biologically based meaning system that gives people feedback about what is important and meaningful for them on a moment-by-moment basis and organizes them for adaptive action. Sadness over loss, anger in the face of violation, and fear in response to threat all are automatic and adaptive responses that produce a readiness to act in a particular way to establish, maintain, or alter the relationship between a person and their intra- and interpersonal environment.

In EFT, we focus on emotion because it is fundamentally an adaptive system (a nonrational system, not rational or irrational) that guides reason and is the means by which people come to know what they prefer and how to choose, from among all possible responses to a given set of circumstances, the options they are willing to pursue. Naming the emotion that one is feeling at the time—anger, frustration, or sadness—has a calming effect. Too often we underestimate the power of this simple action. Because emotion gives us information about our reaction to a situation based on whether our core concerns or goals have been met, knowing what one feels is the first step in a problem-solving process as emotion defines whether there is a problem in goal attunement. People have to symbolize their emotions in awareness to try to make sense of the emotions by reflecting on how to manage them and the triggering situation. EFT research has also shown that becoming an observer of your emotions helps regulate dysregulated emotion and puts one in the position of having the emotion rather than the emotion having you. There is no quick fix, but once people start to acknowledge and revisit hurt feelings, it clears the way to dealing with them and eventually to recalling times when the injurer was more loving and supportive, if that was the case.

Emotions are connected to our most essential needs. They rapidly alert us to situations important to our well-being. They also prepare and guide us in these important situations to take action toward meeting our needs. Emotions set a basic mode of processing in action and are based on survival circuits in our brain (Greenberg, 2002; LeDoux, 1996, 2012, 2015). Clients are helped in therapy to better identify, experience, regulate, explore, make sense of, transform, and flexibly manage their emotions. As a result, clients become more skillful in accessing the important information and meanings about themselves and their world that emotions contain and become more skillful in using that information to live vitally and adaptively. Emotions, as we have said, are central in the process of resolving EI. Forgiveness and letting go involve working through the anger and hurt and arriving at compassion, empathy for the other, or the calm of acceptance and moving on.

In addition, we view affect regulation as a core motive and suggest that we are motivated to have the affects we want and not have the affects we do not want; we evolved this way to aid survival and growth. Much action and interaction is driven by felt satisfaction—by the excitement and joy we feel when relationships are meeting our needs or we attain our goals and the shame, anxieties, and loneliness when we or our relationships fail. In this view, emotion guides us as to what is good and bad for us, and we attach, maintain our identities, and pursue competence because of how these actions make us feel.

It is important to note that although people primarily seek to feel positive emotions, "negative" emotions are highly functional, and people self-regulate emotions with the aim of achieving their goals, not simply seeking pleasure.

People's goals consist of more than "feeling good"; thus, at times, under certain circumstances, they will seek "negative" emotions, tolerate pain, or sacrifice themselves in the service of higher order feelings of virtue or love. Thus, in proposing affect regulation as a primary motivation, we are not proposing hedonism or seeking pleasure and avoiding pain as the primary motivation. In addition to being affect-regulating beings, we also hypothesize that people are motivated to seek meaning and that meaning creation itself brings pleasure (Greenberg & Goldman, 2008). People are constantly trying to make sense of what they feel.

In working with emotion, four distinct classes of emotional response are identified in EFT: primary adaptive emotion, primary maladaptive emotion, secondary reactive emotion, and instrumental emotion (Greenberg & Safran, 1987). EFT intervenes differentially with each class (Greenberg & Paivio, 1997).

*Primary adaptive emotions* are the most fundamental, direct, initial, rapid reactions to a situation, accessed for their adaptive information and capacity for organization. Adaptive emotions have to be symbolized in awareness to provide their information and awareness of their action tendencies.

Once experienced, they have served their function, and they disappear. However, people who have not developed the necessary skills to deal with emotions, frequently because of past EIs, often do not process their emotions at the time and react to reminders of the situation in emotionally maladaptive ways that lead them to treat the self and others badly. These *primary maladaptive emotions* were originally probably adaptive emotional responses, developed as a survival strategy in reaction to fears of loss, destruction of self, or humiliation and neglect or were, in the short term, adaptive but in the long term, maladaptive, such as escaping facing interpersonal difficulties through fear of rejection. Shame, fear, and the sadness of abandonment, as well as anger, are the more frequently occurring primary maladaptive emotions resulting from unresolved EIs.

*Secondary emotions* are emotional reactions to more primary internal processes and may be protections against these. Examples are feelings of reactive anger at the injurer when feelings of hurt or shame are more primary or feeling hopeless when one blocks one's empowering anger or unconsciously worrying to avoid underlying shame. Shame too can be secondary in cases when a person feels ashamed of his or her sadness or anger. Thus, feelings about feelings are secondary.

Finally, *instrumental emotions* are those that a person expresses to achieve an aim, such as crying "crocodile tears" to evoke sympathy. Instrumental emotions are emotional behavior patterns that people have learned to use to influence or manipulate others—for example, expressing shame to convey submission is often a cultural form of greeting, and it also can result from abuse. Instrumental emotions are dysfunctional when they are used rigidly and repeatedly to satisfy unmet needs.

## EMOTION SCHEMES

People come into the world evolutionarily wired with basic emotions. Children are not taught how to be angry or sad or feel fear, but what they become angry and sad about and afraid of is learned through experience. In EFT, this combination of biology and experienced emotion becomes organized into internal mental structures that we call *emotion schemes*. These are seen as the primary source of experience, rapidly and implicitly functioning to produce felt experience and action tendencies automatically. Emotion schemes are based on innate emotional responses, but these are coupled with learning into more complex internal organizations that include cognition. In contrast to a cognitive schema, the emotion scheme includes a large component of nonverbal and affective experience. Emotion schemes form the foundation of the self. The way we find ourselves to be in a situation, the feeling of what happens—such as feeling put down, feeling confident, or feeling shy—emerges from the dynamic synthesis of implicit emotion schemes that produce these changing self-organizations as a felt referent.

The use of focused attention to attend to current bodily feelings, to images of the past, and to a painful experience previously avoided is a central method in EFT. Successful self-change involves the articulation, elaboration, and transformation of the client's life story. Although EFT takes emotion as the fundamental datum of human experience, it recognizes the importance of meaning making and narrative change and ultimately views emotion and cognition as inextricably intertwined.

Dysfunction results when emotion schemes have become maladaptive through traumatic learning and/or when one or more of the elements of the scheme are not symbolized in awareness. The core emotion schemes in EI are anger at violation and sadness at loss and the pain of injury. There also may be shame at violation and fear of insecurity. These are formed by experience and are reactivated by reminders of the experience. The continual activation of these schemes and their synthesis into the states of rage and protests of unfairness and inconsolable hurt and pain and the storying of these feelings into narratives of betrayal, violation, and loss, which in turn reactivate the core schemes, is what has to be changed in therapy.

In individual therapy, the therapist helps clients understand and transform their emotion schematic experience through careful, empathic listening and evocative or expressive interventions; therapists also help clients reflect on and reevaluate emotion schematic memories and expose these structures to more adaptive emotional responses (Greenberg, 2002). In couples therapy, therapists help people reveal their underlying vulnerable attachment- and identity-related emotions and promote corrective interpersonal emotional experiences by exposing the core emotion schematic experiences that are evoked by the injury to new interpersonal experience.

The experience of feeling forgiving or unforgiving is the output of specific emotion schemes. Forgiveness, as we have said, is a highly emotional process, as is unforgiveness. When it is dysfunctional, persistent unforgiveness is accompanied by an affective component of chronic bitter anger or smoldering resentment, as well as sadness, shame, and/or emotional pain, that maintains the evaluation of unfairness. Unforgiveness involves lingering, distressing feelings of bitter resentment, corrosive anger, debilitating sadness, emotional pain, and/or shame and may be accompanied by the desire for revenge, to impose suffering on the one who has made one suffer. These feelings are symbolized in awareness and articulated in narratives of being unfairly treated and rightfully deserving of revenge or restitution.

In contrast, forgiving involves resolving the painful hurt and anger involved in the EI, accepting what happened instead of continuing to fight against the unfairness of it, and giving up the desire for revenge. Forgiveness also involves no longer wishing the other person to suffer for their hurtfulness. The soft affects in forgiveness, such as compassion, promote the ability to see and understand the unfolding of events surrounding the injury from the injurer's perspective, without excusing or condoning the harm done.

We propose that this change in the emotion schematic memory structures is greatly facilitated therapeutically through a recently investigated process called *memory reconsolidation* (Lane, Ryan, Nadel, & Greenberg, 2014; Nadel, Hupbach, Gomez, & Newman-Smith, 2012). The classic view of memory is that immediately after learning there is a period during which the memory is fragile and labile but that after sufficient time has passed, the memory is more or less permanent. The traditional view was that it was only during this consolidation period that it was possible to disrupt the formation of the memory; once this time window passed, the memory might be modified or inhibited, but not eliminated (Lane et al., 2014). Recently, however, an alternative view of memory has been supported in which it has been shown that every time a memory is retrieved, the underlying memory trace is once again labile and fragile, requiring another consolidation period, called *reconsolidation*. This reconsolidation period allows another opportunity to disrupt the memory. Given that maladaptive emotion schematic memories in EIs result in such emotions as fear, shame, anger, and sadness, the possibility of disrupting a previously acquired emotion schematic memory by blocking reconsolidation has important implications for resolving EIs and forgiveness.

We suggest that reevoking the emotion schematic memory and introducing new emotions, as well as reducing the previous injury-related emotions, allows the memory to be reconsolidated in a new way. Thus, in a betrayal when the offending partner is eventually seen with more compassion than anger and the situation is experienced with sadness at loss rather than shame of humiliation, the memory changes. With feelings of forgiveness, the emotion schematic memory is changed, and now the amygdala is no longer activated by memories of the offending incident. The feeling of resolution, of a weight lifting, in forgiveness is probably due to muscle relaxation caused by the cessation of a low-level fight-or-flight response initiated by the amygdala and mediated in part by the sympathetic nervous system. To achieve this change, it is necessary to readmit the memory of the betrayal without the attendant pain and fear and with some new feeling such as anger or compassion. Instead of looking at forgiveness and reconciliation as a triumph of reason over instinct, we have to begin to see that it is the emotional mechanisms involved that lead to change.

As well as focusing on the central role of schemes, the EFT view of human functioning proposes that we are in a constant process of making sense of our emotional experience (Greenberg & Pascual-Leone, 1995; Greenberg, Rice, & Elliott, 1993; Greenberg & Watson, 2006). An ongoing circular process of making sense of experience—symbolizing bodily felt sensations in awareness and articulating them in language—leads to the construction of new experience. What we feel influences and points to paths of meaning, and we virtually create the self we are about to become by how we explicate what we feel. We thus are in a continual process of simultaneously discovering and creating who we are. Although in EFT emotion is the fundamental datum of human experience, the importance of meaning making and narrative change is recognized, and emotion and cognition are viewed as inextricably intertwined. Although forgiveness is a felt orientation toward the injurer and the injury, it ultimately manifests as a meaning and involves a new conscious narrative.

## EMOTIONAL INJURIES

In psychotherapy in general, we have found that many clients often experience unresolved hurt and anger from interpersonal wrongs, and we call these *emotional injuries*. The unresolved emotions in these injuries are the cause of a significant amount of distress. We define interpersonal EI as a perceived betrayal of a cherished aspect of a relationship or a perceived violation of some aspect of a person's identity by another person. In the same way that a physical injury threatens life or causes damage to the integrity of one's body, EIs threaten or cause damage to the integrity of one's identity and/or to the strong, loving connection with another person. Forgiveness has been proposed as an important aspect of emotional recovery following interpersonal EIs of this type (Worthington, 1998a, 1998b, 2001).

Physical injury threatens life or causes damage to the integrity of one's body. Similarly, EIs threaten or cause damage to the integrity of one's sense of healthy self-identity. They can also threaten or cause damage to one's secure attachment with the injurer. Precisely because people are most open and vulnerable to those they care about, the significant people in our lives have the greatest potential to injure us emotionally. Our loved ones, by neglecting us, not responding to our needs, or being insensitive or judgmental, can intentionally or unintentionally injure us emotionally, leaving us wounded and scarred. For example, a man who withdraws from his wife emotionally when she turns to him for comfort and reassurance after their baby is stillborn sends the irretrievable message that he cannot be counted on to be there for her when she most needs him.

More severe injuries such as date rape violate a person's body and can leave that person with an overwhelming fear that being sexually responsive could lead to another experience of hearing an intimate partner declare that they are only doing what they know she or she wants while they violently take what they want. Repeated unwarranted, harsh verbal or physical punishment from a parent teaches a child that no matter how hard he or she tries, he or she is bound to disappoint and be rejected, that only those who are perfectly pleasing deserve affection and validation for their efforts. These experiences become stored in emotion schematic memory and can be activated by cues at any time and produce feelings related to these past situations in the present.

The attention given to processing the emotional impacts of hurtful experiences is the signature of EFT. One of the premises of the EFT approach is that helping clients to access and experience the whole range of feelings associated with the past EI within the safety of the therapeutic relationship is crucial to successful forgiveness-oriented EFT with individuals. Instead of having to go on endlessly fighting against such powerful emotions because they feel overwhelming and dangerous, EFT enables clients to accept, tolerate, and work with their feelings.

An EFT therapist also lends strength and support to their clients as they consider their role in the unfolding of events surrounding the hurtful events. Done effectively, appropriately assigning responsibility and taking ownership of their part in the unfolding of events generates a sense of personal power that helps a client move from being a helpless victim who somehow caused or was too weak to prevent another's hurtful behavior to being someone who has suffered and yet still has the personal resources and resilience to recover well enough to take an active role in influencing how things will unfold in the future.

Fully resolved emotionally hurtful experiences are marked by an emerging sense of the rightness of the anger, pain, and sadness associated with the injury that strengthens and validates the hurt person. These negative emotions, once accepted and experienced, shift and give way to the possibility of closure and a new narrative that includes hope for the future and a sense of the way forward into that future. Sometimes that new narrative is about asserting oneself to gain a healthy emotional distance from the hurtful other. It may even be about finding a way to live at a distance physically to ensure safety. Other times, when the client wants it, compassionate understanding and forgiveness are possible.

## EMOTION-FOCUSED THERAPY: CLINICAL EMPHASES

In EFT, emotions are viewed as centrally important in the experience of self, in both adaptive and maladaptive functioning and therapeutic change. It takes emotion as the fundamental datum of human experience while recognizing the importance of meaning making. In EFT, emotion and cognition are inextricably intertwined, and optimal adaptation involves a synthesis of affect and cognition in which cognition is brought to emotion to make sense of it. EFT is based on the importance of the therapist–client relationship as well as work on specific emotional-processing tasks.

EFT involves a style that combines both following and guiding the client's experiential process and thereby emphasizes the importance of both relationship and intervention skills. *Being* (being fully present and bringing specific relationship qualities to bear) and *doing* (guiding the client through a process of change) are combined in a synergistic flow. Relationship qualities include empathic attunement, communication of positive regard, genuineness, and acceptance and validation of the client's experience (rather than evaluating that experience, interpreting or defining the meaning of it for the client or advising him or her on how to behave or fixing the problem or situation that brought them to therapy). These relationship qualities are the means by which the working alliance is established and maintained, as well as the means by which the therapist "earns the right" to guide clients' awareness and facilitate their engagement with particular kinds of emotional processes that will help resolve the EI.

A major premise guiding EFT intervention in producing emotional change is that one cannot leave a place until one has arrived at it. A person has to feel a feeling to change it, but change involves more than just feeling an emotion. Given that one has to experience an emotion viscerally before it changes, therapists work to enhance clients' emotion-focused coping by helping them arrive at their core emotional experience. This is done by overcoming avoidance of emotions; approaching and becoming aware of them; symbolizing them in awareness; regulating, tolerating, and accepting them; and then reflecting on them to make sense of them. In forgiveness, one has to feel the anger, hurt, and pain and any core maladaptive feelings underlying the hurt and anger, such as shame, fear, envy, and desire for revenge, to transform these. Having experienced and understood the emotions in need of change, the therapist helps transform them by facilitating the generation of alternate emotional responses, such as grief, compassion, and love, and helps in the construction of new narratives based on these feelings.

EFT therapists do not direct or advise clients as to what they should feel. Rather, they offer clients their expertise as process facilitators who know how to help people arrive at and process what they feel at their core. EFT therapists help clients meet their goals by offering expertise in the process of facilitating change; they are not experts on what the client is experiencing but on methods to facilitate experience. They offer this expertise by listening carefully, being empathically attuned, and knowing how to guide systematic exploration. Their expertise includes skill in directing clients' attention to internal experience, helping clients search the edges of their awareness, differentiating global and general experience, elaborating experience, and stimulating and transforming experience. To do this effectively, EFT therapists have to establish a highly supportive and collaborative environment.

The most characteristic style of responding in EFT is *empathic exploration*. Here, the therapist imaginatively enters the world of the other to help make explicit what is implicit. In addition, the therapist identifies markers of different types of in-session processing difficulties to make momentary process diagnoses to identify the types of intervention most likely to be useful at that particular moment in therapy. The use of markers and tasks is probably the most distinguishing aspect of EFT. Thus, the therapist working within the context of EI and forgiveness identifies markers of the unresolved injury and suggests an empty-chair dialogue, as well as markers of conflict or guilt related to the injury, and suggests dialogues between the opposing sides of the self. Therapists also help clients identify key treatment foci, such as feeling like damaged goods, and help them work on these over several sessions. To do this, therapists begin treatment by identifying a core painful emotional condition, identifying markers within each session of current problem states, and offering clients different ways of working on their in-session states that best suit these states.

A variety of in-session therapeutic tasks have been identified, each designed to help resolve a particular type of processing difficulty and to facilitate an ongoing focus on underlying dysfunctional emotion schemes that prevent healthy affect regulation and dysfunctional meanings. As we have said, empty-chair dialogues are most helpful in resolving unfinished business. They facilitate access to maladaptive emotion schemes containing painful and disowned emotional memories and make these amenable to new information and reorganization. Two-chair dialogues for splits help clients integrate opposing aspects of the self involved in any conflicts or self-interruptions involved in resolving their unfinished business to create a more unified sense of self (Elliott, Watson, Goldman, & Greenberg, 2004; Greenberg, Rice, & Elliott, 1993). Focusing is helpful in facilitating deeper experiencing when the client has an unclear felt sense and is confused and unable to get a clear sense of their experience. Markers signify not only particular types of affective problems but also their amenability to particular interventions. The therapist, therefore, notices when a marker emerges and intervenes in a specific manner at that time to facilitate resolution of that type of processing problem.

EFT therapists are thus process diagnostic. As well as assessing different problematic emotional states (unfinished business, splits), they also assess different types of emotions being experienced and expressed and make differential interventions depending on which emotions are being felt. In the assessment of moment-by-moment emotions, the four distinct classes of emotional response are identified in EFT (primary adaptive emotion, primary maladaptive emotion, secondary reactive emotion, and instrumental emotion; Greenberg & Safran, 1987), and interventions differ with each class.

In EFT, the central mechanism of change is emotional processing and the meaning-making process that ensues from emotional change. From the EFT perspective, change occurs by making sense of one's emotions through awareness, expression, regulation, reflection, transformation of emotion, and corrective emotional experience, all in the context of an empathically attuned relationship that facilitates these processes. These six empirically supported principles of change that guide differential intervention are discussed next and related to forgiveness.

## Awareness

Clients' ability to articulate what they are experiencing in their inner world when working through an injury is a central focus of this treatment. The therapist works with clients to help the client approach, tolerate, and regulate, as well as accept, their emotions of pain, hurt, anger, and rage. Accepting these emotions rather than avoiding them is the first step in awareness work. Having facilitated the client's acceptance of the emotions, the therapist then helps the client in the use of emotion. What is the information and action tendency in each of the emotions? In the sadness that lasts from the injury, what is the loss and what is the need? Is it a loss of trust, esteem, position, or status, and is the need for comfort, support, or reconciliation? One has to discriminate in the anger what the unfairness or frustration is and what the anger prompts the client to want to do. Is it informing the client of a violation of a sense of self or a violation of safety or trust, or was one robbed of dignity or something else equally precious? Is there a desire for revenge, for balancing the wrongs, "an eye for an eye"? Is the anger moving one to protect the self from future harm or destroy the wrong-doer? In pain, what is it that is shattered? Is the need for self-repair or relationship repair? Emotional awareness helps clients get at the idiosyncratic meaning of the injury. Clients are helped to make sense of what their emotion is telling them and to identify the goal, need, or concern that it is organizing them to attain. Clients thus learn how to use the emotion they have become aware of and accepted to improve coping. Emotion is thus used both to inform and to move.

## Expression

There is a strong human tendency to avoid painful, injury-related emotions, and this is often the root cause of the inability to resolve EIs. Cognitive processes such as beliefs, assumptions, and attributions about the danger of emotion often distort emotion and transform adaptive unpleasant emotions, such as sadness and anger, into dysfunctional behavior, such as self-medication and substance abuse, designed to avoid the dreaded feeling. To cope effectively with avoided emotions, clients must approach them by attending to their bodily felt experience. This often involves a first step of changing the cognitions governing emotion avoidance. Then clients must allow and tolerate being in live contact with their emotions. These two steps are consistent with notions of exposure. There is a long line of evidence on the effectiveness of exposure to previously avoided feelings (Foa & Jaycox, 1999). From our perspective, however, approach, arousal, and tolerance of emotional experience involved in mere exposure are necessary but not sufficient. Optimum emotional processing involves the integration of cognition and affect (Greenberg, 2002; Greenberg & Pascual-Leone, 1995; Greenberg & Safran, 1987). Once contact with emotional experience is achieved, clients must also cognitively orient to that experience as information and explore, reflect on, and make sense of it.

The effect of emotional arousal in forgiveness-oriented EFT, however, also depends on the quality of the working alliance. Iwakabe, Rogan, and Stalikas (2000) documented that high arousal predicted a good session outcome only when there was a strong alliance. It is important to note that there can be no universal rule about the effectiveness of arousing emotion or evoking emotional expression. The role of arousal and the degree to which it is useful in therapy depends on what emotion is expressed, about what issue, how it is expressed, by whom, to whom, when and under what conditions, and in what way the emotional expression is followed by other experiences of affect and meaning (Whelton, 2004). Arousal is necessary but not sufficient for therapeutic progress. Auszra, Greenberg, and Herrmann (2013) found that it was the degree of productivity of processing of aroused emotions, rather than arousal alone, that distinguished good from poor outcome cases. Thus, in dealing with unresolved EIs, some form of expression is needed, but not all expression is necessarily productive. Disintegrating into a passive sense of helpless or hopeless, for example, is not productive. Greenberg and Malcolm (2002), however, showed that moderate to high arousal of a primary emotion, such as the shame of worthlessness or the anger at violation, was predictive of a change in view of the other, an essential step on the path to resolving unfinished business and to letting go and/or forgiveness. It thus appears that expression of primary emotions is an important component in dealing with EI.

## Emotion Regulation

Facilitating the ability to tolerate and regulate having an emotional experience related to the injury is another important change process in dealing with EIs. Sometimes it is the overregulation (overcontrol) or suppression of powerful emotions, such as anger at betrayal, shame at violation, or sadness of loss, that is a contributing factor to the inability to resolve an EI. In others, it is the underregulation of emotion that is the problem. Important issues in any treatment of injury are what emotions are to be regulated and how they are to be regulated. Underregulated emotions that require down-regulation are either secondary emotions, such as despair and hopelessness, secondary anger or primary maladaptive emotions, such as the shame of feeling worthless, or the anxiety of basic insecurity and panic. Overregulated emotions, such as sadness, grief, and adaptive anger, often have to be up-regulated.

The provision of a safe, validating, supportive, and empathic environment helps regulate automatically generated underregulated distress by interpersonal soothing (Bohart & Greenberg, 1997) and helps strengthen the self. Often people with interpersonal EIs have experienced trauma, and regulation of the overwhelming trauma-related emotions of fear and shame is needed. Emotion-regulation skills involve identifying and labeling emotions, allowing and tolerating emotions, establishing a working distance, increasing positive emotions, reducing vulnerability to negative emotions, self-soothing, breathing, and distraction. Kircanski, Lieberman, and Craske (2012) showed that putting feelings into words (affect labeling) diminished the intensity of the response of the amygdala and other limbic regions to negative emotional images (Lieberman et al., 2007).

Creating an appropriate working distance is particularly important when working with maladaptive emotions of core shame and feelings of shaky vulnerability produced by the injury, which can easily become overwhelming for the client. Forms of meditative practice and self-acceptance often are most helpful in achieving a working distance from overwhelming core emotions. For example, one client, a mother of five, after a tumultuous divorce 10 years earlier, had been rejected by her daughter and experienced a breakdown and panic because she had not been able to deal with the injurious loss of having "a living daughter who was dead to her." During therapy, she benefited greatly from a safe place in which to exercise to calm her distress when she became overwhelmed while telling her imagined daughter in an empty chair the pain of being shut out of her life.

Clients working on overcoming the pain of their injuries often benefit from learning to tolerate their painful emotions and to self-soothe. These emotions can be down-regulated by developing tolerance and by soothing at a variety of different levels of processing. Self-soothing involves, among other things, diaphragmatic breathing, relaxation, development of self-empathy and compassion, and self-talk. Physiological soothing involves activation of the parasympathetic nervous system to regulate heart rate, breathing, and other sympathetic functions that speed up under stress. At the more deliberate behavioral and cognitive levels, promoting clients' abilities to receive and be compassionate to their emerging painful emotional experience is the first step toward tolerating emotion and self-soothing. The ability to regulate breathing and to observe one's emotions and let them come and go are important processes to help regulate emotional distress. Mindful awareness of emotions coupled with awareness of breathing is helpful in regulating symptoms of depression and anxiety related to EI (Greenberg, 2010).

Soothing also comes interpersonally in the form of empathic attunement to one's affect and through acceptance and validation by another person. Being able to soothe the self develops initially by the internalization of the soothing functions of the protective other (Sroufe, 1996; Stern, 1985). In EFT, therapists thus help clients experiencing EI contain and regulate emotional experience by providing a soothing environment. Over time, this is internalized and helps clients develop implicit self-soothing, the ability to regulate feelings automatically without deliberate effort.

### Reflection

In addition to recognizing emotions and symbolizing them in words, promoting further reflection on emotional experience helps people make sense of their injury experience and promotes its assimilation into their ongoing self-narratives. What we make of our emotional experience makes us who we are. A client whose alcoholic father abused him was able to grieve the loss of the father after expressing empowered anger at how he was treated. However, it was many more months before the client understood that although the father's own abuse had made him incapable of healthy parenting, this did not mean that he did not love his son. This type of exploration of emotional experience and reflection on what is discovered is another important process in change. The meanings of situations that have evoked emotion are made sense of in a new way. Reflection helps make sense of the anger and hurt from the injury. In this process, feelings, needs, self-experience, thoughts, and aims of different parts of the self are identified. Recognizing how their never-ending experience of blame and complaint leaves them feeling unsatisfied and powerless helps people let go of trying to change the past.

### Transformation

Probably the most important way of dealing with emotion in therapy involves the transformation of emotion by emotion. This applies most specifically to transforming primary maladaptive emotions such as fear and shame (Greenberg, 2002). Rather than reason with emotion, one can transform one emotion with another. In time, the coactivation of the more adaptive emotion along with or in response to the maladaptive emotion helps transform the maladaptive emotion. Thus, maladaptive rage can be transformed by the sadness of grief. In EFT, an important goal is to arrive at the maladaptive injury-related emotion, not for its good information and motivation, but to make it accessible to transformation.

The key to transforming maladaptive emotions is to access alternate healthy adaptive emotions to act as resources in the self (Greenberg, 2002). In an emotion-focused treatment, feelings related to unforgiveness, such as anger, contempt, and pain, are eventually changed by accessing feelings of compassion, empathy, and concern. Emotion schematic memories are changed by evoking emotional memories and facilitating their reconsolidation with new emotional input.

It is important to note that the process of changing emotion with emotion goes beyond ideas of catharsis or completion and letting go, exposure, extinction, or habituation, in that the maladaptive feeling is not purged, nor does it simply attenuate by the person feeling it. Rather, another feeling is used to transform or undo it. Although exposure to emotion at times may be helpful in overcoming affect phobia, in many situations in therapy, change also occurs because one emotion is transformed by another emotion rather than simply attenuating it. In these instances, emotional change occurs by the activation of an incompatible, more adaptive experience that undoes or transforms the old response. In addition, we have already discussed the role of evoking emotional memories and facilitating their reconsolidation with new emotional input in changing emotion schematic memories. With new emotional input, memories change by changing the emotions associated with them. In forgiveness, not only do people who were stuck in sadness, powerlessness, or shame access anger to move beyond the sadness or people who were stuck in rage and resentments access sadness or shame to move out of the anger, but people also access positive feelings of compassion and love to move to forgiving.

This principle applies not only to positive emotions changing negative ones but also to changing maladaptive emotions by activating dialectically opposing adaptive emotions (Greenberg, 2002). Thus, in therapy for injury, maladaptive fear from abuse, once aroused, can be transformed into security by the activation of more boundary-establishing emotions of adaptive anger or disgust or by evoking the softer feelings of compassion or forgiveness. Similarly, maladaptive anger can be undone by adaptive sadness. Maladaptive shame of humiliation can be transformed by accessing both anger at violation and self-comforting feelings and by accessing pride and self-worth. The tendency to shrink into the ground in shame can be transformed by the thrusting forward tendency in newly accessed anger at violation. In depression, a protest-filled, submissive sense of worthlessness can be transformed therapeutically by guiding people to the desire that drives their protest, a desire to be free of their cages and to access their feelings of joy and excitement for life. Withdrawal emotions from the right hemisphere of the brain are replaced with approach emotions from the left hemisphere or vice versa (Davidson, 2000). Once the alternate emotion has been accessed, it transforms or undoes the original state, and a new state is forged.

## Corrective Emotional Experience

Finally, a key way of changing an emotion is to have a new lived experience that changes an old feeling. A new lived experience with another provides a corrective emotional experience. Experiences that provide interpersonal soothing, disconfirm pathogenic beliefs, or offer a new success experience can correct patterns set down in earlier times. A client who faces the shame of having been ostracized and denigrated by a bullying brother experiences acceptance from the therapist, rather than the expected disgust or denigration, which has the power to change the feeling of shame. Corrective emotional experiences in individual EFT occur predominantly in the therapeutic relationship, although success experience in the world is also encouraged. In working with couples, it is both the expression of vulnerability by one partner and the responsiveness of the other that generate a corrective emotional experience and represent a key process of change.

## HOW ARE NEW EMOTIONS ACCESSED?

In EFT for EIs, transformation comes from the client accessing a new emotional state in the session that undoes the old maladaptive emotion. How does the therapist access new emotions? The therapist attends to subdominant emotions that are being expressed "on the periphery" of a client's awareness and helps the client attend to and experience the more adaptive primary emotions and needs that provide inner resilience. Accessing agentic needs is a key way of accessing new emotions. Activating the need for boundary protection evokes anger, and accessing the need for missed love evokes sadness. Other methods of accessing new emotions involve using enactment and imagery to evoke new emotions, remembering a time an emotion was felt, changing how the client views things, or even expressing an emotion for the client (Greenberg, 2002). Once accessed, these new emotional resources begin to undo the psycho-affective motor program previously determining the person's mode of processing. This enables clients to challenge the validity of perceptions of self and other connected to a maladaptive emotion, weakening its hold on them.

The difficulty in changing emotional experience, and restructuring emotional responses, is that emotional change cannot occur through a rational process of understanding or explanation but, rather, by generating a new emotional response. EFT works on the principle that people must first arrive at a place before they can leave it. Maladaptive emotion schemes must be activated in the therapy session to change them by accessing other more adaptive emotions.

## FORGIVENESS AND THERAPY

Looking at forgiveness in therapy, we see that forgiveness issues are typically set within the context of relationships with an extensive history, where individuals have struggled long and hard to make sense of the offense committed by a person with whom they have had a significant relationship, and they have to come to a resolution of how to continue to deal with him or her. Bass and Davis (1988), for example, counseled survivors of sexual abuse that at some point they will have to give up trying to get anything back from their abusers.

In letting go of previously unmet interpersonal needs, the forgiver is released from the traps of (a) trying to make the offender understand the magnitude of harm done and (b) trying to get the offender to take responsibility.

A number of theorists (Brandsma, 1982; Fitzgibbons, 1986; Hope, 1987; Human Development Study Group, 1991; McCullough, 1997) have identified the capacity for empathy as a crucial element in successful forgiveness. McCullough, Worthington, and Rachal (1997) proposed and investigated an empathy model of forgiveness, and McCullough, Rachal, Sandage, and Worthington (1997) concluded that empathy and forgiveness are intimately, maybe even causally, linked. *Empathy* can be defined as an active effort to understand another person's perception of an interpersonal event as if one were that other person, rather than judging the other person's behavior from the perspective of one's experience of that event.

McCullough and his colleagues have shown that empathy for the perpetrator mediates successful forgiveness (McCullough, Rachal, et al., 1997; McCullough, Worthington, & Rachal, 1997; see also Sandage & Worthington, 2010). When accessed, empathy involves understanding another's feelings and is a complex cognitive–affective state that facilitates forgiveness of an interpersonal injury. *Affective empathy* is best understood as a means of imaginative entry into the world of the other, which generates a bodily felt sense of understanding what the other person may have been feeling, without actually sharing the same experience (Greenberg & Rosenberg, 2002). Berecz (2001) suggested that the task for the injured person is to imaginatively transpose him- or herself into the other person's place in an attempt to understand the unfolding of events from the injurer's perspective. As Rowe et al. (1989) pointed out, empathy toward the injurer involves being able to see the other person as acting in a quintessentially human manner, which flows out of the context of his or her self-focused needs and perceptions. It includes (but does not require) the possibility of recognizing that what the injurer did was similar to something one has done or could do under the same circumstances. In addition to assisting in the revision of how one sees the injurer, cognitive perspective taking sometimes allows the injury itself to be recast within a broader understanding of the context of the unfolding of events.

However, cognitive perspective taking of this nature does not have to involve warm, benevolent feelings associated with forgiveness. Something more is required for forgiveness, and this appears to be compassion for the injurer, or affective empathy. In addition, different processes are needed in individual therapy, where the other is not present, than in couple therapy, where the other is a part of the process.

## FORGIVENESS AND EMOTION-FOCUSED THERAPY

Although there are a number of approaches to working with forgiveness in therapy, EFT is unique in focusing explicitly on how to work with emotion in this process. EFT for forgiveness works on the principle that to change, people have to experience that which is to change, to make it accessible to new input and then to have new emotional experience. Clients, therefore, have to reclaim the disowned painful feelings related to the injury, including at least the sadness at loss, the anger at violation, and the pain of betrayal before they can change these feelings. In this process, it is not that people simply discover things they did not know but, rather, that they experience in a bodily manner aspects of themselves they have not consciously felt or may have previously disclaimed (Greenberg & van Balen, 1998). In working on EIs, clients thus are helped to experience what they are talking about so that they can become aware of the feelings of anger, sadness, fear, and shame involved in being injured and the idiosyncratic hurtfulness of the injurious events. In this way, the message or significance of injury can be clearly and powerfully experienced so that it can later be transformed by new emotions and reflected on to create new meaning. In working on EIs, clients have to acknowledge the anger, which informs them of the violation, and allow the pain and hurt, which allow them to grieve and protest the loss. Any maladaptive shame or fear associated with the injury has to be acknowledged and undone by accessing internal resources of self-soothing, a sense of pride and self-value, and/or positive feelings toward and from the imagined injurer.

Forgiveness is viewed as an affective task that ultimately involves integration of reason and emotion, head and heart. Some investigators—Enright (2001), for example—have proposed that decision or choice is the central element of forgiveness. Although we see meaning and the development of a new narrative as important in the process, we see forgiveness as centrally involving the processing of painful emotion. Cognitive forgiveness also is not enough. We have seen too many people in our psychoeducation groups say that they forgive, out of cognitive reflection, ideological or religious commitments, or change in some other belief, without feeling forgiving. In the long run, this rational process does not lead to lasting forgiveness or positive feelings toward the other. In this book, we present an approach on how to facilitate the feeling of forgiveness, viewing feeling as the fundamental way of changing and that it is change in feeling that leads to thinking and acting in a forgiving manner. EFT thus focuses on forgiveness as primarily a matter of "how I feel about you" and not as much on "how I think about you" or even "how I treat you."

Clinicians have reported that the injured partner experiences intense emotions, including rage toward the injurer, coupled with shame, feelings of powerlessness, victimization, sadness, abandonment, and depression, whereas the injurer typically experiences intrusive, persistent ruminations about the event, which often leads to difficulties concentrating on everyday tasks (Spring, 1996). Without exception, everyone who writes about forgiveness in the face of deep interpersonal hurt acknowledges that strong emotions such as anger and sadness are endemic to the forgiveness process. Acknowledgment of resentment and self-protecting anger in the face of personal injury is an appropriate response to a situation of feeling unfairly treated or violated.

Experiences of the sadness of hurt and grief are also important. These may concern both the loss of what was and/or could have been and, on a deeper level, the loss of a particular way of viewing oneself and the world. Expressions of core emotions like these are biologically adaptive expressions that promote healthy emotional processing (Frijda, 1986; Greenberg & Paivio, 1997).

Processing and letting go of unresolved emotions over time are crucial in forgiveness. Forgiveness-oriented EFT involves helping people process and ultimately let go of many emotions, central of which may be hurt, sadness and pain, loss, anger, revenge and resentment at violation, and shame at humiliation. Letting go means coming to accept what has happened, no longer ruminating or feeling bad about it, and being able to move on rather than looking backward and feeling pain. Beyond letting go, positive feelings of compassion, love, and caring result from arriving at forgiveness, which in itself is a core feeling. Once one feels different, one acts differently. Other positive effects that come with a feeling of forgiveness are the prosocial changes in one's motivations toward the offending person.

Forgiveness appears to involve three important emotional processes: resolving the painful hurt, shame, and anger involved in the injury; possibly generating positive feelings of compassion and loving-kindness; and finally, feeling empathic concern for the injurer. We found that over and above empathy for the injurer, and possibly the route to it, was the ability of the injured people to imagine that the injurers feel compassion or empathy for the pain caused by their actions. This is what seemed crucial in being able to forgive the other in individual therapy. In couples therapy, we found that it was the expression of shame by the injurer over and above guilt or apology that seemed important in leading the injured to be able to forgive the injurer. These findings are elaborated in later chapters. Overall, we can see that people resolve EIs through forgiveness by reducing their bad feelings and by increasing positive feelings.

At the same time, certain behaviors are important in the forgiveness process. The more pragmatic or behavioral elements of forgiveness are often of far more importance to perpetrators than whether victims succeed in experiencing a change of heart. In addition, the acceptance of an apology highlights important ritualistic or performative aspects of forgiveness. Such performances may be significant to the participants in and of themselves and may furthermore cement commitments to change attitudes and behavior and reaffirm moral values. We therefore treat the act of apology in therapy, when the other is present, as an important aspect of the change process.

Forgiveness in EFT involves overcoming initial feelings of rage, resentment, and anger and coming to feel loving compassion, generosity, and goodwill to the other, coming to see the wrongdoer as potentially more than his or her acts toward the injured. Overcoming suppression of adaptive anger appears important in coming to forgiveness. It conveys self-respect and self-worth (Greenberg, 2010). This is an assertive form of anger, as opposed to a more "payback" type of anger. The latter is destructive and rejecting and involves desires to get revenge and belittle or hurt the other. Through assertive anger, we voice our protests. And without protests, there are just silence and grudges. The healthy way of dealing with anger is to express assertive anger while recognizing that the other person to whom one is attributing the hurtful deeds and motives is someone one still respects as a person or cares about. Once one has accepted one's anger and grieved the loss, one lets go of any desire to engage in any retaliatory behavior, articulates words of forgiveness, or participates in some equivalent ritual, with sincerity and good intentions, sincerely accepting an apology and possibly, if one reconciles, moving on to a new, positive relationship.

## CONCLUSION

A key element of therapist skill in forgiveness-oriented EFT resides in the therapist's ability to be empathically attuned to their client's emotions as they process the impact of an unresolved EI. In essence, the difficult lingering emotions a client struggles with are seen not as problematic feelings that have to be controlled but, rather, as the path to accessing and transforming underlying maladaptive emotion schemes. The therapist must be skilled in assessing primary and secondary and adaptive and maladaptive emotionality and in helping clients to tolerate, reflect on, and synthesize previously denied primary experience and feelings, so they may assist clients in their efforts to transform maladaptive responses to the EI. Thus, the blaming anger and the complaint or the quest for answers to the key question of why the injury happened are recognized as secondary responses to the more primary pain of brokenness, the sadness of loss, and the primary anger of having one's goals thwarted. Self-respecting primary, adaptive anger is promoted because this organizes the person to assert and maintain healthy boundaries. Primary sadness is promoted because there is grief work involved in regard to loss of innocence, trust, love, and possibly loss of a relationship. In injury, experiences of grief may concern both the loss of what was and/or could have been and, on a deeper level, the loss of a particular way of viewing oneself and the world.

It is this ability to help clients attend to new adaptive responses that helps clients notice bodily felt shifts or changes that support the emergence of newly constructed meaning, which in turn helps articulate and consolidate change in previously held dysfunctional emotions schemes.

# 3

# Emotion-Focused Therapy and Forgiveness for Individuals

Our research on forgiveness in individual emotion-focused therapy (EFT) has been conducted using Gestalt empty-chair dialogues for resolving unfinished business embedded in a relationship based on the Rogerian person-centered conditions of empathy, positive regard, and genuineness (Rogers, 1959). *Empty-chair dialogue* is an intervention that is used to help clients engage in imaginal dialogue with those who hurt them to find new ways to come to terms with their unresolved bad feelings. This type of imaginal confrontation with the other in an empty chair forms the centerpiece of the emotion injury treatment. Unresolved feelings of anger and hurt that come with the experience of feeling wronged, betrayed, or violated, are usually the basis of a lot of unfinished business centered on an emotional injury (EI) with a significant other.

Empty-chair dialogue in which the client expresses these unresolved feelings to an imagined other in an empty chair has been found, in a number of research studies, to be effective in helping people access these feelings and resolve unfinished business (Greenberg & Malcolm, 2002; Paivio & Greenberg, 1995). Over the past 20 years, this program of research (described in Greenberg, 2010; Greenberg & Malcolm, 2002) has led to the articulation of a model of the resolution of EIs that maps out a path to forgiveness.

http://dx.doi.org/10.1037/0000144-004
*Forgiveness and Letting Go in Emotion-Focused Therapy*, by L. S. Greenberg and C. Woldarsky Meneses

In this chapter, we focus on presenting the theoretical underpinnings of the therapeutic tasks that are crucial to successful forgiveness-oriented EFT in individual therapy. We also provide a treatment outline for this work. We discuss the markers of readiness to engage in the work of resolving a past EI and also look at how to handle the difficulties clients may have in engaging in the imaginal enactments that are at the heart of forgiveness-oriented interventions. We then address different interventions that help people access the painful feelings that have to be processed to make them accessible to transformation, as well as the difficulties clients may have in accessing and tolerating their emotionally laden painful memories of the injury.

One of the premises of the EFT approach to EI is that the interruption or blocking of primary biologically adaptive emotions subverts healthy boundary setting, self-respectful anger, and grieving, which are necessary for overcoming EIs. For that reason, this chapter emphasizes the importance of helping clients overcome blocks to these emotions and to accessing and expressing the emotional pain and distress and the primary feelings of anger and sadness associated with an EI. The expression of underlying emotion is one of the therapeutic tasks crucial to successful forgiveness-oriented EFT with individuals to resolve their injuries. In all phases of the therapy process, there is an emphasis on heightening the intensity of primary emotional experience to access previously unacknowledged core emotion schemes related to the injury to make them amenable to change.

For example, instead of discouraging clients from expressing their revenge fantasies, the desire to retaliate is normalized as a sign of how damaged the injured person feels. Such expressions of anger also teach clients to accept and tolerate their anger and work with rather than against it. The potential forgiver's feelings of anger and resentment and desire for revenge or restitution are of considerable importance. This generates a sense of self as a person of worth who has been treated unfairly and deserves to be treated differently and helps form new adaptive emotion schemes that contribute to the transformation of the client's ability to respond. Although initial resentment and self-protecting anger in the face of personal injury are appropriate and are even positive responses that convey self-respect and self-worth, a transformation of these feelings is required if forgiveness is to take place. Such transformation leads to revisions in the self-concept and self-identity narrative. What has to be targeted in therapy is not the initial animosity but excessive, misplaced, or vindictive resentment that may become "brooding" resentment. This first has to be expressed and validated, but over time, it is transformed into more assertive anger and sadness at loss.

In encouraging the client to speak from inner experience, the therapist promotes the client's ownership of the emotional experience and empowers him or her to appropriately assign responsibility for harm done, rather than remaining stuck in rumination, brooding anger, and the victim role. This promotes a change in identity narratives. This is another of the therapeutic tasks crucial to successful forgiveness-oriented EFT with individuals and leads the client to a changed understanding of him- or herself. For example, a client may change from being a helpless victim who somehow deserved, caused, or was too weak to prevent the other's hurtful behavior to someone who has the personal resources and resilience to recover from the EI.

## MARKERS OF EMOTIONAL INJURIES

In our studies of the resolution of EIs, we operationalized an *emotional injury* as hurt and anger carried for at least 2 years resulting from some action by another person that was experienced as a betrayal or a violation of trust that led to an attachment rupture or an identity insult. An *attachment injury* has been characterized as a perceived abandonment, betrayal, or breach of trust in a critical moment of need (Greenberg & Goldman, 2008; Johnson, Makinen, & Millikin, 2001). An *identity injury* has been characterized as involving invalidation or diminishment of self-esteem resulting from a criticism or insult at a time of vulnerability (Greenberg & Goldman, 2008). The injurious incident leads to a change in the relationship. This in turn creates an impasse that blocks relationship repair and leaves identity damage. Unresolved injuries lead people to withdraw internally or change their view of the other or the relationship in some fundamental way that ruptures the bond of trust and respect or love between people and results in disruption to the integrity of the self.

The injuries that clients brought to treatment in our studies were both emotional and interpersonal; they were emotional in that they involved intense lingering unresolved feelings of hurt or anger and betrayal, and they were interpersonal in that the injurer was a significant person in the injured person's life. Injuries in individual therapy involved abandonment, betrayals, or violations by significant others, such as friends, family members, intimate partners, or bosses. There were many unresolved injuries by parents, such as being neglected or abused, being given up for adoption, being denied paternity, and being left out of a parental will.

In couples therapy, we encountered situations or life events in which partners had been unable to resolve specific disappointing attachment- and identity-related incidents that had a deleterious effect on their relationship bond. Incidents that constituted injuries in couples were such things as a husband being inattentive to a wife's needs during or after childbirth, one partner not accompanying the other to visit a dying parent, a wife criticizing her husband's ability to provide for her in front of his family, one partner ignoring or disparaging a major success of the other, or a partner mocking the other's sexual performance in front of others. Betrayal of marital vows of fidelity with affairs, whether real or virtual, was a special type of injury that resulted in a partner feeling that the other had violated a fundamental aspect of the relational bond on which the partner could depend. Unresolved emotional wounds of this nature for the injured person led to a loss of trust in both a partner's reliability and supportiveness. Although some couples successfully resolve these incidents, for others the incidents remain as EIs that affect the foundation of the relationship for years.

Parmagent, Magyar, Benore, and Mahoney (2005), working in a spiritual framework, differentiated between loss or violation of what was held sacred, resulting in two forms of EIs. A *loss* was predictive of intrusive thoughts and depression, whereas a *violation* was tied to more intense intrusive thoughts and greater anger. Furthermore, loss was linked to greater posttraumatic growth and positive spiritual change; in contrast, desecration, the violation of what was sacred, was associated with less posttraumatic growth. People experience severe consequences when precious aspects of their lives they hold as sacred are lost, but they are more likely to lash out against the perpetrators of the injury when they feel violated. Whether an EI is experienced as a loss or a violation affects the response to the injury and the process of resolution. Violation involves far more rage, and it is far harder to reach forgiveness.

Being left out of a parent's will or feeling judged as not good enough by a parent could be experienced by a client as a loss or violation. Learning that a spouse was not a virgin at the time of marriage or has had an emotional affair during the marriage could be seen by the partner as a loss or violation. A person's beliefs about what is held sacred are a critical ingredient in what will constitute an injury and what will represent a loss versus a violation to that person. For some partners, fidelity is sacred, and its shattering is a violation, whereas for others this may be more of a loss.

## EMPTY-CHAIR WORK

Gestalt empty-chair work (Perls, Hefferline, & Goodman, 1951) is designed to assist clients in processing their unresolved emotions and in finding new ways to come to terms with past hurts instead of dwelling on them in unproductive ways that only serve to entrench the clients in chronic, maladaptive unforgiveness. It is important to remember that empty-chair work is a way of helping clients come to terms with hurtfulness that happened in the past and is not recommended when current hurtfulness is taking place in the present in the context of an important ongoing relationship. In the latter case, clients, if asked to engage in an empty-chair dialogue, may mistakenly see the intervention as a way of figuring out how to respond to the other in the present to make the other person stop being hurtful or use it as an opportunity to rehearse the elements of a confrontation and, in so doing, may unwittingly escalate the risk of the other's continued hurtfulness. Empty-chair work should be reserved for its intended use in resolving unfinished business from the past. Forgiveness and reconciliation work is best facilitated after the hurtfulness has ended and when there is good evidence that the hurtfulness is unlikely to reoccur.

Working with unresolved EIs in empty-chair work begins with the client's expression of a lot of secondary, reactive emotions, especially protest, blame, or complaint. For example, one client in the first session expressed both blame and resignation about her father, stating,

> He was a terrible father. He still is, just never there. I've given up on trying to have a relationship with him. He always told me I would amount to nothing. I have nothing to say to him now. I'll never forgive him for what he has done.

At the therapist's suggestion, in the third session, she imagined him in the empty chair, and this dialogue began with her expressing her blame and resignation. After two sessions of this type of dialogue, the client was able to contact her rage. She said, "I hate you. They should have castrated you in the concentration camp. You shouldn't have been allowed to have children." After this acknowledgment and expression of her rage and after grieving the loss of the father she never had, she began in the dialogue to soften toward him, acknowledging his difficulties in his life and his inabilities, and she went on to forgive him and have a closer relationship with him in reality.

Empty-chair work is based on the principle that you have to arrive at a place before you can leave it. Not only are significant feelings and unmet needs identified, experienced as valid, and voiced such that the emotions are symbolized and the action tendencies are completed (Perls et al., 1951) but also new feelings that change the old feelings are activated and reorganized. When hurtful others are no longer available to be spoken to or have distanced themselves from the client and made it clear that they are unwilling to hear what their past behavior has done to the client, the client can still be helped by engaging in a dialogue with the imagined other, as if that other person were in the therapy room, sitting in an empty chair. The painful emotions and unmet needs are expressed to the imagined other in the expectation that this will lead to a new way of experiencing the self. Sometimes, once the client acknowledges the underlying shame of violation or sadness of loss, it is as if the other (i.e., the internal representation of the other) can hear what the client needs to say and recognizes, and is responsive to, the legitimacy of the client's feelings and needs in regard to the hurtful experience. Then compassion and comfort transform the hurt and shame.

Even if the hurtful other is imagined as unable or unwilling to acknowledge or accept responsibility for the harm done, mobilizing and asserting the unmet needs and acknowledging the pain of what happened produces a new way of being and helps the client make sense of what happened, sorting out what each person was responsible for and grieving over what was lost and can never be recovered. A virtual reality is created in which memories are activated and can be reconsolidated with new input so that one's experience of the past changes. This is likely to free the client to let go of the negative, painful emotions and to relinquish the hope that things can be put right with the hurtful other, which in turn will enable clients to step back from the relationship (whether remembered or currently ongoing), recognize the legitimacy of their need, and begin to explore which of their other meaningful relationships or projects might meet their needs and engender hope for the future.

One client who had discovered the body of her mother, who had died by suicide, had horrifying memories whenever she thought of her mother. Her memory was filled with that terrible picture of her mother as she had found her. Whenever she thought of her mother, it was this image that came to mind. It left her feeling cold and clammy, with awful feelings of fear and empty abandonment. After working through her anger, shame, and sadness, and after finally empathizing with and forgiving her mother, she talked about being able to transform this awful memory with previous happy memories of her mother. These memories, by contrast, left her feeling warm and cozy. She reported later that when she thought of her mother, it was this warm, loving memory that she now accessed. Ultimately, a full restructuring of emotion memory occurred, and she thought of her mother as the loving mother she had known before the suicide, and she had good warm feelings whenever she thought of her.

New emotion memories form help change narratives. No important story is significant without emotion, and no emotions take place outside the context of a story. The stories people tell to make sense of their experience and to construct their identities are to a significant degree dependent on the variety of emotion memories that are available to them. By changing their memories, or the accessibility of different memories, people change the stories of their lives and their identities. Thus, the client's access to positive memories of her mother and a new lived experience in the session now supported a view in which she saw her mother as loving and caring rather than as recklessly abandoning her, as she had previously seen her.

## RESOLVING EMOTIONAL INJURY

Our research has demonstrated that there are two distinct forms of resolution (Greenberg & Malcolm, 2002). The first form involves a process of client self-validation and self-assertion, which permits the client to step back from the attachment bond to find the strength to hold the other accountable for harm done. It is commonly the form of resolution sought by individuals who have been victims of traumatic abuse or violence at some time in the past when they were too vulnerable or too dependent on the hurtful other to prevent the hurtfulness successfully. It is also likely to be a safer, more appropriate form of resolution for clients who are dealing with the pain of being in a current ongoing relationship with someone (e.g., a parent, a spouse) who was hurtful in the past and either denies their hurtfulness or acknowledges what happened but insists that they were not responsible for the client's suffering (often by blaming the client or some feature of the situation they see as having caused them to behave hurtfully).

The second form of resolution involves working toward a new view of the hurtful other such that the client comes to understand what may have motivated the other person's behavior and, without minimizing or dismissing the hurtfulness, also possibly comes to see the other as forgivable. This becomes possible because, in the process of enacting self and other in the empty-chair dialogue, the client can imagine and believe that if the hurtful other fully grasped and understood the pain and suffering the client had experienced, she or he would take responsibility for the harm done, would be remorseful, and would be willing to participate in the process of repairing the attachment bond and making changes that would make the relationship safe and trustworthy. Wanting to find a way to understand and forgive the hurtful other is usually motivated by the desire to come to terms with hurtfulness that is no longer being inflicted within a current ongoing relationship or by the desire to retrieve a sense of psychological attachment to someone the client cares about but has been separated from (by here-and-now distance or by the death of the hurtful other).

Regardless of the type of resolution attained—holding the other accountable or understanding and forgiving the other—assisting clients to imagine the hurtful other in the empty chair and facilitating a dialogue with the imagined other serve to bring alive clients' representation of the other in ways that create opportunities for clients to make changes in how they experience themselves and the other. Changes in how clients experience themselves could include a shift from weak and vulnerable to strong enough to take care of themselves and cope with the suffering that derived from the hurtfulness or enraged impotence to a grounded and self-respecting assertion of boundaries. With shifts like these, clients are helped to experience themselves as free to choose how best to respond to the other and as capable of taking responsibility for those choices, independent of what the other does. Or clients may shift from feeling lonely and unloved to feeling cared for and comforted.

As clients' experiences of themselves shift and become more adaptive, their view of the hurtful other will also shift. For example, a person who as a child might have believed a harshly critical parent's assertions that he was only pointing out flaws and shortcomings because he loved the child and wanted her to do well might as an adult client come to understand that the parent was unable or unwilling to value the client in her own right and was therefore truly insensitive and invalidating. A shift like this could enable the client to set about the work of differentiating her goals from the parent's goals for her. This frees the client to pursue the goals she sets for herself for the satisfaction of enjoying her achievements instead of trying to live up to her parent's expectations in hopes that this will somehow satisfy the parent and make him willing to acknowledge and affirm the client's effort and abilities. Or the client may come to understand that it was not that the parent was not loving but rather was overwhelmed or so wounded that he was unable to express the love that was felt or that what felt like control or intrusion came from parental anxiety and protectiveness.

## WHEN EMPTY-CHAIR WORK IS INADVISABLE

Before we move into a description of the therapist and client tasks involved in successful empty-chair work, note that empty-chair work could be unwise and possibly harmful when the unresolved experience was severely traumatizing and there is a risk of retraumatization or when the client has a recent history of behaviors that are self-harming (e.g., self-mutilation, suicide attempts) and/or other harming (e.g., aggressive and violent acting-out behaviors, impulsive risk taking that puts others in danger). When such behaviors have become part of the way the client responds to intense distress or arousal, it is strongly recommended that the therapist use less evocative interventions, initially at the very least delaying introduction of interventions such as an empty-chair dialogue until after a particularly strong therapeutic relationship is well established and a safe place that the client can go to internally has been established as a resource. Establishing sufficient internal and external support to face an imagined hurtful other is essential before introducing empty-chair dialogue.

Trauma-based empty-chair work is typically more intense than the unfinished business related to neglect or poor parenting. In trauma-based injury, the person is fragile and experiences unwanted memories and debilitating emotional pain. To promote enduring change, it is important to deal with the dysregulated emotion. People with this type of problem, however, are often ambivalent about whether they want to return to face the source of the trauma or engage in an empty-chair dialogue. On the one hand, they present the issue in an attempt to rid themselves of the intrusive memories, but on the other hand, there is significant pain that threatens to retraumatize the person. As a result, the empty-chair work should only be suggested when safety has been established and the clients feel ready to "face" their abusers (Paivio & Pascual-Leone, 2010).

## CONDUCTING FORGIVENESS-ORIENTED EMOTION-FOCUSED THERAPY

What follows can be thought of as a road map for the steps of forgiveness-oriented EFT. The steps are laid out in the following five phases, all embedded in a person-centered relationship: creation of an alliance, evocation and exploration, interruption, empowerment and letting go or forgiving, and termination. In describing the flow of key sessions that move each phase forward, we provide our clinical insights in the form of instructions and suggestions for professionals who intend to incorporate this therapy into their practice.

Empty-chair work is not a means for hurrying clients toward a therapist's outcome goals. Rather, it relies on a person-centered relational stance of empathy, acceptance, and genuineness on the part of the therapist. Likewise, a person-centered relational stance is characterized by genuine empathic positive regard that is typically communicated to the client by way of the therapist's gentle and caring tone of voice. EFT therapists establish safe and validating relationships by being authentically present as caring people who are able and willing to hear and fully appreciate the client's whole story. Therapists convey their ability to do this by being nonpossessively welcoming, empathically attuned, and skillfully attentive to the client's moment-by-moment experience as clients recount their stories. They accept what the clients say without judging or challenging the truth of what happened, ready to reflect back the emotional essence of what clients have been describing when they pause to see how the therapist is receiving their story.

This experience of being empathically and respectfully listened to and understood shows clients that the therapist is prepared to provide the emotional safety net they need in order to risk paying attention to their bodily felt emotions as they reenter and reprocesses the full depth and magnitude of the hurtful events involved in the EI, aspects of what happened that have been excised from clients' initial accounts because those parts of the experience have evoked intolerable responses either from other people or from the clients themselves. The more significant the unresolved experience has been in forming the client's view of her- or himself and of the hurtful other, the longer and slower the process is likely to be. Client and therapist will have to work together to confront and address experiential obstacles and impasses, often going over the same material several times before a fundamental shift occurs in the client's self-organization and perceptions of the hurtful other.

The therapist has to demonstrate that she or he knows and accepts clients' expertise about their experience and, when the time is right, has to explain that the expertise the therapist brings is in the way she or he helps clients work with their experience. Clients have to come to know that their therapist has the skill and is willing to collaborate, working alongside them to identify and reach for their goals of recovery, and that they do not have to concern themselves with externally set objectives that do not fit their experience of what it means to make peace with the past. It is appropriate, however, for the therapist to briefly describe empty-chair work as a possible way of working with the unresolved hurt the first time the client describes such hurts.

### Phase I: Creating an Alliance

The first phase of treatment, which unfolds over the first two to three sessions, involves creating a safe relationship and developing a working alliance. In this stage, while getting acquainted with clients, the therapist hears the narrative of the injury that brought the clients to therapy and empathically understands why they are coming to therapy at this time. It can be safely assumed that if clients are seeking therapy because they have been struggling for a long time to make sense of and recover from a deeply hurtful EI, the therapist will be meeting someone who is experiencing chronic, maladaptive unforgiveness of the sort described in the first chapters. A bond is established with the client by empathically responding to and validating the client's pain and emotional experience of the interpersonal injury. This stage also entails helping clients to articulate and clarify the most problematic aspects of the injury.

In all likelihood, clients may not have told the story of their EI to anyone, or if they have, they have become used to family and friends doing one of two things: either withdrawing from them and signaling that they do not want to hear the story again or energetically moving in and offering clients advice about how to get over the hurt and how they should get on with their lives. Clients come to therapy hoping that things will be different when they recount their story to someone trained to listen and help. At the same time, they will be protecting themselves against the probability of disappointment, ready to resent and be discouraged by the therapist's failure to understand how hard they have been working to get over what has happened to them. This being the case, the first crucial task an EFT therapist must focus on is establishing a hopeful and positive alliance based on a safe and validating relationship that soothes some of the pain of trying but not being able to get over the hurt. All the debates and controversies about forgiveness discussed in earlier chapters may play a role in and can be essential to establishing a good working alliance in a therapy of EI; that is why therapists should have already thought about their views of forgiveness and be able to dialogue about it respectfully.

## Session 1

Begin by introducing yourself and, if appropriate, say that you know from the assessment process (or perhaps a brief telephone intake interview) that the client has an EI or unresolved feelings toward Person X, but you would like to hear more about it and understand how he or she feels about it now or whether there is something else he or she would rather start with. Work to define the injury, at least in part, in this session and the nature of the current relationship with the offending person. Make sure you respond to the pain or emotional experience of the injury. In this and the next session, gather any historical information you deem relevant to help contextualize the injury and the person, such as family relations and previous and current relationships. It may be that the person does not see the unresolved issue with Person X as the focus of therapy (i.e., they may be aware that it is part of their personal history, but they may be seeking therapy to address another issue). If this is the case, the therapist will have to work collaboratively with the client to get an agreement on the focus of the therapy and discuss how the suffering inherent in unforgiveness may be interfering with his or her well-being. In other words, the therapist will have to consider how and where working to resolve the EI fits within the conceptualization of this therapy (Goldman & Greenberg, 2015).

By the end of the session, provide a rationale along the following lines:

> I'd like to say a little about what we will do here. First, I see our relationship as an important part of the treatment that will help you feel comfortable and safe

> enough to deal with the injury. So, if at any time you start to feel uncomfortable with me or what we do, it is important to let me know so we can address what is making you feel too uncomfortable.
>
> What we will do is first try and clearly define what about the injury has made it so hard to resolve, as we have already begun to do today. Then we will attempt to deal with your unresolved feelings about the injury. Many core feelings give us information about what is important to us, so we will work to become aware of core feelings and what it is you need to move on. [Possibly say something such as, "We will need to acknowledge the anger and face the shame and pain and other feelings and understand how the injury has affected your view of self, other, and the world."] We will look at what stops you from moving on and find ways to overcome this so that you can. This will involve us both talking together and exploring your experience as we have been, and at some time, when you seem ready, I will probably suggest we try some dialoguing with the imagined other or try some other form of intervention to help you deal with your unresolved feelings.

At the end of the first session suggest that starting a diary may be helpful as homework between sessions. Ask clients to start keeping a diary of what they are feeling toward the other. The diary helps clients process their feelings by writing about them (Pennebaker, 1995) and also helps them track their change. Guide clients to write about their feelings, especially those regarding their injury. Suggest they may start the diary by clarifying the nature of the injury. Ask them also to write in their diary any time they have strong feelings toward their partner or about the injury and to try to name specifically the feeling in the diary. In addition, suggest they may write about what happened in the session to affect their feelings toward the other.

### Session 2

Empathic work to consolidate the bond, plus exploration of the nature of the injury, continues. The therapist asks about the diary homework but does not overstress that it must be done. If there is a clear marker of unfinished business with the injurer, with a readiness indicator (i.e., the person is experientially engaged and feeling what is being talked about), and it seems appropriate, you can introduce chair work in this session. Otherwise, begin chair work in the third session.

***Identifying Markers for Empty-Chair Dialogue.*** The signature marker of an unresolved EI is the current and recurrent experience of the distressing pain, anger, sadness, and vulnerability that clients feel every time they are reminded of what happened or think about the person who hurt them. As we have said, it is important in applying empty-chair dialogues to distinguish between *unfinished business* (UFB) and current interpersonal conflict. In UFB, material comes from the past. This differs from a current interpersonal difficulty in which the person is currently struggling with someone in their environment. In current interpersonal difficulty, if, for example, there is current spousal conflict about childrearing practices or ongoing physical abuse, the empty chair is not the intervention of choice. Here, if one wanted to use a chair dialogue, role-play or assertiveness training might help in promoting new ways of behaving in the interpersonal interaction. UFB differs in its purpose in that it is about unresolved past feelings, and the goal is not how to handle the person in the present but to resolve painful emotion. A key indication for empty-chair dialogue for UFB is whether there is a lot of interrupted emotion. There are, however, mixed situations in which a current interpersonal difficulty evokes UFB—for instance, a young adult client who is having some current difficulty with his mother, who he complains nags him about not keeping his room tidy or washing the dishes (current situation) but also experiences her behavior and attitude as evoking what has been happening since the death of his father when the client was 9 years old, (e.g., "Ever since he passed she has expected me to be her support"). He is in current interpersonal conflict but also has UFB.

***Beginning the Dialogue.*** When clients show that they are ready to work on their unresolved past hurts (by producing or reproducing verbal and expressive markers of the hurt), validate these feelings and begin to move the process toward setting up a dialogue. Ask the client to imagine the key other in the empty chair. At the beginning of this dialogue, ensure that the client is making contact with the imagined other. Evoking the sensed presence of the other, making sure the person is currently experiencing the imagined presence of someone or something in a direct and immediate way, is important in evoking the emotion schematic memory. If clients are having difficulty sensing the other, you may say, "Can you see the person here or sense them in some way?" or suggest, "You may want to close your eyes during imagery work." If the client cannot imagine the other in an emotionally provoking way, you might say, "Can you think of a time when he or she hurt you most?" If clients initially have a positive or nonaroused initial response to the other in the empty chair, ask them first to express this current feeling, and then focus on the unresolved feelings by saying, "So, now tell her how she wronged you."

Enacting the other person performing the hurtful behavior also is important in evoking the emotional reaction to the person. Have the client move to the chair where they imagined the other person sitting so that they can role-play the part of the other. Differentiate what the "other" did that was injurious by guiding the client to enact in the empty chair what the other did (e.g., ask what the other said or did specifically, and ask the client to do this; get the details of their "insults," "neglects," or "hurtful behaviors" toward the client). Enacting the significant other is not to promote a debate between self and other in the chairs but to arouse emotions. The goal of playing the other is to heighten the stimulus value of the other's behavior to in turn evoke the client's affective reaction to it. Once the client has portrayed the negative actions and attitudes of the other, the client's affective reaction to this becomes the focus. Ask the client to move to the self chair and enquire, "How do you react or what happens inside in response to [the person in the other chair]?" With your careful and attuned tracking and reflection, relevant feelings toward the other will emerge.

You might introduce a dialogue with, "Let's bring her in here and tell her this" or "I hear that you have a lot of lingering feelings toward her. Let's try something: Can you put her in the chair and tell her what you feel?" or "I'd like to try a helpful method to try to resolve these feelings." Once you have identified a marker and want to introduce empty-chair work, do not talk about the injury too much because this often reduces the emotional arousal level. Soon after you identify a marker, place a chair in front of the client and say, "Imagine her there; say this to her." If the injury was not traumatic, do not be overconcerned about getting historical background information about it. The client will provide the information in context if it is important.

It is important to evoke the client's feelings and tease apart the different causes of the injury. Have the client play the role of the other a number of times to evoke more feeling. Guide the person to enact what the other did and flesh it out. The memory begins to unpack slowly. Repeat this as many times as is necessary.

The more clearly the wrong is defined, the better (e.g., "Tell him what he did that hurt the most"). It can also help to have the client phrase the wrongdoing as an accusation or a charge. This begins the initial anger phase. The client usually starts with attacking anger (e.g., "You're a jerk") but then shifts to owned anger, such as "I'm angry at you for violating me" or "I resent you for that."

Help clients both make contact with their feelings and put these feelings in contact with the object of the feeling. There thus should be (a) an awareness of the feeling and (b) an expression of the feeling. If the client is too reluctant to face the other, do not force the client to do this. Rather, explore the reasons for not wanting to face the other. You can turn the chair away or put it far away at first (progressive approximation to contact with the other) or identify and explore the blocks to contact.

Do not set the expectation of positive feelings toward the other too early in therapy (if at all) because you could mistakenly foster the idea that negative emotion has no place in the experience of the forgiving person. This is particularly true in those instances in which abuse is the focus. Such expectations would short-circuit the healthy adaptive process of being in touch with feelings of anger and resentment and can put the client at risk of future harm not only regarding the original offender but also potential future relationships of a similar kind.

***Ways of Engaging the "Other."*** It is important to distinguish between different ways in which one can work with the other in the empty chair, only one of which is UFB. In UFB work, the "other" in the empty chair should be the negative other engaging in giving their negative message. Working with the introjected other in split work (i.e., in a two-chair dialogue between a critical voice and an experiencing self) differs from UFB work with the other. Split work involves a different process (see Greenberg, Rice, & Elliott, 1993). Sometimes the distinction is fuzzy, and you do not have to know definitely which it is to start because it will be clarified as you work.

The other is an *introject* when there is no specific episodic memory of the other engaging in the action, but rather the person has a generic memory and has internalized the function of the other as part of the self—that is, having internalized expectations such as "you're only valuable if you're a success." This statement will appear in the form of a "should," and it is not emotion memory of shame or longing, or its interruption, that is central in the distress. In working with the introject in a split, you often have to get at the "should" in the form of the other because this is how it is experienced most powerfully and gets the strongest emotional reaction. In UFB, it is more a case of the client having unresolved feelings and specific memories (e.g., "I'm carrying this feeling toward you"), whereas, in a split, it is the other's voice saying, "You're not good enough" that has been internalized and is most problematic. In splits, it is as though the clients have their parents in their head as part of them. So, splits involve being colonized by the other, whereas in UFB, it is the painful emotional memories and the unresolved sadness, anger, and so forth, that are troubling, and the person is pained by actual experiences that led to EIs to attachment and identity. As we have said, splits and UFB often are intertwined, but one aspect is generally more salient than the other.

Splits also may occur in UFB work in a variety of ways—for example, when the client experiences internalized shame. If the other was contemptuous and sent messages such as "Get away from me; you're disgusting," this is now internalized, and a negative attitude and feeling toward the self are formed. Resolving this involves working with the introjected other, and resolving the self-split sometimes helps resolve the UFB. The reverse is also true: Resolving the UFB resolves the self-split. Another type of intervention involving another person in the empty chair that is not UFB but a split involves working with the "other" as a projection (i.e., clients' constructions of reality or attributions to the other based on their hypersensitivities). For example, a client may say in a distressed or indignant manner of a shop assistant or friend, "The way he said what he said really got to me." There is so much affective charge in this expression that it appears that what the other did had a unique meaning to the client as a function of the client's sensitivities, and it was this that got to the client. The other may have done something minor, but the strength of the reaction probably comes from the client, and this is not the same as the view that "my father abandoned me," which evokes unresolved painful memories. In the former instance, the other is more of a projection of some internal voice onto the other, rather than the other being an object of unresolved anger or hurt. So, it also is important to distinguish UFB from working on aspects of the self projected onto others.

***Who Takes the Lead?*** An important issue, especially in early sessions in working with UFB, is managing what we can call the *dance of initiative*. The goal is for the balance of initiative to be weighted in favor of the client leading and you following—that is, for you not to take too much initiative too early by leading too much; rather, you want the person to become engaged in a self-motivated experiential process. If the client sits back expectantly with an attitude of "Okay, now 'treat' me or tell me what to do," you want the client to understand that the task is to coexplore his or her issues. The initial task is to get the client engaged in an experiential process. Do not use the intervention because it seems as if you are expected by the client to "do something" to solve the problem or because the client seems disengaged. If the client is conceptual, it is better to use empathic exploration or a focusing intervention to try to deepen the process first. Often empathy or focusing interventions will help develop an experientially based focus for the treatment.

However, you also do not want the client taking too much initiative, often in the form of external storytelling, which prevents access to inner experience. If the client takes all the initiative and you are left in a passive role, you have to work to regain a balance of initiative for your presence to be felt. If clients are fully directing the process, they probably will get stuck as they have in the past. Therapy has to involve a true coconstruction, and both partners have to contribute to achieve a resolution.

For Session 2, again ask clients to keep a diary of what they are feeling toward the other and of what happened in the session to affect this. Inquire somewhere in each session, often near the beginning of the session, if anything of interest came up in the diary. But again, do not make the homework the focus of the session or a chore the client must do.

## Phase II: Evocation and Exploration

The major task in this phase is arousal and exploration of emotions and needs. This phase involves acknowledging, experiencing, and expressing the anger, sadness, pain, and other distressing feelings associated with the EI. There will continue to be an empathic focus in all sessions, but at least each alternate session in this phase will contain a chair dialogue, if possible. The key inner experience that has to be worked on is the resolution of what has remained unfinished about the injury.

### Session 3

This is the session in which empty-chair dialogue is hopefully introduced if it has not already been used. It is important to try to get the client engaged in the dialogue in this session. The therapist evokes the other and makes sure contact is established. Contact evokes experience by forming a figure. It heightens the stimulus, and this evokes an emotional reaction. One client remarked that she was aware of regulating the intensity of "contact" with the imagined other as a means of managing her affect. Given this, therapists should be aware of fluctuations in the quality of the sensed presence of the other and the affects associated with this and intervene to maintain contact and arousal.

As mentioned previously, when clients talk about unresolved past EIs, they typically first express a "fused" combination of hurt and resentment. The outrage or protest against the unfairness of what happened comes out as a complaint. A sense of defeated resignation and hopelessness are possible as well. The client's feelings are currently felt, but they are expressed in the form of intellectualized or inhibited primary emotions or constricted secondary, reactive emotions such as hopelessness rather than full, uninterrupted expressions of primary adaptive emotion. For example, clients may express resentment through gritted teeth instead of a grounded, self-respecting anger, or they may talk about what happened with a hopeless longing that the past be undone instead of fully expressing the grief they feel about the innocent trust and unquestioned sense of safety that is now irreparably gone from the relationship as a consequence of the injury. Such interruptions or restrictions may signal an effort to minimize or stop the overwhelming intensity of feelings about which the client is afraid of losing control. They may also signal that the clients are clamping down on their feelings because others have hurtfully communicated that they do not want to hear the distress anymore and think they should stop focusing on what happened so they can get on with their lives.

***Encouraging Expression of Primary Emotions.*** Throughout the dialogue, the therapist focuses on encouraging the expression of clients' concrete experience and emotions toward the other in the empty chair. Once the client's experience of the other has been sufficiently evoked, the goal of the dialogue is to move beyond these initial reactions into differentiating underlying feelings and meanings and encouraging the expression of primary emotional states. For example, a complaint must always be separated into its more fundamental components of anger and sadness and be experienced, symbolized, and expressed separately. The typical secondary emotions expressed in the empty-chair work of hopelessness, resignation, depression, and anxiety are often expressed in an outer-directed manner and a blaming tone. The therapist acknowledges and helps clients work through these secondary emotions.

The aim is to encourage the direct expression of a primary emotion such as "I resent you" or "I missed having you around," rather than "You were a bastard" or "Why did you neglect me?" Primary emotions are often first experienced and expressed in a jumbled manner, all mixed together. For example, the fused anger and sadness of complaint often come out in question form: "Why couldn't you be more . . . ?" or "Why did you . . . ? I just want to know why." It may take two or three sessions to help clients move beyond secondary reactions to expressing their primary sadness, anger, fear, and shame to the imagined other. Phase II cannot progress to Phase III unless this happens. In cases of abuse, combinations of maladaptive fear, shame, and disgust have to be accessed, validated, and reprocessed to the point where the client is later able to access primary adaptive anger and sadness (Greenberg, 2002), and this will likely take longer.

In working with anger, it is necessary to distinguish between secondary and primary anger. *Primary anger*, or anger in response to violation, is essential and must be validated and its expression encouraged. In UFB, this anger may have been disavowed because it was unsafe to express it in the original relationship. In not being able to access primary anger, people lose access to healthy resources that can promote adaptive behavior. Thus, the expression of anger and standing up to the other by saying, for example, "I am angry at you for hurting me like that—even though you were sick, I did not deserve to be treated like that" is empowering and healing. To distinguish primary anger from secondary anger, therapists use the criteria that adaptive anger is in response to violation; it involves an assertion of self and is empowering. In contrast, *secondary anger* has a more blustery, destructive quality to it, and it serves to push the other away or obscures the expression of more vulnerable emotion. Its expression does not bring relief or promote the working through of experience.

Once emotions have been differentiated and interruptions dissolved, the emotional arousal that is a necessary precondition for resolution of the injury emerges. Emotional arousal has been found to be an important precursor of the next step toward resolution, a change in view of the other. Without arousal, this step is far less probable (Greenberg & Malcolm, 2002). In working with emotions at this stage, therapists have to know that once primary emotions are fully and freely expressed, they move quickly. Anger and sadness tend to follow each other in sequence and are circularly related in diminishing spirals. Finally, when primary sadness is fully expressed, primary adaptive anger emerges rapidly and boundaries are created. Conversely, the full expression of adaptive anger allows clients to acknowledge the pain of losses and betrayal and fully grieve for what they missed.

***Moving From Past to Present.*** The therapist at all times brings the process back to present feelings with "I feel" statements (e.g., "What are you feeling now?"). Ask, "What do you feel as you say this? Tell her." Change "I was" or "I felt" statements focused on the past to "I am" or "I feel" statements centered in the present. The purpose of this is to help people learn to tolerate their painful emotions, to accept and stay with their emotions rather than rushing too quickly into change. This involves approaching the emotion, being able to focus attention on it, and experiencing the emotion rather than avoiding it. Tolerance also may occur through the process of getting an observer's perspective on an emotion one is currently feeling, somewhat like standing a little distance outside the emotion to have what may be likened to a metarelationship with the emotion (an attentional allocation shift is required). The person has to have the emotion rather the emotion having the person. This helps create a working distance from the emotion and enables the person to symbolize the emotion rather than be overwhelmed by it, which are key indicators of productive emotional processing (Auszra, Greenberg, & Herrmann, 2013). It is useful to note that worrying is often a way of avoiding emotion and is helped by accepting the underlying emotion.

Homework related to the chair work may be assigned after this session. At this early stage, homework will usually be of an awareness nature, to highlight any discoveries already made in the session—for example, "Become aware of this feeling of anger whenever you see him during the week" or "Become aware of how your anger collapses into sadness." Ask clients to note how they experienced their emotions during the week and what they did to stop themselves from feeling emotion, and be aware of attempts to regulate problematic emotional experience and what happens when they do this. Connect this to the emotions that came up or did not come up in the session. These observations may be part of the ongoing diary of feelings toward the other and of what happened in the session to affect this. If the person is cut off from feelings, offer a simple structure for the diary writing. For example, ask them once a day to write down at least three emotions they felt that day. From there, they can expand, describing what the situation was when they felt the emotion, what happened in their bodies, and what they wanted to do.

### Session 4

Start by checking where the person is now and how the week was. Then ask them about how they felt after the empty-chair dialogue in the last session. It now is a matter of clinical judgment whether to use another dialogue. If you do not, the next session should use a dialogue. Inquire about the diary. This session will deepen the exploration of the injury and the context and also look for possible past links to the present injury. If the injury is with a recent relationship, such as a spouse, does this mirror any earlier relationships? Does the injury relate to relationships with parents, an earlier marriage, a past loss? This exploration of links to the past may not take place specifically in this session but is part of a general gathering of information about the narrative context that will take place in the first half of the treatment.

Dialogue with an injuring spouse or boss often reverts to dialogue with parents or other attachment figures. Listen carefully, and if a past scene comes up, guide the client into the scene and go for what is most salient. During guided visualization or imaginal confrontation, when you ask a client to go back to the original scene, the client can either go back with the current feeling and meaning (I'm angry) or contact what it was like then (I'm afraid or lonely). When putting the other in the chair, you can ask the client "What comes up now? What do you want to say?" or "What was it like for you? Be the little boy—what do you feel as the little boy?"

***Differentiating Among Forms of Anger.*** Sometimes the anger a client expresses is instrumental in quality, as in the following statement: "I deserve it because I've always been a good girl, so give it to me!" This type of anger often is tied to low self-esteem. Instrumental anger is like that of a spoilt child, as opposed to primary adaptive anger, which is part of the deeper grieving process involving both the sadness of losing something important and anger at one's needs or goals being thwarted (e.g., "I'm angry that you are not the father I wanted you to be"). If anger and sadness are both present, be sure once they are differentiated, to keep them separate and distinct as much as possible. They often occur together because clients are angry at not getting what they wanted and sad at what they are not getting. As we have seen, fused anger and sadness leave people stuck in disempowered hurt that is expressed as complaints.

Often, anger can be secondary. It can be destructive or rejecting anger, or anger can be based on the motivation of payback to get even. Secondary forms of anger like these mask core powerlessness or hopelessness or helplessness, as in, "What's the point of talking?" Powerless anger is a difficult phenomenon: It is anger that has nowhere to go. There is often a lot of frustration at anger that has no impact. Therapists can reflect how bad it feels to have all this anger and to feel it can have no impact. When the question of how to overcome the anger arises for someone who is stuck in anger that has no impact—"I don't want to feel this anger. How do I stop?"—an important new place has been reached. The client realizes this anger is useless and potentially destructive to the self. Keep this question alive, and ponder it together.

Sometimes it is difficult for the client to stay with either emotion—for example, a client oscillates too quickly between anger and sadness, and when the client starts to get angry, she collapses immediately into sadness; when she gets sad, she flips into anger before elaborating on the sadness. If she is not able to stay and differentiate her feelings after you attempt to help her do so, then follow the oscillation of anger and sadness and bring the oscillation to her awareness. Make the oscillation that is occurring automatically deliberate to deautomatize it.

In working through EIs in abusive relationships, anger has to be expressed to the abusive other. Often, however, it is better not to express sadness to the abusive other. Each emotion has to find its appropriate object, so sadness may have to be expressed to the therapist or to someone else in the person's life, such as a protective other, rather than expressing it to the abusive other.

In situations of past abuse and terrorization, the core fear felt in the original situations, which often remains coded at a body level, has to be countered with adaptive anger. As long as the anger remains buried beneath the fear, the person can protest forever but will not improve and will continue to feel helpless. What is needed for transformation is a mobilization of the protective adaptive anger that could not be expressed in the original situation. This often is best expressed as an embodied action by hitting, screaming, or extending the arms forward to allow the pushing away to be experienced at a body level.

People who have been trapped in traumatic experiences have been unable to perform any of the actions they needed to save themselves. What is needed in these cases is the promotion of the action tendencies and the ultimate feeling of triumph over oppression. They have to experience themselves as able to vanquish the perpetrator to overcome the feeling of being vanquished. The anger has to be directed outward rather than toward the self and to be differentiated from the other emotions of sadness and shame and pain, so it is clearly felt and the action tendency to set a boundary felt. In addition, the anger has to be expressed assertively with a full sense of agency and ownership rather than an as a victim, at a level of intensity appropriate to the situation. Finally, there needs to be some exploration, symbolization, and elaboration of the meaning embodied in the anger.

***Managing Expressions of Sadness and Anger.*** The following are sample steps in a dialogue to convey a prototypic sequence of expressing sadness and anger:

1. Establish contact. Ask clients to imagine the other and to express what they feel to the other.
2. Access the feeling. Ask the client, "What do you feel in your body?" The client might respond, "I feel sad." Help clients "sink into" this experience by asking them where in their body they feel this and inviting them to stay with the feeling. The client might respond, "I feel it in my chest, here, and I feel so alone." Ask, "What did you miss?" This intervention helps unpack sadness with a suggestion such as, "Tell the other what it's like, what you missed." Validate the hurt (even if you hear subdominant anger).
3. Access need in the feeling.

   **THERAPIST:** Tell him what you needed.

   **CLIENT:** I needed you to tell me you loved me.

4. Once the need has been expressed, anger often emerges. You may say, "Tell him what you resent." Anger and sadness can be reversed in these steps.

This type of sequence will lead eventually to a new view of the self and other. Access to the need and feeling entitled to the need changes the person's sense of self from unworthy to worthy. Expressing the need assertively to the empty chair creates a sense of agency, which transforms the previous more passive victimized experience into a more active one. Often, at the heart of the injury is the fact that the trusted other either insensitively failed to recognize the hurt person's needs, or hurtfully withheld what he or she needed in the relationship. Often there is a change in view of the other that allows the need to be responded to in this virtual reality, in the therapy situation. If, however, the imagined other is nonresponsive, people have to let go of wanting what they cannot get.

At this stage it is necessary to start focusing on what type of individual processing style may be preventing the person from accessing feelings. Is the person stuck in a complaint with fused anger and sadness? Is the person predominantly conceptual, unable to focus inward with consequent low depth of experiencing? Does the person speak in an external or limited voice, and is he or she unable to turn inward and attain a focused vocal quality? Is the person contracting muscles or tightening the chest or fists? Interventions are adjusted to match processing styles. If inner focus is low, use focusing interventions. If there is constriction, work with the blocking and avoidance process.

### Session 5

If a dialogue was not used in the previous session, it is important to do so now. The goal now is to move forward to the arousal of more intense emotion and to encounter any interruptive processes that block this expression. This will be the continued focus of the treatment. When a marker emerges in the session, implement the dialogue. If by 20 minutes into a session the UFB has not become a focus, you should introduce it, unless what you are currently doing seems more important. You might inquire into how clients are doing with their injury with the other or with their hurt or anger and attempt to steer them toward, focusing on what is unfinished. The work is now focused on getting the primary emotions aroused and getting to the unmet need. This work and dealing with the interruptive processes will probably occupy the next five sessions.

***Evocation Interventions.*** When a client is enacting the other in the empty chair, to get a sense of the impact of the other on the self, ask, "What was the message she gave you? What did her face or voice say?" Too much concern with the content of the client's narrative takes the therapist away from the affective tone. Stay attuned to the emotional tone that is evident in the discourse. Listen to its music. Check in with clients to determine whether they are "feeling" what they are saying. Ask, "As you say this what do you feel?"

As a basic style, we recommend following a reflection with a suggestion. For example, the therapist might respond to the self chair, first reflecting "Feeling really hesitant" reflection and follow this with a suggestion, "Tell her again, 'I'm hesitant to say this'" direction. Remember that the therapist's tone of voice used in empathic attunement is important. However, it is not always gentle. It must match the client's emotion. If anger is the emotion being highlighted, the attuned voice should have an intensity to it, especially when giving directions for the expression of anger, such as "Tell her, 'I resent . . .' with some volume and emphasis."

If the intensity of affect or experiencing wanes in the self chair, the client should take the part of the other briefly to restimulate the affect. Spend time enacting the negative other, highlighting what is negative, so it becomes clearer what the insult, injury, or offense is. Get to the nature or the quality by which the client felt betrayed by observing his or her particular manner. It may not be what was said that hurt so much but how it was said. For example, if it seems like it is being said with "disdain" or "a scolding tone," you might reflect that to the client and then ask him or her to do some more of it, or you may ask, "What's the core meaning of what the other did to you that so upset you?" Get at the metamessage delivered by the other. Use the other as a stimulator of affect, not as a debater.

It may also be sufficient merely to ask the client in the self chair what the other looks like now—facial expression, body posture—to reevoke the emotion. Ask, "What does his face look like now? What would he say to that?" Pay attention to what appears most alive to the client at the present moment and follow and heighten that.

Generally, "why" questions do not deepen experience. "How" and "what" questions are better. Analyze how this person is expressing him- or herself, then turn the process into content. The manner of expression is what is important, not the content. Thus ask, "As you're doing this, how are you saying it?" or "What are you expressing in your manner?" Pay attention to body language. How the person delivers the message shifts toward being the message—for example, if the style or manner of the client is contempt, direct him or her to tell the other "I feel contempt for you." An advantage of using chair dialogue is that it adds the expressive dimensions as it brings out "the how": timid or hostile. Track the emotional process, not the content. Notice present nonverbal expressions and feed them into the dialogue—for example, if a client's hand has gone up as a shield, it may be a bodily sign that perhaps there is a need for protection from the other (e.g., "I see you put your hand up to cover yourself, as if you need protection? Tell him that").

Interventions should elicit a present-tense stance. As noted earlier, do not ask questions in the past tense; instead, bring the client into the present to evoke feeling now. Link the content or story with the feeling at the moment, focusing on the latter—for example, "How are you feeling now as you tell this story?" "What's happening in your body?" Then direct the client to express this to the other. It is true that all emotions are embedded in an important story; likewise, all important stories are based on significant emotions. However, people are more used to listening to and telling stories as manifestations of the emotion; we want to privilege the emotion over the story.

In working with the injury, validate the legitimacy of the feeling of being wronged with interventions such as, "Tell her, 'I was wronged . . . you violated my boundaries.'" Validate anger and intensify emotions by saying, "It's okay to feel anger." At the crescendo of the anger ask, "What did you need?" or "Is there something you want from the other to finish this?" It is important to get a sense of whether clients' statements such as "I need" or "I deserve" are grounded enough in heartfelt loss or empowered anger or feeling of legitimacy. If not, promote empowered anger or heartfelt grief.

When giving instructions to the client in the chair, try not to say "I want you to" because this implies you, the therapist, want something, and the client may be reluctant to oppose you if it does not fit. Rather, it is a collaborative process; use language such as "Let's try something" or "Try putting your father in the chair," but do not be too tentative when giving directions. However, be tentative when you are offering a conjecture about the client's experience.

Ask clients to be where they are not where they are not. If the client does not want to tell the other about his or her experience, of the affect associated with the injury, he or she should be encouraged to express the unwillingness to tell: "I don't want to tell you." However, when working on letting go of an unmet need, you have to heighten the loss. For example, with a client who has difficulty accepting that the other was "not there" for her and is unable to give up hoping for what will never be, say, "Tell the other what died that night for you. Tell her about the pain of facing up to the fact that she won't ever be available. Tell her how hard it is to give up the wish."

Help clients distinguish different between emotions: "What's the most important feeling right now? What's the most alive for you? What's the strongest?" Feed clients a sentence to help identify and express what is felt: "Can you say, 'I despise you' or 'I miss you?'" Treat this as an experiment—that is, "Try this and see what happens. Does it fit? What does it feel like?" Try to catch where the client is at with a word of correct intensity (e.g., *resent, angry, furious, hate*): "Tell him, 'I'm angry that you . . .' Tell him what you hate. Tell him what you resent." Say, "Puts words to the tears," "It really hurts," "I missed having a father who cared." To promote the making of distinctions in experience you can use a contrasting sentence—for example, try "I love you" and then "I hate you," or say "I won't" rather than "I can't," and then ask, "What do they each feel like?" To address guilt feelings over an expression of anger or hate toward a parent it is sometimes helpful to split the parent into the "good parent" and the "bad parent" and express the negative to the bad parent with the knowledge that that is not all there is. You also can combine feeling sentences to promote integration (e.g., "Say one thing you resent and one thing you appreciate about what you resent").

***Connecting and Boundary Setting Needs.*** Anger is often best symbolized by saying, "Tell him what you resent." The word *resent* carries a flavor of the past in a way that anger does not. When working with unexpressed anger, start with outward anger (e.g., "You're a jerk"), but shift to assertive anger (e.g., "I'm angry at you for violating me," "I resent you for that"). Moving to the need helps clients move from destructive anger to empowered anger. Note that anger is the "separating," "boundary setting" emotion, and its goal is to empower and legitimize.

Sadness, however, is the "connecting" emotion. Its goal is to receive comfort or withdraw to recuperate. With sadness, it is best to say, "Tell him what you missed or how you were hurt." You are looking for primary emotion to mobilize the need. Validate the hurt, even when the anger is there.

To get through the anger, it first must be accepted. You cannot leave a place till you arrive at it. Recognize that resignation often is the inability to be angry. Shame and fear may also arise. Anger is a major antidote for both of these emotions. In sadness, attention often is directed inward, whereas in anger expression is often directed outward. Expression to the other often is best promoted through graded experiments (building up to the expression of intense feelings using gradual steps). You can also pump up the expression by telling the client to say it again louder; sometimes you can override a block to expression by intensification (e.g., "Tell her I'm furious. . . . Tell her again"). Asking what clients need also can be used to heighten the feeling.

Note that expressing feelings, especially dramatically, sometimes can interfere with the experience of the feeling. So, after someone expresses sadness, focus the client inward (e.g., "How does that feel to weep?"). After expressing anger, ask, "What do you feel?" Encouraging intense expression often serves an interpersonal validation function rather than inducing catharsis. The idea is not to get rid of the anger or pain—rather, to legitimize it and its intensity.

***Learning From the Client's Perspective.*** Meaning making is important at the end of an intervention. Get the client's perspective on the meaning they are making of the experience they had in the empty-chair dialogue. This helps to consolidate session gains. However, it is important not to start with meaning making too early; instead, do this after the client has experienced emotional arousal. This emphasis on making meaning from aroused emotional experience is what distinguishes EFT from more purely interpretive and cognitive approaches.

It may also be important to talk about the therapeutic relationship (e.g., "How are you feeling with me [the therapist]? I'm not sure whether when I said that it felt diminishing?"). A balance of following and leading also is important. It is best to follow the client's experience and lead only when necessary. However, you should see yourself as a coach who offers guidance, not only as purely a follower. You can be half or one step ahead of your client but never too far ahead. Stay in the client's proximal zone of development. Always see whether the client can use what is offered, and use your client's response as feedback to recalibrate your next response. Be coexplorative; do not be too interpretive or project one's feelings onto the client. It is important to be accepting and nonjudgmental. Homework may continue as described in previous sessions.

## Phase III: Self-Interruptive Work

The third phase of therapy involves interventions at client markers of interruption, such as emotional constriction, resignation, or hopelessness. These interventions are aimed at turning the passive, automatic process of interruption into an active one. This phase, which is not independent of the evocative phase and often precedes it, aims to heighten clients' awareness of how they interrupt themselves and undo these interruptive processes so that emotions inhibiting resolution can be accessed and processed. Self-interruption is essentially giving oneself the instruction "Don't feel. Don't need." Interruption involves complex physiological, muscular, emotional, and cognitive processes that inhibit experience and expression.

A particularly helpful intervention for working with blocks to emotion is one in which we have clients enact the process of interruption in an imaginary dialogue between both sides of the personality (Elliott, Watson, Goldman, & Greenberg, 2004; Greenberg, Rice, & Elliott, 1993). This enactment of the interruption of emotion involves a slightly different use of the two-chair dialogue than the one for self-criticism. A *two-chair enactment* is implemented when the person begins to experience or express an emotion or associated need or action but is interrupted by a suppressing part of the person that attempts to prevent the expression or experience. In comparison to self-critical splits, markers of self-interruptive splits typically have a larger nonverbal, bodily aspect and are sometimes purely nonverbal, such as a headache or tightness in the chest, and may be completely automatic. The therapist's goals in self-interruptive work are both to heighten awareness of the interruptive process and help the client access and allow blocked or disavowed internal experience.

### Initial Elements of Sessions 6 to 8

Exploring and overcoming interruptive processes are important subgoals of a therapy of EI, and collaboration has to be established between therapist and client to do so and on the means by which it will be done. By definition, facing what is dreaded can be threatening. Collaboration to do this provides safety and minimizes the development of opposition, misalliances, or treatment impasses.

***Helping Clients Recognize Blocks.*** In a two-chair enactment, clients are encouraged to enact how they stop themselves from feeling, to verbalize the particular injunctions used, or exaggerate the muscular constrictions involved in the interruption (Greenberg, Rice, & Elliott, 1993; Greenberg & Watson, 2006). Eventually, this provokes a response from the suppressed aspect, often a rebellion against the suppression, and the experiencing self challenges the injunctions, restraining thoughts or muscular blocks, and the suppressed emotion bursts through the constrictions. This undoes the block.

As blocks to experience and expression emerge in empty-chair dialogues, therapists have to focus on them and help clients become aware of and experience how they interrupt their feelings or needs. Interventions have to explore the various ways clients block experience in the session. Blocks range from dissociation to stifling tears to deflecting. Helping people first become aware that they are blocking and then how they are blocking helps them become aware of their agency in the process of blocking their emotions. This, in the long run, helps them allow the emotional experience that is avoided.

In working with interruption, the therapist cannot know what is being suppressed but only that something is indeed being suppressed. Working with self-interruption has to be approached "from the outside in." This task requires three essential steps:

1. Bring the client's attention to the fact that she or he is interrupting or suppressing (i.e., by noting that the client looks away whenever she or he mentions certain things, such as changes the topic or smiles).
2. Turn the passive to active and the automatic to deliberate by inquiring and ascribing personal agency to the client (e.g., "How do you stop yourself or interrupt yourself?"). This is an awareness task and can be used to elaborate conscious experience and specify what the interrupters are (e.g., "What do you say to yourself?" "What do you do muscularly?" "How would you do it to me?").
3. Eventually, what is being suppressed becomes evident to both client and therapist.

   Examples of standard interventions to access blocks are, "How do you make yourself feel helpless?" or "How do you prevent yourself from feeling angry or sad?" If a client is interrupting anger or tears, ask the client to change chairs: "Stop her now. How do you do this? Stop her from being angry" or "How do you squeeze back her tears? Do it now".

Resignation and deadness are often the result of squashing and suppressing emotional arousal. "What's the use" often captures this feeling. "I don't care" is often an expression of cynical resignation in the face of UFB. A client may say, "He never gave me or never will give me what I want, so what's the use of feeling or needing it?" This is worked with as an interruptive process.

An example of work using two chairs for interruption is as follows:

**CLIENT:** I'm so angry at him (referring to imagined father in the empty chair).

**THERAPIST:** Tell him.

**CLIENT:** I couldn't do that. I just hold it all in.

**THERAPIST:** Come over here and stop him from being angry.

**CLIENT:** (Sitting in the chair that represents his father.) Who am I here?

**THERAPIST:** Be a part of yourself that stops him.

**CLIENT:** Well, my father just seems so superior, so powerful, I just retreat.

**THERAPIST:** Okay, as yourself, make yourself retreat. How do you do that? What does this voice inside you say?

**CLIENT:** It says, "Well, you have no legitimacy. Don't get angry." I get scared. It's not okay; it's dangerous.

**THERAPIST:** Make him scared. What do you say?

**CLIENT:** "Watch out. You won't be able to speak."

**THERAPIST:** Make him not able to speak.

**CLIENT:** "Well, you're stupid. You don't have what it takes. Also, you'll get too emotional and you'll cry, or you'll damage the relationship. So just retreat."

**THERAPIST:** Yeah, tell him this again.

**CLIENT:** "Retreat, just shrink away, disappear."

**THERAPIST:** Change chairs now. What do you say to that?

**CLIENT:** (In self chair) But I do feel like I have a valid point of view. And I just feel so angry.

**THERAPIST:** (Redirecting to the father) Put your father there; tell him, "I'm angry at you."

As shown in this example, after working on a self-interruption—for example, of resignation—once a client gets to the point of feeling more deserving and says, "I do deserve it; I didn't do anything wrong," the therapist now directs the newly accessed feelings and needs back toward the other.

It is essential to ensure that clients have sufficient internal support for making contact with emotions before the blocks are undone and emotions are evoked and experienced. Some clients become tense at the prospect of encountering their feelings. At these times, the therapist has to empathize with the fear and understand that the block is a protection and provide more support. On the one hand, more relational support in the form of validation and trust building is indicated. On the other hand, the building of internal supports by a slower approach to emotion, in small steps, helps clients deal with their anxiety. A type of graded exposure or desensitization process is most useful in helping clients to approach and tolerate their emotions. The therapist also helps clients mobilize internal support by suggesting, for example, that clients breathe, put their feet on the ground, and describe what they are experiencing to increase contact with sensory reality.

***Focusing on Hopelessness as a Self-Interruptive Process.*** Hopelessness or resignation often is a key self-interruptive process. When something is being suppressed, and this results in hopelessness, you have to identify the suppressing agent and find the underlying feeling or need being suppressed. Suppressing agents are either (a) fear producing or (b) sadness producing. When fear is at work, it says, "If you speak up, others will retaliate." In this fear-based interruptive split, one side is a catastrophizer or an agency that makes the person fear the consequences, and the other side is the feeling of being stuck or resigned. When sadness suppresses, it says, "It's no use; you will never get what you need" or "No one will be there to receive your sadness; nobody cares." Here, the therapist has to access the dysfunctional beliefs blocking expression and notice that the motivation driving these interruptions and beliefs is often protective.

A standard intervention to work with hopelessness or resignation is as follows: First, help the client symbolize the feeling of "What's the use?" in words. Then ask the person to change chairs and ask, "How could you make her feel it is no use? Make yourself give up. What do you say?" Alternatively, when faced with resignation about unmet needs, the therapist can empathize with the client's pain and explore further, saying, "Stay with this feeling. What is this like for you?" thereby eventually leading the client from resignation to disappointment to sadness, thus achieving a deeper grieving of the loss.

To identify the need or goal being blocked or thwarted, the therapist can ask, "How do you stop yourself from achieving your goal?" or "What is it that you'd really like?" This can provide motivation for moving ahead rather than simply providing protection. Note that a person must be experiencing hopelessness before one can get at the need and use it to get out of the hopelessness. Here you have to listen for nuances. When a bit of the need is implied, focus on it because it gives a sense of direction. Say, "Tell him what you need."

In working with hopelessness in contexts of relational closeness, the nature of the situation is relevant. In situations of the other distancing or rejecting, the situation may be hopeless. If the person recognizes this and then lets go of the goal of being close to the other, the feeling of hopelessness can be a primary adaptive emotion that leads to giving up the goal and grieving the loss when all is lost. Sometimes, however, it is more a case of losing resilience rather than the situation being hopeless. This hopelessness is more a function of self-disempowerment through interruption of anger and sadness than adaptive hopelessness. In other words, one's assertions have not been fully thwarted; rather, one has given up on trying to assert oneself. When it is this form of self-disempowered hopelessness, the therapist activates the agency in the personality that produces the stuckness and brings it into awareness and under deliberate control.

To use an interruptive intervention when working with hopelessness, you may have to step back from the client's hopeless state and reframe the situation. It is often difficult to ask, "How do you make yourself feel hopeless?" and it is better to say such things as "How do you keep yourself hoping (hanging on) after feeling disappointed?" "How do you keep the hope alive?" or "How do you make yourself need him exclusively?" or more fully, "I hear how hopeless you feel. I guess it's really hard hoping he will come through and always being disappointed, but I guess it's really difficult to give up hoping he will be responsive (or stop drinking, etc.)."

When it is a case of being truly hopeless, as in situations when there is anger but no hope of fairness or justice or when there is sadness or loss with no hope of reconnection, you have to help the client grieve the loss. When the person cannot accept that and deals with it with protest and stuckness, you have to get at the agency in the personality that produces the stuckness. There are two main aspects of this agency: (a) the emotional or motivational aspect, which involves hanging on to the unmet need and to the hope that it will be met; and (b) the cognitive interruptive process in the form of negative self-statements. To address the emotional or motivational aspect, it often is helpful to have the client while in the self chair express feeling stuck in ways that capture the paradox of hopeless hope and heighten awareness of the futility, such as "I won't give up trying to get from you what is impossible; I will keep trying to change you." To address the negative self-statements, as in a standard self-critical split, have the client voice them aloud: "Nobody has ever loved you; why should you get it now? You don't count. You'll never be good enough."

To intensify the hopeless feelings in the self chair, you also can ask the client to be the imagined frustrating other. This is not making "yourself" feel hopeless but heightening the hopelessness through the frustration of the need by the other. Then you help articulate and differentiate the hopeless feelings produced in the self to get at the yearning underlying the need. When it is truly hopeless, it often is best to get at the need with questions about what you missed or had wanted or what it was that you will never get. The client may say, "I missed feeling loved; you didn't love me, but I still needed you to." This gets to the sorrow and grief, to what it was like to need and to never be able to get what was needed. You have to go into the deep grieving underlying the hopelessness to resolve it. It is important to support entitlement to the needs, to promote self-assertion: the fact that it was okay to need and that the client deserved to have the needs met and to help the client find another source of need fulfillment.

***Validating Clients' Unmet Needs.*** Letting go often requires some separation of the need from the particular other in question. Therapists promote, allow, and validate the need but redirect it to alternative sources. Ask, "Who else could meet this need?" Ultimately, the client must accept that the need is okay and healthy and that she or he is deserving of it but that the particular relationship is inadequate to support the need.

Therapists help people feel entitled to their need, but this entitlement should be to their need being legitimate, not to the legitimacy of having the other person meet their need. The latter is an unproductive form of entitlement. Healthy entitlement is supported by clients' expressions being made through "I" statements. This helps in the taking of responsibility. "I deserved more" is better and emphasizes agency more than "Why did you do this to me?" which is more of a complaint. Once the person experiences "I deserve," the person is empowered, and the question "What do you need to do to get what you need?" is viable. Note the need is not always interpersonal or from the other, but at times, can also be from the self, so you can say, "What do you need from the other or from yourself?"

A question that may arise once you have identified a marker of self-interruption is whether the client might not benefit more from continuing with the empty-chair task, as opposed to working on the self-interruptive split. If the client is ready or wanting to "speak out" to the other, let the self-interruption be in the background, but if it is preventing the client from "finding a voice," it may be necessary to work on it before continuing the UFB. Continue in these sessions to work with feelings and needs as the central elements of this change process.

### Later Elements of Sessions 6 to 8

Episodic memories also are important for promoting change. Rework the original memories by reentering the scene, reenacting the experience, and undoing original emotional responses with new ones. First, promote the experience of what happened and was not previously symbolized. Provide empathy, acceptance, and attuned responsiveness to the pain of having been injured and being so alone. Then access adaptive responses that were not able to be experienced or expressed then, and transform the maladaptive emotions with the adaptive response. For example, if a person who was physically abused froze or ran away, with fear or shame predominating over anger, you now help access the anger or the sadness at violation, and this transforms the fear (Greenberg, 2002).

As well as fear, shame is produced by abuse. Often, the abused child, to maintain some connection to the powerful abuser, feels an essential badness from being beaten or treated badly. In addition, the child's anger is often turned against the self instead of directed at the abuser, especially when the abuser is an attachment figure on whom the child is dependent for survival. Probably the most damaging aspect of a parent's abuse is that the child comes to feel he or she deserved the beatings or the maltreatment because he or she was bad. First, there is guilt—"I did something bad," and this transforms into shame—"I am bad." Inside, the child's adaptive biological response of rage, hatred, or desire to destroy the parent only confirms the child's feeling that the child is bad and defective and deserves punishment. All this is so painful that it is disowned, but it has to be reactivated in therapy to introduce new adaptive emotions to change these feelings of shame and unworthiness. The ability to stand up for oneself in therapy against the perpetrator is needed to transform the bodily held fear and shame, and this is what helps develop a healthy sense of self-worth.

## Phase IV: Empowerment and Letting Go or Forgiving

This final working phase entails accessing previously unexpressed adaptive primary emotions, mobilizing and promoting the entitlement of unmet needs, and supporting changes in the way the client views the injurer. The shift in the view of the other is facilitated by emotional arousal in the self and mobilization and a sense of entitlement to previously unmet needs. Elaborating the worldview of the other by enacting the other aids empathy toward the injurer, and the therapist helps the client to understand the other better or hold him or her accountable. This phase also involves helping clients grieve and let go of unmet needs when there is no change in view of the other.

Evoking emotion involves not only expressing emotion but also expressing and validating the unmet interpersonal needs for attachment or separation or validation. These are needs that were never expressed in the original relationship because people felt they were not entitled to do so or that their needs would not be met. For therapy to be productive, needs must be expressed as belonging to and coming from the self and with a sense of entitlement, rather than as a protest about deprivations or as accusations of the other. They are an assertion of entitlement to the need rather than expressions of desperate neediness. This step is crucial in helping people establish their sense of the self as agent, separate from the other, and as existing in their own right.

At this stage, the therapist encourages the expression of both emotions and needs. In addition, the therapist helps clients symbolize and assert boundaries, to say "no" to intrusion, for example, or to reassert their rights. Therapists are aware that in early experience people often have found it necessary to disavow their basic needs and that as a result they do not automatically attend to or express those needs. Therapists, therefore, listen for needs to arise and, when they do, quickly validate them and encourage clients to express them. A thorough exploration of feelings is typically followed by a statement of related needs.

A key to forgiving is developing some form of empathy toward the other. This involves seeing the world from the other's point of view and having some compassion or understanding of this view. A shift in the view of the other or a new experience of the other is an important part of the change process. In promoting a change in view of the other, work has to be done on elaborating and understanding the worldview of the other. This work is somewhat more cognitive because it involves perspective taking and elaborating what it was like inside for the other. Taking the view of the other involves the development of empathy for the other and letting go of the expectation that the other will change.

### Grieving Unmet Needs

In situations in which the need cannot or will not be met by the other, clients must still come to recognize their right to have had their needs met by the other in the past. This often allows the important process of letting go of the unmet need. At this point in the dialogue, the therapist supports and promotes the letting go of the unfulfilled hopes and expectations. When letting go does not naturally flow from the expression of primary emotions, therapists can help clients explore and evaluate whether the unfulfilled expectations can and will be met by the other, and if not, therapists can help clients explore the effects of hanging on to the expectations. In this situation, therapists can consider asking clients to express to the significant other "I won't let you go" or "I won't let go of the hope you'll change."

Letting go often produces another round of grief work in which the client works through mourning the loss of the possibility of getting the need met from the attachment figure. This is often the most poignant and painful experience of the process. For example, once people can truly grieve the parent they never had, they can let go and move on.

The fullest form of grieving involves integrating the good aspects of the relationship to be able to carry the love for the other after the loss. But often the anger and rage prevent a fuller grieving. This is especially true in the death of a person who has injured you. If the internal representation of a parent who has died remains persecutory and is seen as hating or abandoning, the parent and the loss of what was needed can never be mourned. One cannot take in the good that was there and allow the good other to live on.

Although each bereavement has to be unique to each person, and there are many forms of grief, if one is to come to terms with one's injuries it appears that mourning the loss caused by the injury is crucial. The biggest block to the process of mourning is unresolved anger. Once the person's anger and the suffering of the injury is witnessed and arousal decreases, this makes way for memories of the more benign or loving aspects of the other. Even though the other had injured, abandoned, neglected, or persecuted the self, there is likely also a good part when the other had been caring, loving, supportive, or validating and was doing the best he or she could. Being able to retrieve these memories and become aware of the positive as well as negative broadens the person's view of the other and the context. This allows one to move on and create a new memory and new narrative and allows one to see the other as more human.

### Forms of Letting Go and Resolution

Through arousal and direct expression of emotions and a strong sense of the legitimacy of their needs, clients begin to let go of previously salient but overly constricted perceptions and to expand their view of the other. Resolution occurs when clients reach a sense that they are worthwhile and can let go of the previously unfinished bad feelings. This letting go is accomplished in one of three major ways: through holding the other accountable for the injury experienced and affirming the self, through letting go of the unmet need and moving on, or through increased understanding of the other and possibly forgiving the other for past wrongs. In nonabuse cases, the client is able to understand the other better, view the other with empathy, compassion, and, sometimes, forgiveness. In abusive or trauma-related situations, letting go most often involves holding the other accountable and moving on, but empathy and forgiveness may also occur. In Chapter 4, we delve more deeply into resolution and provide two in-depth examples of the different forms it can take.

### Sessions 8 to 10

Letting go is part of forgiving. But what is it that clients are letting go of? They are letting mainly anger and hurt go, but they are also letting go of the wish that a need be met by the other. If clients cannot let go of unmet needs and, for example, still need a parent's love, the therapist can ask, noncritically and empathically, "Will you still need this when you are 65 years old?" This confronts the hanging-on tendencies. Putting the person in the other chair helps empathy and letting go, and it is in this chair that often the shift takes place. When you move the person to take the role of the parent you can test for a softening in view of the other by saying, "Come over here. What do you say to her need?" When facilitating this, do not be overly leading by saying "Come over here. Can you feel compassion for her?" because this may result in mere compliance. Empathy for the other can be facilitated by playing the role of the other in a sympathetic or empathic manner or playing the self as empathizing with the other. This can be promoted by accessing what the child has longed for or missed versus what the child received, as in the following example.

**THERAPIST:** What would you have wanted your mother to realize?

**CLIENT:** That she was so cruel and horrible to me!

**THERAPIST:** How would you want her to feel as she realizes this?

**CLIENT:** Pained, guilty, sorry.

**THERAPIST:** And how can she express this pain and guilt and sorrow to you?

**CLIENT:** By saying, "I'm sorry."

Having expressed emotions, at least a moderate level of arousal and mobilized unmet needs have been found to facilitate a softening in the other toward the self. The other expresses guilt, shame, sorrow, regret, and compassion for the pain caused to the self. After imagining compassion in the other, the client experiences relief, soothing, grieving, letting go, and possibly, forgiveness. If, however, the other does not soften, and the client says something such as, "I'd want her to feel sorry, but she never would! She'd never get it!" You could say, "How sad it must have been for you that she is so unable to respond, that you got so little from her." This helps to get to more feeling to reprocess and provides soothing through therapist empathy.

The shift in the other can occur on one of two major dimensions: a shift from a neglectful other toward a more affiliative loving other or a shift from the other being a powerful figure to the other being weak and pathetic. The latter is often the case in an abusive context in which the client says, "Now I'm an adult, and I see what kind of a sick person you really were." Here, sensing the other as less powerful is empowering to the client. So, the shifts are either on an affiliative dimension, from disaffiliative to affiliative, or on an influence dimension, from powerful and controlling to weak and submissive. Once a person does shift, you facilitate elaboration and consolidation by asking them as the other to "tell yourself more about what life was like for you." Help the client to get more into the shoes of the other.

While role-playing the other, if the other remains negative, keep suggesting the client return to the self chair and repeat the expression of feelings and needs to ensure completion of the processing of all that was felt and remembered. If after some time, if there is no shift in the other, you may have to confront the client empathically with a question such as, "Will you go to your grave still wanting this?" You then reflect the client's dilemma, that they so deeply want the other's love or approval, but to want it when it will never come leaves them stuck. The concept of dilemma is useful here because it offers the client an empathic confrontation with the problem they need to resolve. Having explored the dilemma, one may need to go back and keep reworking the problem until a resolution arises.

We have found that when people have difficulty letting go of trying to get the other to meet the unmet need, deeper grieving often is needed to promote the letting go. Here, the person has to grieve the loss of the primary attachment figure to let go. In letting go of unmet interpersonal needs, what was missed or lost has to be acknowledged, grieved, and relinquished. Letting go is giving up the hope that you are going to get what it is that you want. It also is giving up on trying to change the past. A sense of relief may ensue.

Hanging on to the negative other provides security because it is all one had and what one understands love to be. To let go of it feels like the self will shatter. This desperate fear of annihilation must be recognized as such, and all the things the client does to avoid that anxiety must also be brought to light. Articulating and considering a yearning such as, "If mommy is not there, then I'll die!" might make more meaning out of the experience than just feeling desperate, as they may have in the past. At this point, you encourage the client to do some cognitive reorganizing and to work on affective regulation, especially self-soothing. This can be done by having the client consider "What do I need to survive?" Finally, concretizing the loss may make the grieving less overwhelming. A therapist could say, for example, "Say goodbye to the things you are going to miss" and "What do these things do for you?" This is complemented with, "How can you integrate the positive and take it with you" or "How can you do it for yourself?"

Somewhere in the last third of treatment, if there is not a spontaneous resolution, you might try the following highly structured sequence in an empty-chair dialogue as a type of summary of the process. Ask the client to

1. tell the other how they injured you (what is the injury);
2. say what you are angry about or resent and what you have lost;
3. tell the other about what hurt most (the idiosyncratic impact of the injury);
4. tell the other what you hold them accountable for or responsible for;
5. tell the other what you cannot forgive; and
6. tell the other what you can forgive, let go of, or accept.

Make sure you also at some point (not necessarily in conjunction with the previous sequence) have the client take the role of the other and express the inner experience of the other. This is often a difficult step, but it is important that you do it at some point in the latter part of treatment and try to get the inner world of the other elaborated so that the client describes what was happening for the other, their reasons for their actions, and their difficulties in life. This may help develop empathy for the other.

In this phase, develop a piece of homework that uniquely fits your client's situation and give it in one of the last three sessions after the prescribed homework. Discuss possibilities for homework in supervision or think about what the client would do to help symbolize resolution. Rituals such as burying or burning letters written to the injurer, or other symbols that represent the injurer, or engaging in rituals of freedom, such as dancing on the beach or cleansing, can help symbolize a letting go or forgiving and can be helpful.

***Alternatives to Empty-Chair Enactment.*** Also note that the process of resolving the injury can be worked with without having the person speak to an empty chair. You can follow the resolution process by empathically following and guiding without enactment by saying such things as, "What would you say to him if he were here?" or "What kind of things did he say?"

Imagery also can be used in a variety of other ways to evoke the unresolved emotion. The visual system is highly related to emotion, so imagination can be used to evoke an unresolved emotion, enact dialogues in imagination to experience a new emotion, or imagine adding people or resources to situations or scenes to help one experience the scene in a new way. Thus, one can ask the client to restructure an originally damaging scene by imagining him- or herself as a child expressing what was needed or by bringing one's adult self into a childhood scene. The adult protector can offer the protection that was missing or bring in aids that will empower or protect the child version of the self, such as a lock and key to secure their room or a cage in which to put the feared person (Greenberg, 2002, 2015).

In this type of imaginal transformation process (Greenberg, 2002, 2015), the therapist might say,

> Close your eyes and remember the experience of yourself in a situation. Get a concrete image if you can. Go into it. Be yourself as a child in this scene. Please tell me what is happening. What do you see, smell, and hear in the situation? What is going through your mind?

After a while, the therapist asks the client to shift perspectives and says,

> Now I would like you to view the scene as an adult. What do you see, feel, and think? Do you see the look on the child's face? What do you want to do? Do it. How can you intervene? Try it now in imagination.

Changing perspectives again, the therapist asks the client to become the child:

> What as the child do you feel and think? What do you need from the adult? Ask for what you need or wish for. What does the adult do? Is it sufficient? What

> else do you need? Ask for it. Is there someone else you would like to come in to help? Receive the care and protection offered.

This intervention concludes with the therapist asking,

> Check how you feel now. What does all this mean to you about you and about what you needed? Come back to the present, to yourself as an adult now. How do you feel? Will you say goodbye to the child for now?

***Forgiveness.*** To forgive, clients have to give up their claims to restitution in the form of "I'm not going to forgive unless you . . ." For forgiveness to occur, clients also may have to recognize that they are prone to distorting the facts about the offense (as is the offender). Maybe the person will recognize the benefits of holding a grudge, or the perception of the other as "all bad" will shift to a more complex view. However, you should not try to promote this too early.

Note that some of the possible ways the perpetrator may distort the facts may be enacted in the chairs. The perpetrator may play the victim (weakness) or may not feel guilty, for example, about an affair. A perpetrator's lack of remorse is difficult for the betrayed to bear. Or the perpetrator may blame the other person, saying, "I wouldn't have done it if you had been more . . ."

To feel empathy for the other, there must be a more complex view of the other (a shift)—for example, seeing the perpetrator as being motivated by something other than the pure intent to hurt helps to see the other in a new way. Therapists can attempt to stimulate understanding rather than forgiveness per se, and empathy may lead to forgiveness. Forgiveness also is promoted by the realization that the self could do wrong and also that there are benefits of forgiveness to self. You can promote the client's existential awareness of "what it is like to have done wrong in my life and have been forgiven for it" or "there but for the grace of God go I."

In our study, we found that a key process in forgiveness is the clients' ability to imagine the other as being empathic and compassionate to their pain and to imagine the other has having the capacity to feel concern for the client and thereby feel remorse and be apologetic (Greenberg, Warwar, & Malcolm, 2008). This process can be facilitated by asking the person in the role of the other, "Do you hear the pain?" of the self, and "What do you feel or want to say to that?" If the injurer shows empathy or remorse, then promote its expression to the self. Then ask the self to respond to the injurer's empathy by asking, "How does that feel to hear that?" and then "What do you feel toward the injurer?" Another helpful intervention is to ask the person to imagine an injuring parent standing outside the therapy room door hearing what the client in the self chair has been saying and asking the client what the parent would feel. This helps bypass the client imagining what the parent might say defensively to the client's expression and get to how the parent might feel. Often this evokes sadness or compassion in the representation of parents who did not intend to cause the pain they did.

In contrast to the emphasis in the literature on the link between the hurt person's compassionate understanding of the offender and forgiveness, our examination of empty-chair dialogues in individual therapy suggested that it is equally important for the client to imagine the hurtful other feeling and express affective empathy toward the client, taking responsibility for harm done and absolving the client of responsibility for what happened. Early on, Greenberg and Paivio (1997) highlighted how important it is that victims of betrayals of trust believed in their empty-chair dialogues that the offending parties would hear them, take responsibility, and seek to make amends if they could. The victim then can soften and begin to empathize with the other's limitations. Resolution of the injury then occurs either by holding the other accountable or by using empathy or understanding and feeling more affiliative toward the other. Forgiveness will occur with imagined empathy from the other for the pain caused and with empathy for the other—putting oneself in the other's shoes emotionally. Self-affirmation and self-assertion are also a part of the resolution.

***What Forgiveness Can Look Like.*** When a UFB situation is resolved, there is no more negative feeling as one goes back to or thinks about the situation—there is no bad body feeling. This feeling of acceptance may also affect other relationships, or the resolution can generalize to other relationships. An experiment (in session or out of session) might involve trying to see whether any feeling is left when the client imagines seeing the person or target in a future situation. In forgiving and letting go of previously unmet interpersonal needs, the forgiver is released from the traps of (a) trying to make the offender understand the magnitude of harm done and (b) trying to get the offender to take responsibility.

The ideal state of forgiveness is characterized by the absence of animosity and a foreswearing of the desire for revenge and restitution. In therapy, however, it is conceivable that the resentment, which the therapist and client may both perceive to have been expressed and relinquished, might resurface at a later time. We expect this more often in situations in which the individual is working through the unresolved issues of a long-standing relationship rather than in situations in which a single trauma has precipitated a crisis of forgiveness. The surfacing and resurfacing of resentment and animosity may not be symptomatic of a failure to forgive so much as it may indicate that other transgressions have to be forgiven as well.

Finally, injuries are cast as narratives with characters (injurer and injured) and a plot featuring a theme of loss or violation, having a beginning, middle, and an end. As such, events, such as a partner's sexual affair, that result in a violation of what is held sacred are likely to disrupt severely the narrative flow of an individual's life. The old story the individual had planned to live by may no longer be viable, and a new story must be constructed. Losing one's idealized view of a partner or experiencing a challenge to cherished beliefs or what was held inviolable may lead to a loss of trust that results in a change in one's life narrative. Ultimately, the individual may see this unfolding story as one of growth, but the process is still likely to be highly painful.

## Phase V: Termination

A set of principles of termination that best seem to guide the termination process involve (a) viewing the client as an agent, (b) viewing change as a process, (c) dealing with separation and loss, (d) empowering the client, (e) consolidating new meanings, and (f) predicting possible relapse.

### Initial Elements of Termination

In these sessions, the work of previous phases is completed, and termination issues are dealt with. The first principle, viewing the client as an agent, highlights that termination is a collaborative process in which the client's emerging decision to end therapy is discussed as part of the process of terminating. The second principle requires that the therapist discuss that change is an ongoing process and that this process will continue after therapy. Termination is therefore not seen as the attainment of an absolute endpoint.

The third principle focuses on termination as a separation process. With some clients, termination may bring up issues of separation and loss, especially if these issues have been part of the main theme of the injury. Termination then becomes an opportunity to further work through any issues of abandonment or fear. The therapist asks about possible anxiety or sadness about loss and explores the client's idiosyncratic feelings of connectedness, isolation, or dependence.

### Later Elements of Termination

The fourth principle involves empowering the client. As therapy draws to a close, the therapist reveals more and attempts to equalize the relationship as much as possible and to deelevate him- or herself, stepping down from any pedestal the client may have placed the therapist on in the process of treatment. This means self-disclosing more, making sure the client sees the therapist as a human being just like him or her. It also is good to make sure to attribute change to clients' efforts, although if the client attributes change to the therapist, the therapist accepts this humbly.

The fifth principle emphasizes that termination is a time to consolidate new meanings formed during treatment. Themes identified during treatment are clearly symbolized and reiterated. The emerging new narrative about the self and the other that was constructed in therapy is summarized.

The sixth and final principle involves dealing with creating realistic expectations about the effects of treatment, to stave off possible feelings of disappointment or failure if the client falls back temporarily. Thus, relapses into negative states or patterns are predicted as expected and as part of a process change. It is emphasized that falling back into old patterns or reactions is not a problem. Rather, the difficulty is being stuck in these old patterns or bad states without awareness and not being able to leave them. Reentering problem states does not mean relapse and does not mean that no benefits have occurred or that therapy or the client has failed. We suggest that, as long as relapses do not endure for too long, for more than a day or so, their occurrence should not be taken as a sign of failure.

## CONCLUSION

Resolving EIs, in whatever way it is done, is ultimately about changing emotion schematic memory. Emotions are often embedded in relational contexts. They connect self to other in the memory. People have memories of feeling shame in the face of a contemptuous parent, anger at an intrusive other, or fear of an abusive other. Therefore, accessing views of others helps evoke emotion, and accessing alternate views of others and mobilizing new responses to others helps change emotion memories.

Personally relevant events are stored in memory at their emotion addresses. Thus, a current disappointment links to other disappointments, a feeling of shame to other losses of face. Present emotional experiences are always multilayered, evoking with them prior instances of the same or similar emotional experiences. We have to help people have new lived experiences in the session to help them restructure their emotion memories. Accessing a new emotion is one of the best ways to change an old emotion memory. Once a previously inaccessible emotion memory is evoked, the new emotional experience is integrated into it, and when the memory reconsolidates, the new emotion fuses with the old memory and transforms it.

In this chapter, we have outlined a road map for facilitating a process of change based on arriving at emotion and at transforming emotion with new emotions, thereby leading to change in memories by a process of memory reconsolidation. This, we suggest, is the best way to optimize the possibility of the emergence of forgiveness.

# 4

# Case Examples of the Resolution Process for Individuals

In this chapter, we expand on information presented in Chapter 3 about the different forms resolution of emotional injury (EI) can take. To do this, we first present the results of our study on facilitating the resolution of EIs in individual therapy (Greenberg, Warwar, & Malcolm, 2008). Next, we discuss a task analytically derived model that describes the essential components that differentiate successful from unsuccessful forgiveness. This provides both an understanding of how people forgive and a guide to intervention.

In the years since we conducted the study, we have amassed a body of qualitative data to illustrate how the model works. To demonstrate the process and the components of resolution and forgiveness, we present two cases for comparison—one when the client forgave and another when the client did not. Both clients were participants in the 2008 study, and from their cases, we derived several clinical insights we hope therapists will find helpful in their practice of emotion-focused therapy (EFT) for forgiveness. The names and identifying details of the clients have been changed to ensure confidentiality.

## THE YORK EMOTIONAL INJURY PROJECT

In our studies of the treatment of EIs, we began by comparing the effectiveness of EFT involving empty-chair dialogue in individual therapy with psychoeducation in a group designed to deal with these injuries. Results indicated that

http://dx.doi.org/10.1037/0000144-005
*Forgiveness and Letting Go in Emotion-Focused Therapy*, by L. S. Greenberg and C. Woldarsky Meneses

clients in EFT using empty-chair dialogue showed significantly more improvement than the psychoeducation group treatment on all measures of forgiveness and letting go, as well as on global symptoms and key target complaints (Greenberg et al., 2008). We also examined aspects of the emotional process related to treatment outcome and investigated the relationship between letting go of distressing feelings and forgiveness. Once we had shown that the treatment was effective in promoting forgiveness, at least in some people, we then compared in detail the in-session process of those who forgave and those who did not.

In this study, 46 clients assessed as having unresolved, interpersonal EIs with a significant other were randomly assigned to an individual therapy treatment of EFT or a psychoeducation group. Clients were assessed pretreatment, posttreatment, and at 3-month follow-up on measures of forgiveness, letting go, depression, global symptoms, and key target complaints. Approximately one third of the participants were diagnosed with at least one Axis I anxiety and mood disorder from the *Diagnostic and Statistical Manual of Mental Disorders* (fourth ed.; *DSM–IV*; American Psychiatric Association, 1994), and just under one quarter of the participants were also diagnosed with at least one Axis II diagnosis of personality disorder from *DSM–IV*. All the clients had reasonable levels of occupational and social functioning, and the exclusion of clients who were actively suicidal, psychotic, or involved in a current violent relationship suggested that the participants were appropriate candidates for a brief program of psychotherapy or psychoeducation.

An inclusion criterion was that that the injuries had taken place at least 2 years before entering therapy to ensure we were dealing with people who were in chronic states of unresolvedness. The injuries participants described were emotional in that they involved intense, lingering, and distressingly unresolved feelings of hurt, anger, and pain in response to injuries such as abandonment, neglect, betrayal, or abuse. The injuries were also interpersonal in that they invariably took place within the context of an ongoing significant relationship. The most common hurtful experience involved one or both parents, with an ex-partner as the next most common hurtful other. The remaining clients described experiences involving a friend, boss, neighbor, or family member other than a parent.

The individual therapy took place over 10 to 12 sessions. Of key importance in the treatment was empty-chair work, in the context of an empathic relationship. As described in Chapter 3, this aids in expressing and processing the anger and sadness felt toward the injurer and in evoking empathy both for the injurer and the client's emerging awareness of what was needed from the injurer in regard to the pain and suffering the injurer caused. The psychoeducational group (PG) attended six 2-hour workshop presentations that covered information and facilitated discussion about (a) the importance of resolving past interpersonal EIs, (b) how to go about that process, (c) crucial aspects of forgiveness and (d) its potential benefits, (e) the important differences between forgiveness and reconciliation, and (f) a description of the quality of the experience of successfully resolving a past hurt. It was assumed that any positive changes experienced by the participants in the PG would result from the discussion of, and reflection on, the information provided.

An analysis of the outcome measures showed that participants in both the psychoeducational and individual EFT treatment groups benefited from the treatments. The results of this study showed that clients in the individual EFT treatment showed significantly more improvement on all measures of forgiveness, on measures assessing the degree to which clients had let go of distressing feelings and unmet needs in relation to the injurer, and on change in target complaints at termination and follow-up. Greater improvement in the EFT condition was also reported on the Global Symptom Index (GSI) of the Symptom Checklist–90–Revised (SCL-90-R; Derogatis, 1992). The significant change in general psychological symptoms on the SCL-90-R in EFT, with no change in the PG on symptoms, is notable, suggesting that an individual emotion-focused treatment, in addition to enhancing forgiveness and letting go of the EI, has positive effects on a person's general level of well-being that well exceed those of a psychoeducation group. These results supported the hypothesis that working through the emotions of past interpersonal EIs is better facilitated by EFT than by psychoeducation.

Although some of the literature assumes that forgiveness can lead to an emotionally neutral stance toward an injurer, we differentiated between emotional neutrality or letting go (of the negative distressing feelings and unmet interpersonal needs) and forgiveness (letting go plus the development of empathic understanding of and compassionate feelings toward the other). All of the participants who reported that they had forgiven the injurer, regardless of whether they were in the PG or individual EFT treatment, also indicated that they had let go of the distressing feelings and unmet needs previously associated with the injury. This is not an unexpected finding because every discussion in the literature assumes that forgiveness will be accompanied by reductions in the intensity and frequency of feelings of anger, resentment, and hurt. What is noteworthy is that a number of individuals reported that they had let go of the distressing feelings and unmet needs associated with the injury but had not forgiven the injurer. This suggests that letting go of persistent, unresolved, and distressingly negative feelings is a necessary but not a sufficient condition for reaching a stance of forgiveness toward the injurer. If their feelings toward the injurer and/or about what happened were less negative or at best neutral, the participants did not consider themselves to have forgiven, suggesting that forgiveness was marked by something else—positive feelings toward the injurer.

It is also important to note that, in our study, increases in both forgiveness and letting go were related to a decrease in psychological symptoms. Thus, it seems that increases over treatment in forgiveness, empathy, and acceptance toward the injurer and in being able to resolve distressing feelings and, importantly, unmet interpersonal needs are associated with improved mental health. Contrary to what is found in the forgiveness literature (McCullough &

Witvliet, 2002; Orcutt 2006), forgiveness was not initially correlated with the GSI of the SCL-90-R. Clients at the start of treatment who were more forgiving were not psychologically healthier. This, however, may have been due to lack of range on both the sets of measures and because participants were seeking help for presenting problems involving a lack of letting go and forgiveness. In our study pre–post increases in forgiveness and letting go variables, however, were related to a decrease in GSI. Thus, it seems that increases over treatment in forgiveness, in empathy and acceptance toward the injurer, and being able to resolve feelings and needs, were significantly related to improved health as measured by the GSI, suggesting health benefits to resolving injuries both by forgiveness and letting go.

In addition to showing better outcomes, the EFT group was found to involve more client-reported emotional arousal, especially of negative emotions in the mid-phase of treatment, confirming that the EFT treatment was more emotion-arousing than the PG treatment. There was also more negative emotional arousal in the early phase of therapy for the EFT treatment than for the PG treatment. In the final phase, the two groups did not differ in reported emotional arousal on positive or negative emotions. This was probably because EFT clients were more likely to access negative emotions right from the start as a function of therapy, rather than because they entered treatment with more negative emotions than clients in the PG treatment. This finding also suggests that the emotional change processes in therapy are not necessarily simply ones of replacing bad feelings with good feelings in a linear process but that at times feeling bad can, in fact, lead to feeling good. Thus, the idea that working through bad feelings by facing them, allowing and accepting them can lead to change (Greenberg, 2002) was supported.

It should be noted, however, that reported in-session emotional arousal did not relate to outcome in either group. This is likely because not all arousal of emotion is the same. For example, some arousal may be a sign of distress rather than a sign of working through distress (Greenberg & Watson, 2006). Auszra, Greenberg, and Herrmann (2013) showed that arousal alone is not necessarily a measure of productive emotional processing and that it is productive processing of arousal emotion that best discriminates good from poor outcome cases. It is important, however, to note that we observed that some poorer outcome clients who reported high emotional intensity (reported arousal) showed few visible signs of the reported arousal (expression) and were often quite constricted in their expression of emotion in the session. They reported they had felt a lot of anger, sadness, shame, or fear but had not necessarily expressed it, so although the self-reports were indicative of emotion experienced, they were not indices of how much emotion was allowed and expressed in the session and made accessible for further processing. As Greenberg (2010) suggested, emotion awareness and expression are different emotion change processes, and the latter, by revealing the self to the other, overcoming constriction, and altering physiology and neurochemistry, may be what is most therapeutic when dealing with unresolved painful emotions.

After the study was completed, two clients who had participated were chosen for intensive analysis to look at the process of forgiveness. Each resolved their EI, but one did this through the process of forgiveness, whereas the other resolved through self-assertion and holding the other accountable. Both cases had good outcomes. Comparison of these two cases, however, allowed us to distinguish what elements were unique to, and necessary for, forgiveness. Other cases were then studied through this lens to check for the presence of the components unique to forgiveness.

## THE CASES

Melissa was a 36-year-old, unmarried woman who came to therapy with an EI related to her father's emotional abuse, manipulation, and neglect, resolved through the process of forgiveness. At the time of participation, she had been struggling with low self-esteem and feelings of isolation, abandonment, and stagnation. She had grown up in a constant state of fear because she had not wanted to fall short of her father's expectations. What made her father so important to her was that her mother had emotionally abandoned her at a young age. Realizing her mother was not emotionally available, Melissa quickly determined that her only form of parental love would be from her father. Consequently, she began doing things to please her father in the hope of retaining the love she received from him. Although he quite often had said that success was not everything, he often made her feel the opposite by making his paternal love and affection conditional on what she accomplished. This led her to feel as though she was not lovable for herself but only as an extension of her father, as a means to bolster his ego through her achievements.

Because of his self-absorbed nature, she also felt as though he did not care about her as a person and that he was never there for her when she needed his support. Whenever she complained or spoke up about how she felt, her father would tell her that she was being selfish. In response, the client learned to bury her feelings and developed the idea that her emotions did not have any legitimacy. Many of her needs for love, protection, care, and acceptance, as well as her need to be heard, went unmet. As a result, she was left with a great deal of anger and resentment toward her father as well as with feelings of worthlessness because she did not believe she deserved any better. To combat her anxieties, she would self-medicate by overeating and smoking cigarettes, although she recognized these were not effective methods of coping with her negative emotions.

The second client, Kira, was a 31-year-old, married woman who had been struggling with feelings of shame, hopelessness, and low self-esteem. She presented with an EI related to her mother's controlling nature and cruel and critical treatment during her upbringing. She resolved through self-assertion and holding her mother accountable. This client did not forgive. The client reported that the mother was a person who enjoyed the weaknesses of others and controlled those around her by causing crises, playing the victim in life, and belittling others. Essentially, her mother did everything in her power to break the client's spirit so she could remain the center of attention. Early in her childhood, Kira learned from her mother that everything in life was bad and nothing was worth any effort. Noticing her mother was constantly miserable and contemptuous of others, she developed feelings of guilt surrounding her mother's state and felt it was her responsibility to make her mother happy. This arduous task was made more difficult by the fact that whenever Kira showed signs of strength and tried to make things better, her mother would attack her character and tell her how worthless she was and how she could never do anything right. Consequently, Kira grew up feeling she had nothing to offer and that she was not worth being heard.

Lacking support and nurturance from her mother, she immersed herself deeply in her studies, finding that she could get affirmation from her teachers. Although Kira always got the highest grades, she was nonetheless criticized by her mother and reprimanded for attempting to overstep the boundaries her mother had imposed on her. Realizing that she was in a toxic environment, this client, when she was older, decided to separate from her family, which was under her mother's control, and she moved away to pursue academic studies. In retaliation for this act of independence, her mother began sending her daughter hate mail and stated that she wished she had never had her as a daughter. As a result, this client was left with a great deal of anger and sadness in relation to her mother.

*Task analysis* (Greenberg, 1984, 1992, 2007), an investigative strategy aimed at understanding how clients in therapy resolve problems, was used to discern the steps in the resolution of these EIs. The transcripts of each of the sessions of both cases were rigorously scrutinized to ascertain the essential steps of resolution. Each of the events pertaining to the process of the resolution of the injuries was isolated, and themes relevant to this process were tracked throughout the course of therapy. Each of the steps the client took to resolve the problem was identified and described. Categories were then formed to group similar states, and shifts in the sequence of the client's process were tracked to reveal the essential steps in the process of resolution. On the basis of a comparison between the two routes to resolution, the components that distinguished the two cases could be identified. Similarities helped determine steps to resolution, whereas differences helped establish where in the process the two paths diverged. On the basis of these determinations, the essential steps to forgiveness were noted and incorporated into a preliminary model of the process of forgiveness. There were then compared with further cases to check the model.

### Melissa's Therapy

The client's relationship to her father early on in the therapy can be characterized as antagonistic and adversarial, and she did not express the source of her pain, probably out of fear of being attacked, because her father had rejected these expressions in the past. Showing the source of her pain was an act of vulnerability and was an important step in the resolution process. The father's showing compassion and empathy for the pain caused, however, appears to be the most important component that led to forgiveness.

In the initial stages of Melissa's therapy, she expressed many unresolved feelings toward her father. An early empty-chair dialogue was characterized by complaints about her father's insensitive, negligent, and sometimes cruel behavior. Specifically, she expressed distress that her father always used her as a means of bolstering his ego through her achievements, that he never treated her as an individual, and was not supportive when she needed him. She said she had never learned to care about herself and blamed her father for the lack of self-care that she still experiences.

Many of these complaints developed into highly emotionally aroused expressions of anger and sadness. She expressed anger at her father for his negative impact on her and resentment that he treated her like a piece of property and demanded the highest standards from her. This was particularly upsetting because he never achieved any form of excellence himself. However, Melissa knew that her father was treated the same way by his parents. Nonetheless, she experienced sadness because, as a result, she was now an injured child. After expressing her anger and sadness, she was then able to mobilize her needs for understanding, appreciation, and support. However, when this client switched chairs and played the role of her father, she was met with verbally abusive statements.

As the therapy continued, bitter dialogue persisted between the client and her father. However, a shift occurred when the client, enacting her father, elaborated on his experience of being humiliated and abandoned by his parents during his childhood. The father also talked about how he never felt appreciated for the sacrifices he made for his daughter. In response to this shift in the representation of the father, the client displayed the first sign of vulnerability by stating that all she needed was an apology and that validation would go a long way for her. Essentially, this was the first sign that she was shifting from an attacking stance to a softer one where she could show her father the source of her pain.

The following statements are examples of the categories formed from the dialogue of the client. These examples are the parts of sentences that capture the essential meaning of what the client is saying. The words used to describe the categories are close to those used by the client.

This first example illustrates the client presenting her vulnerability because she is showing the source of her pain, which came from needing an apology, acknowledgment of her hurt, and validation. Vulnerability by the self was first expressed in Session 5 after the other stated his view. The father said such things as the following:

- "You never focus on the good things I did for you."

- "I threw my life away to raise the family and did jobs I hated."
- "You never appreciated that."
- "You only talk of how I hurt you."

The self then responded with the following statements:

- "Sorry (sarcastically) I brought it up."
- (Crying) "I need you to say I'm sorry."
- "I need you to acknowledge that it [the hurt] happened."
- (Crying) "Validation would go a long way for me."

Further elaboration of the father's perspective revealed he was distressed at not being able to do more for his daughter to make her happy. He stated that he had failed her as a parent because he never felt cared for himself. He also said he understood how she felt and wished he could take away her pain. His understanding of her pain came from his own experiences because he had gone through the same in his upbringing.

Toward the middle of the therapy, the amount of vulnerability expressed by the client increased substantially. Elaborating on her pain, the client stated that all she ever wanted to do was please her father and that she was always afraid of losing his affection, because losing his love would mean that she would be left with nothing.

In Session 7, following the expression of a need, other expressions of vulnerability emerged:

- (Crying) "I needed to feel good about myself."
- "I never felt good about myself as far as encouragement went."
- "I was always on my own, it seemed."
- (Crying) "I was afraid that you wouldn't love me."
- (Crying) "I had nobody else, just you."
- "You had me right where you wanted me."
- "I was completely dependent upon you."
- "I wanted to be just like you because I knew that made you happy."

And to the therapists, crying, she said,

- "I just needed to feel like I'm good."
- "I heard nothing but what a bad girl I am."
- (Crying) "I heard I was bad from everybody, but you were the only one that said anything that differed."

This vulnerability was a sign that Melissa did not want to continue the struggle and that she was letting go of her confrontational anger. An example of vulnerability by the father came in Session 6 after an elaboration of his experience:

- (Crying) "I'm angry at myself because I can't help her because I'm so needy."
- (Crying) "I'm so vulnerable."
- (Crying) "Nobody's taking care of me."

This vulnerability by the other was an important development in response to the vulnerability by the self. The effect of this expression of vulnerability was that it triggered guilt in her father, and he was now able to hear what she was saying in a nondefensive way. In enacting the other, the client was also able to feel her father's emotions, and this led her to experience empathy for her father. Identifying with her father, she could feel the guilt he felt for his wrongdoings in the past. Examples of guilt and shame by the father were seen in Session 9 after he gave his apology:

- (Crying) "I'm beyond sorry; I'm sick with grief and guilt that I did this to you."
- (Crying) "I just wish I could die."
- (Crying) "Everyone would be better off without me."
- (Crying) "I just can't face it; it'll destroy me."

Guilt and shame were allowed to surface as the father elaborated on his experience in life. An example of empathy by the self for the father was observed in Session 7 after the other had expressed his guilt and apologized. To the therapist, Melissa said,

- "I feel really sorry for him."
- "I can completely feel the way he must have felt his whole life."
- "I really think the way I feel now is the way he felt."

To the father she said,

- (Crying) "I think you experienced all the same pain, but you weren't aware of it the way I am."
- (Crying) "I don't think you ever made any attempt to understand it [the pain]."
- (Crying) "I'm crying for you and me."

Empathy came after the client played the role of her father. Through the enactment of her father, this client was able to experience the emotions her father must have felt. In taking her father's perspective, the client was able to identify with her father's anguish about being told he was bad as a child. Sharing this similar experience allowed the client to understand the source of her father's behavior and recognize him as someone with his own pain.

After seeing the daughter as vulnerable and receiving empathy from his daughter, the father continued to express his understanding and related his experience to hers. This empathy for the daughter from the father was an important step, and it led to a sincere apology from the father and feelings of compassion for the hurt Melissa had experienced at his hands. An example of compassion by the other was demonstrated in Session 6 after the father expressed his guilt: "I wish I could help you," "I wish I could erase the damage I did to you." The tone associated with this wish showed that the father felt deep sympathy and sorrow for the suffering the self had endured. These statements also showed that he had a desire to alleviate the self's pain.

An example of the father's understanding occurred in session after he had talked about his childhood and elaborated his worldview:

- "I feel like I did when I was a boy."
- (Crying) "You think I don't understand, but I do."
- (Crying) "I was always told I was bad too, and then they packed me off to boarding school because I was considered an incorrigible."

In these statements, the father communicated that his understanding went beyond the intellectual level. This dialogue showed that the father's level of understanding came from his experience.

An example of the apology from the father occurred in Session 8 after the other elaborated his view:

- "I did my best."
- "The odds were stacked against me, and it wasn't easy for me."
- (Crying) "I was raised to think I wasn't worth anything more than dirt either."
- (Crying) "I didn't know I was offloading my problems on you."
- (Crying) "I think I'm sorry."
- (Crying) "I'm sorry I made you feel worthless."
- (Crying) "I'm sorry I disappointed you."
- (Crying) "I'm sorry I wasn't who you thought I was."

An example of the taking of responsibility by the father was demonstrated in Session 9 after the other elaborated his view: "I always tried to be the hero to you, but I fell very short of that," "I feel sick about it." In tandem with the apology came the taking of responsibility for the harm he had done.

As the dialogue between father and daughter continued, regret emerged on both sides. Along with the dissipation of the anger between them, both conceded that all the fighting and animosity were futile and a waste of both their lives. The daughter expressed regret at not having been fully aware of what the father had experienced. The father's regret was how he had lived his life and how it had impacted his daughter. In essence, he regretted hurting her and felt compassion for her. An example of regret of the self was observed in Session 8 after the other elaborated his view: "What a waste of your life and mine to have to go through this."

The essence of the client's regret revolved around her new understanding of her father's perspective. She previously saw him as overbearing and cruel, and she now understood him as a human being with tender feelings, and she was regretful about not being able to enjoy the relationship with her father as it could have been. An example of regret by the father was observed in Session 8 after the daughter expressed her regret:

- "Yeah, what a waste."
- "I regret what I did to you as a result of that."
- "I regret I didn't have the courage to change it."

The sense of loss the father experienced came from his feeling that their relationship should not have grown as distant as it had become. Because it was becoming apparent that he had good intentions regarding the way he raised his daughter, the father felt as though he had wasted a lot of his life not getting the result he was after.

The first instance of forgiveness, although only partial, emerged around midtreatment shortly after the father emotionally expressed an apology for all he had done, in addition to expressions of guilt. Later, he affirmed his daughter by expressing his wish that she just be herself, vehemently expressed his love for her, and finally requested forgiveness. After experiencing his pain and receiving this nurturing, the client said she forgave her father for how he hurt her because he was a hurt person himself. However, she was still angry with him for refusing to see the truth and for being so defensive. This signified that although forgiveness had occurred, it was not yet complete, and further emotional work was necessary.

Before forgiveness was complete, Melissa also developed compassion for her father. She wished he had not had the burden he carried his whole life. With this softening, the self also expressed love for her father and absolved him of any failings in his paternal role. In response, the father expressed his relief, happiness, and love. This was followed by him fulfilling her previously unmet needs by affirming and unconditionally accepting her as a person. At this point, she had the strongest emotional outpouring observed throughout the entire therapy because she had received what she had been looking for her whole life. Melissa was overwhelmed with tears of joy and was glad for everything that happened. Consequently, she let go of her hurt, anger, and previously unmet needs. In addition, she uttered the phrase "I forgive you" without any conditions. An example of compassion by the self was observed in Session 9 after the other elaborated his view:

- "My heart is just so heavy for you."
- "I feel so bad for you, and I feel so close to you."
- (Crying) "I forgive you, and I wish that somebody could have helped you."

The client's crying in this part of her therapy signified the sympathy and sorrow she felt for her father's misfortunes. She acknowledged that he carried a burden his whole life and indicated her wish that someone would have been around to help him with his suffering.

At the beginning of her therapy, this client was frustrated and angry with her father because of how he cruelly treated her. He was perceived as someone who was insensitive to her needs. She felt her father did not care about her as an individual and only loved her when she was successful. By the end of therapy, she had changed her view and felt love for him. He was seen as not all bad, and she admitted that he had many good qualities.

In the final sessions of her therapy, Melissa expressed a deep understanding of her father. She said that having experienced some of his experience, by identifying with him in the empty chair and thereby having some of his body felt sensations, she now understood his compulsions, self-abuse, and loneliness. An example of understanding by the self was observed in Session 9 after the self expressed her initial, although incomplete, forgiveness:

- (Crying) "I didn't know that you were going through all this too when I was a kid."
- (Crying) "I didn't see any of that [what father was going through]."
- (Crying) "I just saw my hero who kept hurting me."
- (Crying) "I couldn't understand it [what the father was going through]."

To the therapist, as she is crying, she said,

- "I feel so sorry for my dad."
- "I feel sad for him."
- "I really think he was misunderstood."
- "I think he was a tortured individual."
- "I know what it must be like for him being told he was a bad boy because I was told I was a bad girl."
- "I understand the loneliness of knowing that you're not a bad kid."
- "I understand you get confused as a kid, that you think you are bad."

- "It's a terrible, isolating feeling [being told you are bad]."
- "I know how isolated he was."

The client, in this excerpt, indicated that as a child, she could not understand what difficulties her father was experiencing. When she was a child, she could only comprehend her feelings of hurt in relation to her father. She said that as a child, she got confused into thinking she was bad. Now as an adult, experiencing her father's bodily felt sensations during her enactment of him in the empty-chair dialogue, the client was able to understand the agony and loneliness he felt.

An example of the positive other was observed in Session 10 after the father elaborated his view:

- (Crying) "[I'm overwhelmed] by love, happiness, and also some grief."
- (Crying) "[I'm sad] that this had to happen, and I'm glad that it did."
- "I think you're doing the right thing to take control of your life."
- "I accept you the way you are without conditions, and I never said that before, but I want to say it now."
- "I want you to remember that even if I slip sometimes and revert back to my old patterns of behavior."
- "I want you to remember because it's going to be hard for me to break out of those patterns now at my age."
- "I do love you as you are."

An example of letting go was observed in Session 10 after the client had her primary need met by her father:

- (Crying) "I guess I'm going to try and say goodbye to that part of me that was a hurt child."
- (Crying) "I'm going to say goodbye to the part that was defenseless. (Crying) I'm not that child anymore."
- (Crying) "I'm an adult now."
- "I have control of my own destiny."
- "Goodbye to being a victim."
- "Goodbye to being angry at you."
- "It [the anger] never helped me, ultimately."
- "I'm not interested in being angry with you anymore."
- "I'm really over it [her anger]."

The client in this example had just received unconditional acceptance from her father. Previously, this was the unmet need that gave the client the most distress. As she cried her tears of joy, she began to let go of the defenseless, childlike parts of herself that were a result of not having this need met. As the letting-go process continued, this client also let go of her anger toward her father and asserted that she was over the issue with her father.

An example of forgiveness was observed in Session 10 after all the previously seen states had come to their completion. To the therapist, she said, "I feel forgiving toward my father," and to him in the empty chair she said,

- "I do forgive you."
- "I'm really not angry with you anymore."
- "I really left that behind."

It is important to note that there was no crying attached to the last statement of forgiveness. Previous states of forgiveness were observed while the client was crying. This indicated that although the forgiveness bestowed on her father was genuine, it was not yet complete and required further work. In this last instance of forgiveness, the clear expression of it indicated her emotions had been fully processed, and the process of forgiveness was complete.

### Kira's Therapy

Kira came to therapy with an EI related to her mother, resolved through self-assertion, not forgiveness. In the initial stages of her therapy, Kira began by expressing many unresolved feelings toward her mother in the form of complaint and criticism. Specifically, she complained that her mother had done nothing ever to help her in her life but rather did everything in her power to stifle her daughter, trying to convince her that she was weak and that no one would ever love her. The client saw her mother as cruel and overbearing and felt hopeless that the relationship between her and her mother would ever improve.

As her therapy progressed, Kira got in touch with the sadness she felt concerning her mother. She experienced and processed first the distress and helplessness of never having been seen or nurtured and her shame of feeling worthless. She was sad that her mother might never know who she truly was because she never acted normally in front of her mother. Because her mother would only love those around her when they were weak, Kira never showed any of her talents or strengths, although she had many. Essentially, she was sad that she had to sacrifice herself to please her mother. Kira was also angry because she felt a general sense of discouragement in most of her activities and felt that was because her mother never believed in her. She expressed anger toward her mother about how her mother would intentionally create problems in her daughter's life to fix them. This way, her mother made herself feel needed and important.

Following the client's expression of sadness and anger, the negative mother was enacted by the client in the other chair. The mother attacked her daughter, saying that Kira could not take care of herself and that she expected her daughter to live a life as bad as hers. These enactments made the client believe that her mother would never apologize or take responsibility for how she hurt her. These statements materialized early in the therapy, and an apology or the taking of responsibility never came up in the other chair throughout the course of treatment. This was a direct contrast to Melissa's process in her description, where both apology and responsibility from the imagined other were present in her forgiveness process. Like Melissa, Kira's expressed arousal was high, and she experienced assertive anger and entitlement to her need to progress; however, she did not forgive. Rather she grieved that she would never have the mother she deserved. Following Kira's emotional work, her need for her mother to take responsibility emerged. The client also expressed a need for acceptance and the need for support so she could grow and spread her wings. Neither of these needs was ever met by her enacted mother during the course of her therapy, and the mother never showed any signs of softening.

The enacted mother showed no vulnerability, guilt, compassion, or empathy. Rather, the mother was critical of the daughter for being unlovable. From the mother's perspective, her daughter did not deserve anyone good in her life because she was a bad person. She even expressed anger and disappointment to the point of saying she wished she had never had a daughter. Other utterances by the mother involved attacking the client for trying to grow and become a better person. Even when the mother elaborated on her experience in life, admitting that she had never had a mother, she still failed to take responsibility for any mistakes she had made as a mother herself. This mother asserted that none of her mistakes was her fault because no one was around to teach her how to be a mother. Finally, because she had such a bad life, the mother stated, without any justification, that her daughter deserved a life just as bad.

Toward the middle of the therapy, the client in the mother's role showed no signs of softening. In addition, no other states other than attack, criticism, and elaboration of worldview emerged. Because no new states came up, the self was left in a state of not being able to understand how her mother could treat her in the way she had, especially because she had done nothing wrong. This was another direct contrast to the case where forgiveness occurred because understanding had developed in both roles.

Seeing that she was not able to make any progress in her dialogue with her mother and that she could not get her needs met, Kira began to assert herself and set boundaries. This signified the self's development of her inner strength and foreshadowed her separation from her mother. Some of these assertions revolved around the refusal to be controlled by her mother. In addition, she emphasized that she was not a piece of property to be used in her mother's twisted schemes to create problems. Other statements asserted that she had achieved a great deal on her own, despite her mother's interference. As she continued to grow stronger, the client was able to define who she was and how she wanted her life to be. This life did not include her mother, and she became certain that she wanted complete separation.

After her self-assertion, Kira also began to affirm herself. This was not seen at the inception of therapy. Seeing the toxicity of how her mother treated her, the client was now able to acknowledge and recognize the value and merit of her achievements. She expressed that she was proud of herself for her accomplishments and for the fact that she had become a good person despite being abused. She also expressed self-support for herself by stating that she looked forward to what she would become.

In the final sessions of her therapy, Kira held her mother accountable for all her transgressions. The mother was held accountable for causing trouble within the family and creating distance with relatives. She was also held accountable for trying to continue the cycle of unhappiness across younger generations within the family. Further, she held her mother accountable for not fulfilling the needs a mother should fulfill for her children. Specifically, she stated that her mother never nurtured her needs for encouragement, acceptance, and exploration. Realizing that her mother would never meet her needs, the client finally let go of wanting these needs met by her mother.

Indications that the therapy had reached its conclusion came in several forms. First, the client stated that she had developed the feeling of wanting to protect herself. This was new because in the past she felt threatened in many situations, including ones involving her mother. Second, the view of her mother changed from seeing her mother as powerful to seeing her as someone who was sick. Despite seeing her mother as sick, Kira still maintained that what her mother did was unforgivable. Next, the enactment of the bad mother shifted from an overbearing and controlling tone to a more persuasive one. This was an indication that the mother was losing her hold over her daughter. Last, the client reported feeling good about the choices she made in the dialogues during her therapy.

## A MODEL OF THE FORGIVENESS PROCESS

The model shown in Figure 4.1 displays the path to forgiveness taken by Melissa and other clients studied in this way who achieved forgiveness. The lower path demonstrates the observed states of the self, and the upper path displays the observed states of the other. Besides (a) the initial steps of blame and complaint, differentiation of anger or sadness, in both the self and other positions; (b) the elaboration of the worldview in the other's position; and (c) the expression of a need in the self chair, which is common to both cases, the model indicates those components that were crucial in distinguishing the forgiveness from the nonforgiveness performance. The crucial components that distinguish forgiveness from letting go are indicated by black circles with

**FIGURE 4.1. Path to Forgiveness**

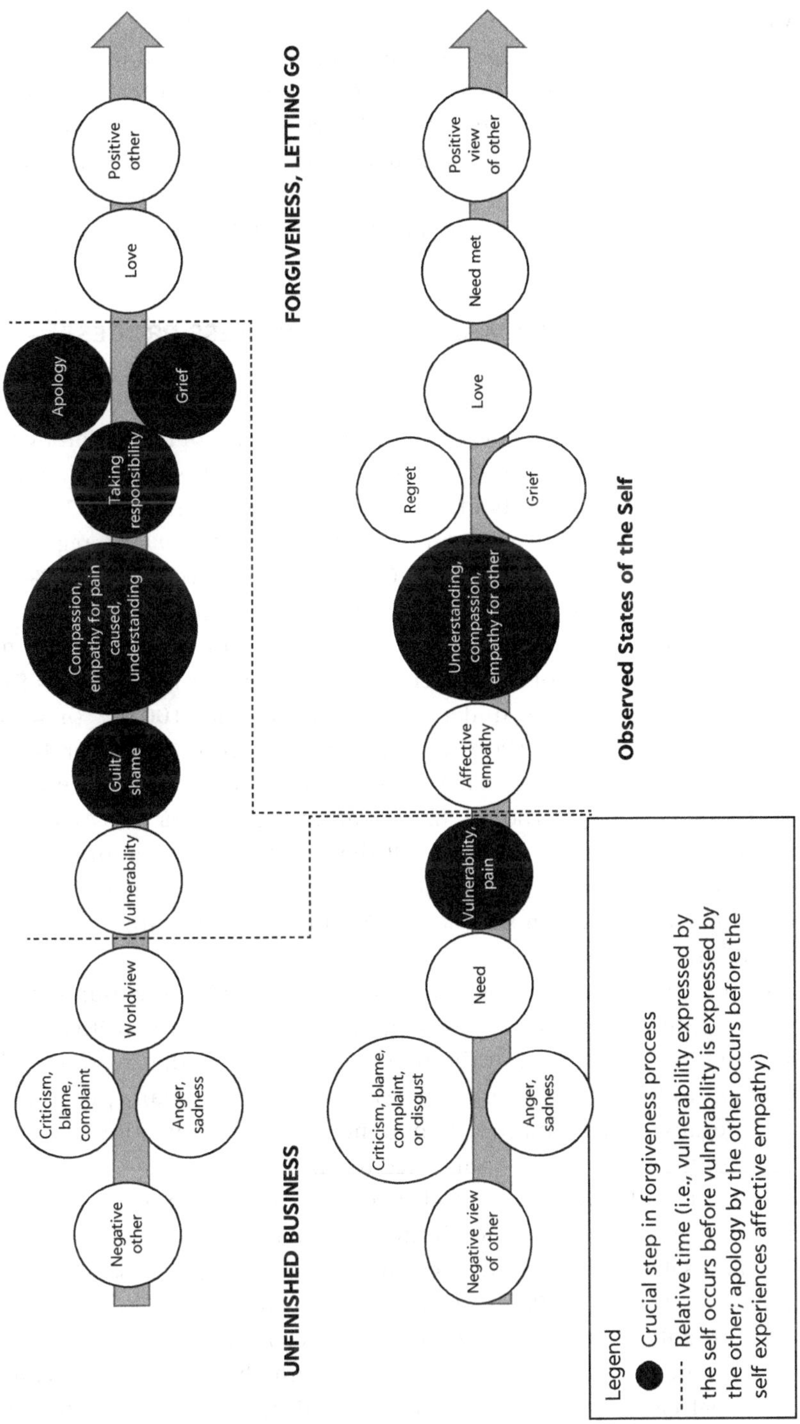

white lettering in the figure. Differences appear to emerge between the two processes after the expression of vulnerability by the client in the self chair. It was the expression of compassion by the imagined injurer and empathy for the pain caused accompanied by grief that seemed crucial to facilitate reciprocal empathy, understanding, and possibly compassion for the injurer. The sequence in time of the appearance of states is also represented in the model. For example, taking the horizontal axis to be a time line, vulnerability by the self occurs before vulnerability by the other. This indicates that in therapy vulnerability by the self emerges before vulnerability by the other.

## ELEMENTS UNIQUE TO MELISSA'S FORGIVENESS PROCESS

The defining features of unilateral forgiveness were identified by comparing the different states arising between Melissa's process of resolution by forgiveness and Kira's process of resolving through self-assertion. The following states occurred almost exclusively in Melissa's self chair: vulnerability 100.0% ($n$ = 14), empathy 100.0% ($n$ = 14), understanding 100.0% ($n$ = 8), regret 100.0% ($n$ = 4), acceptance of apology 100.0% ($n$ = 1), forgiveness 100.0% ($n$ = 8), compassion 100.0% ($n$ = 3), love 100.0% ($n$ = 3), letting go 90.1% ($n$ = 9), and need being met 100.0% ($n$ = 1). The states that occurred uniquely in Melissa's portrayal of her father were vulnerability 100.0% ($n$ = 9), compassion 100.0% ($n$ = 2), understanding of the other 100.0% ($n$ = 2), guilt expressed by the other 100% ($n$ = 6), empathy from the other 100.0% ($n$ = 1), apology 100.0% ($n$ = 15), taking responsibility 100.0% ($n$ = 3), love 100.0% ($n$ = 6), regret 100.0% ($n$ = 4), affirming 100.0% ($n$ = 4), and accepting 100.0% ($n$ = 1). Conversely, all these states, except letting go, did not occur in the resolution of unfinished business through self-assertion. The state of letting go occurred on 12.1% ($n$ = 2) of the occasions from the self's chair in Kira's therapy.

Of the remaining states observed, 67.8% ($n$ = 422) were found to be common to both courses of therapy, and 1.4% ($n$ = 9) were positive states that occurred toward the end of the therapies. The states that were found to be common to both clients' forms of resolution, such as blame, complaint and hurt, negative other, and statement of need, are accounted for in the existing model of the resolution of unfinished business.

Differences were also found between the amount of aroused and nonaroused states visited by each client through the courses of their therapies. High arousal appears in both cases. Melissa's very high arousal (88.3%) compared with Kira's (11.7%) was attributed to an individual difference rather than through distinguishing the process because both were intensely emotional. States of arousal were classified from the transcript as containing nonverbal elements by indications of sniffling, an increase in breathing, a trembling voice, a raised voice, or crying, which were all marked on the transcript. In total, across the two clients, 31.7% ($n$ = 197) of the states observed were accompanied by emotional arousal. Of the states accompanied by arousal, 11.7% ($n$ = 23) were found to have occurred in Kira's case of resolution by self-assertion, and 88.3% ($n$ = 174) were noted in Melissa's case, where resolution had taken place through forgiveness.

## SEQUENCING THE ELEMENTS OF FORGIVENESS

The first state unique to forgiveness emerged as vulnerability by the self in Session 5 after the expression of a need. This was followed by vulnerability by the other, which involved showing the other's pain concerning past developmental trauma that reveals the other to be someone who has been hurt. For example, the client, as the other, cried when talking about being shipped to boarding school as a child. This state was not observed in the case of self-assertion. Following the development of vulnerability in the other, the client was next able to access feelings of compassion as the other. Emerging next was the state of compassion by the other. Compassion by the other involved the other feeling sympathy and sorrow for the suffering the self had experienced. Sympathy and sorrow are also accompanied by a desire to alleviate the suffering. For example, in one part of the therapy, the other expressed, while crying, a desire to help his daughter with the pain she had experienced. Compassion by the other was not observed in the case of self-assertion.

The next state to arise in the other's chair was understanding by the other. This state was not observed in the case of self-assertion.

The next state to emerge was guilt or shame in the other's chair. The main characteristic of this state involved the other feeling bad for his actions. The distinguishing feature of guilt is an action tendency of wanting to make amends, and the distinguishing feature of shame is a tendency of wanting to sink into the ground. To reiterate, however, the main characteristic of this state is the other feeling bad for past behavior. For example, during an enactment in the other chair, the father stated, while crying, that he was beyond sorry and felt guilty for what he had done to his daughter. Furthermore, he wished that he would die. Guilt or shame was not observed in the self-assertion case. Empathy by identification was observed several times while the client enacted the role of the other. This type of enactment allows the client to experience the other's emotions and body felt sensations by embodying their expression. Empathy by identification by enacting the other is different from empathy by the self for the other or the other for the self because it is a phenomenon that occurs when the client enacts the role of the other at an emotionally aroused level. Empathic identification was not observed in the self-assertion case.

Continuing on the path of the other, the state of empathy by the other was next observed. The state of apology next emerged from the other's chair. The apology involved the other expressing remorse or sorrow for having injured or wronged another. Following the apology, the other took responsibility by admitting he had made mistakes and owning up to any wrongdoing.

Returning to the self's chair, the next state observed was empathy by the self. This state was not seen in the case of self-assertion.

The state of regret by the self next occurred in the case of forgiveness. Regret by the other immediately followed regret by the self. Compassion by the self was the last state to emerge before the forgiveness process moved into completion. A shift in view of the other was predominantly observed in at least two sessions. A shift in view of the other is defined as a change in the opinion the self has about the other. For example, at the beginning of therapy, the other was seen as someone who was bad, cold, and overbearing. By the end of therapy, the client saw the other as someone who was hurt and not all bad. This state was observed only once in the case of self-assertion. All shifts in view of the other, except the last one, were followed by a reversion to a negative view of the other. Only the last shift in view of the other was followed by positive dialogue, indicating a full shift in view of the other had occurred.

The positive other emerged near the end of therapy in Sessions 9 and 10. This state was not seen in the case of self-assertion. The positive other is defined as the other, demonstrating the qualities of nurturing, affirmation, and caring that meet the needs of the self. For example, at the beginning of therapy, the other was harsh and highly critical of his daughter. At the end of therapy, the other affirmed his daughter and accepted her without conditions.

At the conclusion of therapy, forgiveness emerged as the first state of resolution. *Forgiveness* is defined as the state of excusing past transgressions or renouncing resentment against another for an offense. For example, at the end of therapy, the client stated she forgave her father and uttered the statement without any anger or emotional arousal. Although forgiveness was first observed in Session 8, it was not complete and required additional work. All early statements of forgiveness absolved the other for specific things while holding the other accountable for others and retained some resentment toward the other. Some of these early statements of forgiveness were also uttered with emotional arousal. These indications demonstrated that further emotional processing was required for forgiveness to be complete. Unconditional forgiveness was not observed until its last appearance in Session 10.

Accompanying forgiveness at the end of treatment, letting go was the other state to emerge at the point of resolution and was only observed in Session 10. *Letting go* is defined as the process of saying goodbye to past pain and distress related to the EI.

## IDENTIFYING THE ESSENTIAL COMPONENTS OF FORGIVENESS

Many states, such as complaining, the expressions of anger and sadness, the articulation of needs, as well as others, were common to both the self-assertion and forgiveness paths to resolution. There were, however, also many unique states present in the forgiveness path that were not present in the self-assertion path to resolution. It is these distinguishing features that are thought to possibly be the essential components of the process of forgiveness.

The client who resolved through forgiveness experienced a significantly higher amount of states in the other chair. Especially important because emotional arousal has been linked to better outcomes in psychotherapy is that the client who forgave attained considerably more of these states at an emotionally aroused level than the client who asserted. Emotional enactment of the other in dialogue with the self seemed to be paramount to the process of forgiveness for two reasons. First, because the initial element unique to forgiveness was presented as aroused vulnerability by the self in Session 5, it appeared necessary for the other to respond similarly to lay the groundwork for other states to arise. Vulnerability by the self, which involved the showing of the self's pain in relation to the other, represented the first move toward reconciliation because it signified a desire to end the conflict. In Kira's case, whenever the self displayed sadness, the other responded in an attacking manner. Because it was not safe to even express emotion to the other, it was unlikely that vulnerability by the self would be expressed. In fact, Kira never expressed vulnerability. Both cases illustrate that some sort of reciprocity or an appropriate response is necessary for the process of forgiveness to begin and progress to other states. Essentially, Melissa illustrated that a reciprocal response to vulnerability by the self leads to the development of other states in the other chair necessary for forgiveness, whereas a negative response to vulnerability by the self inhibits the development of other states necessary for forgiveness.

Second, it was necessary that the client spend a considerable amount of time enacting the role of the other because many states in the other were required before the self could move from the state of vulnerability to the state of empathy. It makes sense that the injuring party would have to develop the dialogue and make reparations for the inflicted pain before the injured party could begin to soften their defensive stance further and allow other, more adaptive states conducive to forgiveness to surface. These states also had to be enacted at the emotionally aroused level for the client to experience all the body felt sensations the other would have felt. Because of their absence in the self-assertion case and high incidence in the forgiveness case, the self's vulnerability, empathy, understanding, compassion, regret, and acceptance of the apology seemed to be the necessary states required for letting go and forgiveness to occur. In addition, guilt and shame, apology, and taking responsibility by the other were the states necessary for forgiveness to occur. This supports the assertion that the emotional work in the role of the other is necessary for forgiveness because guilt and shame, apology, and taking responsibility only came from the other's position.

The process of resolving past EIs is nonlinear and unfolds over time. The phases of the EFT process are intended to be a road map rather than a prescription to facilitating change because there is often recursive looping back through the phases within one session and from one session to another. In the beginning, it is important to help clients figure out what it is that they hold against the other—forgiveness that is specific and accurately addresses the meaning of the injury (e.g., did it damage or destroy the client's willingness or ability to trust others or their sense of being able to trust themselves and/or alter their worldview from a belief in a just world to one that recognizes that life is not always fair even if one behaves well toward others?). The timing of forgiveness also is important—not immediately in the wake of hurtfulness and not when there is self-work that has to happen first.

In all phases of the therapy process, there is an emphasis on heightening the intensity of primary emotional experience to access previously unacknowledged core emotion schemes related to the injury and make them amenable to change. The potential forgiver's feelings of resentment and desire for revenge or restitution are of considerable importance. It is important not to set the expectation of positive feelings toward the other too early in therapy (if at all) because one could mistakenly foster the idea that negative emotion has no place in the experience of the forgiving person. Such expectations would short-circuit the healthy adaptive process of being in touch with feelings of anger and resentment and can put the client at risk for future harm. This is particularly true in those instances when abuse is the focus of the client's work, not only regarding the original injurer but also potential future relationships of a similar kind.

Part of what is needed to achieve the primary, adaptive, and complex feeling of forgiveness is a shift from viewing the self as wholly injured and other as wholly bad to a view of self as "not all good" and other as "not all bad" (Akhtar, 2002). There is a connection between such shifts and the emotion work and emerging feelings of empathy and compassion. When people permit themselves to feel their resentment and acknowledge their desire to hurt the other as he or she was hurt or access their intense feelings of loss, shame, or fear, the groundwork is laid for the necessary shift in view of self and other.

In terms of facilitating unilateral forgiveness in the absence of the injurer, unresolved interpersonal injuries are characterized by negative self–other schemas that are part of the individual's role-relationship model (Horowitz, Rosenbaum, & Wilner, 1988). These models involve schematic memories of highly significant, emotion-laden interactions of him- or herself with the other. Episodic memories and attitudes toward the self and other become set as inner representations of the self and other (Greenberg & Safran, 1987) and may include the failure to integrate the experience of the other fully. This can be understood as an introjection of a negative experience of the other without assimilation. As a result, rather than seeing the other person as someone with both positive and negative aspects, the other is seen as all "bad," whereas the "good" aspects of the other are relegated to the background of the individual's perception of the other.

This shift in how the other is represented and viewed is crucial to forgiveness. Greenberg and Paivio (1997) highlighted how important it is that an injured person in therapy come to believe that if the injurer were present in the room, he or she would be able to hear and empathize with the client's emotional pain and distress, take responsibility for harm done, and seek to make amends if they could. Only then can the client soften and begin to empathize with the others' limitations. One client in the York Emotional Injury Project explained during his posttreatment interview that he could never forgive his father for being harshly critical and rejecting when the client was a child because his father had never been able to acknowledge the wrongfulness of or apologize for his hurtful behavior toward the client. Because his harshly critical father was still present in the client's life, the client could not revise his inner representation of his father to incorporate a remorseful, empathic father with whom he, in turn, would be drawn to empathize. This highlights that the connection between apology, empathy, and forgiveness found by McCullough et al. (1998) may operate in both interpersonal and unilateral forms of forgiveness.

Emotion-laden memories of self and other are at the heart of unilateral forgiveness, and part of the function of dialectic imagination in empty-chair work is to facilitate the client imaginatively projecting him- or herself into an enactment of the other as empathic. This, in turn, fosters an empathic response within the client, thereby opening up the possibility of revising his or her representations of the other from inhuman monster to "not all bad" and therefore forgivable.

A shift in view of the other (being able to imagine the other as feeling sorrow and regret for harm done) and enacting the other as having affective empathy is important, but it is possible that self-work (self-validation, self-affirmation, and self-strengthening) will take priority over feeling forgiving toward the hurtful other.

When accessed, empathy is a primary and adaptive complex feeling that facilitates forgiveness in the face of an interpersonal injury. The ability to feel empathy for the injurer, however, appears in our sample to be preceded by the process of helping clients to access and face their pain, which in turn enables them to imagine that the injurer could see and understand it too. Only when a client experiences him- or herself as someone who is strong enough to own and express painful and distressing emotions can he or she envision another who is similarly strong enough to hear and take responsibility for harm done. Engaging in imaginary dialogues with the injurer, in an empathic therapeutic environment, seems to facilitate these processes.

## CONCLUSION

Empty-chair dialogue with the injurer has been shown to be effective both in letting go of troublesome feelings and moving on and in promoting forgiveness. It appears that activating painful emotional feelings and bringing cognition to bear to make sense of these feelings are helpful in promoting forgiveness. In addition, accessing a representation of the other as empathic and compassionate to the pain caused to the self seems important in promoting forgiveness. This emotion work leads to a change in the view of the other and the construction of new narratives.

# 5

# Overview of the Emotion-Focused Therapy for Couples Framework

Emotion-focused therapy for couples (EFT-C) involves entering into primary emotion and forging new experiences between partners in-session (Greenberg & Goldman, 2008; Greenberg & Johnson, 1988; Johnson, 1996). This is what gives the approach power; it is the up and running live emotion in-session that generates powerful change. Johnson and Greenberg (1988) found that EFT-C was more effective than a cognitive behavioral approach and that the presence of partners experiencing primary emotion and sharing these with each other via in-session enactments mediated therapy outcome.

## EMOTIONS IN SYSTEMS: THE ROLE OF AFFECT IN COUPLES INTERACTIONS

Relationships are intrinsically linked to emotions. We choose to enter an intimate relationship with another person because this person helps us feel calm, secure, valued, and excited, and we strive to keep these feelings alive as the relationship evolves. We immediately know that our relationship is in trouble when we feel anxious, insecure, invalidated, or bored. At a fundamental level, we seek relationships because we seek emotion. In our view, seeking emotion is an important motivating force, and affect regulation is a major motive that exists in relationships. Taking care of others also regulates our feelings and those of our partner while liking and being liked elevates our vitality and

http://dx.doi.org/10.1037/0000144-006
*Forgiveness and Letting Go in Emotion-Focused Therapy*, by L. S. Greenberg and C. Woldarsky Meneses

purpose. As Greenberg and Goldman (2008) suggested, relationships are primary affect regulators: As adults, we bond with partners because this gives us the feelings we want, and we break the bond when we receive too many of the feelings we do not want.

It is also important to note that, as we discussed in Chapter 2, we come into the world with a differentiated set of basic psycho–affective–motor programs. Many of these emotion programs are interpersonally oriented and lead us to seek out and react to the other. According to Panksepp and Biven (2012), there are at least seven emotional patterns with subcortical deep brain stimulation in mammals, each linked to a unique form of arousal. These neurophysiological processes are either *rewarding* (seeking, lust, care, and play) or *punishing* (rage, fear, and panic). Unfortunately, behaviorism, with its stimulus–consequence paradigm, rendered emotions outside the realm of scientific investigation. This has led to a serious neglect of emotion in psychotherapy (Greenberg, 2010; Greenberg & Safran, 1987). Not included in the behaviorist paradigm is the consideration that all mammals feel and that any stimulus can be rewarding or punishing depending on how they lead the organism to feel (Panksepp & Biven, 2012). For example, we avoid a given stimulus because we avoid the fear associated with that situation, whereas we approach a stimulus because we associate the stimulus with feelings of comfort and ease. Thus, feelings have a primary effect on whether we approach or avoid our intimate partners.

From the EFT-C perspective, Greenberg and Goldman (2008) viewed affect regulation as the process that governs the motivation to couple. Affect regulation is neither monomotivational (e.g., we are not exclusively motivated to attach as per Bowlby, 1968, or to self-actualize as per Rogers, 1959) nor bimotivational (libido and aggression as per Freud, pleasure-seeking and pain-avoiding as per behaviorism). Instead, affect is seen as motivational and goal directed, promoting behavior that is diverse and extensive (Greenberg & Goldman, 2008). For example, we seek the feelings of pride, satisfaction, and joy that come with mastering a new skill. This is what drives us to take on the challenge of learning something new, more than the practical consequences of acquiring the new skill. The motives considered important for successful coupling attachment—establishing coherence and identity, exploration, control, and achievement—are all motivated by how these make us feel. As discussed in Chapter 2, we seek to have certain emotions because the goals in these emotions—to approach, withdraw, push away, run away, cuddle, or seek out—were central to our survival as a species (Greenberg & Goldman, 2008).

Emotion is a central component of coupling and marriage; no other context is so infused with and responsive to the ebb and flow of human emotion. Without our conscious awareness, we attend to nonverbal cues from our partner, cues such as facial expression, gestures, and tone of voice, and we are exquisitely sensitive to minute signals that inform us about closeness and distance and dominance and submission. Therefore, emotion is at the forefront of our approach to working with couples in therapy.

An important emotional process between couples is the notion of emotional injuries (EIs), which are dependent on emotional memories and the creation of meaning. Over the course of their relationship, couples often respond to one another in ways that damage or threaten to damage their intimate relational bond. These experiences can lead to a loss of basic trust in either the partner's ability to be there when needed or ability to see and validate the other partner when this support is needed. These are cases when letting go and forgiveness are potentially most relevant.

## EFFECTS OF THREE BASIC AFFECTIVE AND MOTIVATIONAL SYSTEMS ON INTIMATE RELATIONSHIPS

We seek to feel a set of core emotions in close relationships: soothed and calm as an antidote to fear and sadness at loss of the connection; pride and joy in being recognized and validated as an antidote to shame and diminishment; and interest, joy, excitement, and passionate love that are involved in affection. The need to regulate our emotions motivates us to engage in specific behaviors vis-à-vis our partner (Greenberg & Goldman, 2008). For example, when we feel sad or afraid, we reach out for comfort and soothing and feel more secure when we receive it; when we feel disrespected or attacked, we lash out to protect ourselves and feel more powerful. Greenberg and Goldman (2008) posited that this central need, to regulate our affect, governs the following three primary motivational systems important in intimate relationships: attachment (related to contact and comfort), identity (related to territoriality), and attraction and liking (related to warmth and intimacy).

Other theorists have recognized these three dimensions as important to interpersonal functioning. The first two dimensions have been previously described by Bakan (1966) as the need for communion and agency, whereas the dimension of attraction and liking has been described by Gottman (2011) as the fondness and admiration system, which enhances the relationship and promotes healthy functioning, arguing that interest in our partners and attraction to them generates positive feelings that are important to the well-being of the couple.

Although feelings of attraction and liking are important in intimate relationships, this motivational system is not treated as central as the other two in EFT-C. Interestingly, pleasant feelings of attraction and liking are often seen to resurge once difficulties related to the dimensions of attachment (i.e., security, closeness, and responsiveness) and identity (i.e., validation, acceptance, and recognition) have been resolved. This emphasis on attachment- and identity-related feelings is apparent in working with an EI and forgiveness in couples. Greenberg and Goldman (2008) argued that if these two sets of affective needs are not met by our partners, negative feelings arise (e.g., fear at loss of connection, shame at feeling diminished) that motivate us to behave in a particular way in an attempt to have these feelings or to not have them. (e.g., to approach or to avoid, to submit or to dominate). These emotion-motivated behaviors are then generally met by complementary responses from our partners and result in escalating conflict. Part of what fuels couples' conflicts is the difficulty partners have in expressing their vulnerable emotions to one another and the tendency to express hostile emotions (e.g., anger, contempt) instead or indifference that elicit defensiveness or a counterattack from the other partner. This circular view of emotion in close relationships (Greenberg & Goldman, 2008; Greenberg & Johnson, 1988) highlights that interactions are influenced and maintained by the emotional expressions of both partners and by both partners' ability to regulate each other's and their own emotions. For example, a husband's request for increased closeness goes unmet and results in him feeling alone and rejected, which is uncomfortable for him, so instead of revealing his vulnerable feelings, he expresses anger toward his wife in a critical and persistent manner. She, however, feels attacked and inadequate in response to his criticism and rather than sharing with him what she feels, she retreats further to avoid his anger, which only leads him to become more persistent with her. In distressed couples, misguided efforts to get the emotions one desires from the other and the inability to soothe one's own emotions evolve into a rigid, repetitive, and cyclical way of interacting.

## Negative Interactional Cycles

*Negative interactional cycles* develop when each partner's efforts to have the other respond to his or her needs generates a response that is contrary to what each partner hopes for and seeks. A classic example involves one partner pursuing closeness and approaching the other partner, who perceives this as invasive and thus distances him- or herself, which results in the first partner increasing his or her pursuing behavior. The EFT-C therapist frames each partner's problematic behaviors not as being the result of one or both partners' failings but rather as attempted solutions to problems, which have now become the problem. This framework shifts the "blame" onto the interaction rather than on the individuals so that rather than attempting to change one another, the partners join forces and work toward changing their problematic interactional patterns. When there has been an EI, the couple likely develops a negative interactional cycle that stems from the unresolved feelings related to the injury. Therapists have to be mindful to attend to both the cycle that developed post-EI and the one that predated it because it is in the original cycle that the injury occurred.

In EFT-C, the focus is on understanding how both partners' emotional experience contributes to the negative interactions in the couple. The interactional cycle that is established between the partners is a consequence of them expressing secondary rather than primary emotions. According to Goldman and Greenberg (2013), couples' interactions take place along two dimensions: affiliation and influence. Negative behaviors can be understood as counter-productive attempts to manage or shift the dynamics of closeness in the relationship or those related to power and influence in the relationship, respectively. All behaviors occur on a continuum, and affiliative behaviors range from expressions of love, warmth, and nurturance at one end of the continuum to hostile, indifferent, or withdrawn behaviors at the other end. Similarly, behaviors on the influence dimension range from attempts to control, override, or dominate to submissive, deferential, and yielding behaviors at the other end of the continuum. Greenberg and Goldman (2008) identified attachment- and identity-related needs as being the two fundamental concerns driving negative interactional cycles.

## Attachment Cycles

Variations of attachment-related cycles include pursue–distance, demand–withdraw, and cling–pull away, all of which are attempts to manage proximity and responsiveness. The pursuing partner's anger typically obscures primary fear and/or sadness, whereas the distancing partner's defensiveness or withdrawal typically obscure fear and/or shame.

In this type of cycle, the pursuing partner's "approaching" behavior is typically driven by a need for greater closeness, security, availability, or responsiveness from his or her partner. Rather than welcoming more closeness, the withdrawer experiences closeness as uncomfortable, or even dangerous, potentially leading to boundary intrusion, engulfment, and/or increased pain in the event of future abandonment. Although the pursuer manages his or her anxiety by approaching the withdrawer—perhaps lovingly at first and then perhaps with hostility after "failed attempts" to receive more closeness—the withdrawer regulates his or her anxiety by keeping his or her distance (e.g., responding in an indifferent and detached manner, withdrawing to another room, and avoiding spending time together). This type of behavior is likely to evoke further anxiety or anger in the pursuing partner, who may escalate his or her efforts to have these attachment needs met, which result in the withdrawer distancing even further. It should be noted that the cycle can emerge regardless of who "takes the first step," such that it may be the withdrawer's need for more distance that may be unsettling for the pursuer and lead to him or her increasing his or her attempts to seek closeness.

## Identity Cycles

These types of negative interactions involve dominating or controlling behavior by one partner and deferential and submissive behavior by the other. They may also take the form of an overfunctioning or underfunctioning dynamic. The partner in the dominant position typically makes the decisions, defines reality, and views him- or herself as knowing what is best or right and thus takes on the "lion's share of the work." These behaviors reflect a need to regulate feelings of shame (difficulties with self-esteem) by attempting to get the other partner to provide them with validation, respect, and appreciation and also speak to an underlying fear of losing control or feeling dominated. The partner in the submissive position typically follows, defers, and looks to the other partner for direction. The primary emotions underlying the submissive partner's interactional stance include fear, shame, and anger.

Partners can function in this type of cycle for years without conflict arising until the day that the partner in the submissive position grows resentful of the unequal dynamic and begins to resist or stand up to the dominant partner. This typically activates great anxiety in the dominant partner because he or she experiences his or her status or sense of self as under threat and feels a loss of control over the other partner. Rather than acknowledge that he or she was wrong and be open to negotiating a new type of arrangement with the submissive partner, the dominant partner regulates his or her negative affect through the use of persuasion or coercion, maintaining the one-up position and sense of being right or superior. Dominant partners often rely on intellect and rationality to convince the other that their views or actions are the correct ones (i.e., they "define reality"). When intellectual arguments fail to sway their partner, they may resort to expressing anger and contempt to achieve acquiescence.

For both attachment and identity cycles, helping partners to access and express vulnerable underlying emotions, such as shame and fear, is viewed as central to generating new types of interactions. In working with submissive partners, however, the expression of primary anger is seen as adaptive and important for the renegotiation of roles in the couple.

## PRINCIPLES OF CHANGE IN FORGIVENESS-ORIENTED EMOTION-FOCUSED THERAPY FOR COUPLES

The key principles of change in EFT-C include working with expressions of vulnerability and having partners be responsive to these expressions, thereby promoting corrective interpersonal emotional experiences (Greenberg & Goldman, 2008). All these elements hold true when working with couples wishing to resolve an EI.

In EFT, we understand that a secondary emotion masks or overshadows the primary emotion, and once the latter can be accessed and explored (a process that is facilitated by the EFT therapist), the previously unacknowledged core emotion schemes related to the injury are activated and are now amenable to change (Elliott, Watson, Goldman, & Greenberg, 2004; Greenberg, 2002; see Chapter 4, this volume). In working with couples to facilitate forgiveness, the therapist helps partners move from secondary, reactive emotions to primary, vulnerable emotions and works at having them be responsive to each other's vulnerability while at the same time promoting the necessary tasks that invite forgiveness, which will be elaborated on in Chapter 7.

Witnessing one's partner express vulnerability, where there is an openness to revealing what one feels without any guardedness or defensiveness, is a powerful experience that has a significant impact on the couple. Early research conducted by Greenberg and colleagues (Greenberg, Ford, Alden, & Johnson, 1993; Johnson & Greenberg, 1988) consistently found that when an expression of vulnerability evokes a compassionate response from the other partner, the relational dynamic changes dramatically and there is a "softening" between the partners, which is associated with success in EFT. Research by McKinnon and Greenberg (2013) revealed that couples rate EFT-C sessions in which vulnerability is expressed as being more "productive" than sessions in which it is not expressed. Follow-up research by McKinnon and Greenberg (2017) showed that the expression of emotional vulnerability among couples seeking to heal an EI predicts greater levels of improvement at the final outcome. The resolution of an EI is most likely to occur when (a) the offending partner shows a high level of supportiveness in response to the injured partner's expressions of vulnerability, and (b) the offending partner expresses a high level of vulnerable emotion him or herself (McKinnon, & Greenberg, 2017).

In working with couples who wish to resolve an EI, the principle of working with emotional vulnerability holds true; however, it is a specific type of vulnerability that will promote forgiveness: The offender's expression of other-focused remorse, such as shame or empathic distress, elicits a different stance from the injured partner (i.e., feelings of concern, compassion, or empathy) and makes forgiveness more likely.

## INTERVENTION STRATEGIES

In EFT-C, expression of primary vulnerable emotions is considered to be the key to transforming the couple's rigid cycle of relating and bringing partners closer together (Greenberg & Goldman, 2008; Greenberg & Johnson, 1988). The EFT-C therapist aims to help each partner realize that what they typically express to each other in conflict situations are secondary or instrumental emotions, which serve to keep them trapped in a negative interactional cycle. The aim is to have partners be able to express the primary underlying attachment- and identity-oriented emotions (e.g., fear underneath anger or hostility, shame or inadequacy underneath withdrawal or contempt) that are beneath the harsh emotions or indifference they typically express. Emphasis is placed on understanding each partner's underlying vulnerabilities in the relationship and individual sensitivities that predate the couple's union (e.g., feeling sensitive to abandonment or criticism). These sensitivities may stem from unmet childhood needs and/or emotions linked to the dimension of identity (e.g., shame) that cannot be soothed by a partner's reassurance and depend instead on self-focused work that may enhance the capacity to self-soothe. Thus, Greenberg and Goldman (2008) included individual-based work to promote self-soothing and address unmet needs that originated in childhood, in addition to assisting couples to develop proficiency in responding to each other's primary emotions and associated needs.

## STAGES OF TREATMENT

Greenberg and Goldman (2008) proposed a five-stage treatment model, which is presented next, along with details of how to adjust this approach when the focus is on the resolution of an EI. It should be noted that the treatment protocol used in the York Emotional Injury Project (Greenberg, Warwar, & Malcolm, 2010) out of which our research is derived, included the use of homework (see Appendix 5.1). At Session 6, the couple was presented with three handouts and asked to reflect on how the information outlined pertained to them, and they were asked to write a letter to their partner. Chapter 8 includes a case example that helps illustrate the treatment model outlined here.

### Stage 1: Validation and Alliance Formation

During this stage, the therapist aims to form a collaborative alliance with both partners by validating their individual emotional experience, as well as their shared suffering. It is paramount that the therapist maintains an empathic stance toward both partners even if it there may be a personal inclination to side with the injured partner over the offending partner. This means validating the injured partner's pain without shaming or blaming the offending partner. The therapist can do this by clearly stating his or her intentions:

> I want to understand and help you both understand what happened so that we can work toward healing this rupture that is creating so much suffering for you both. I can see how painful this is for you, [injured partner], and I imagine it must also be difficult for you, [offending partner].

Creating an emotional bond with both partners fosters the safety that is needed for each partner to reveal themselves emotionally and process their experiences freely in therapy (Greenberg, 2006; Greenberg & Goldman, 2008). The therapist is also seeking an understanding of the couple's narrative: their relational history and the contextual factors that favored the EI (i.e., the therapist is attentive to current and past difficulties related to the domains of attachment and identity).

### Stage 2: Negative Cycle De-Escalation

It is essential to reduce the emotional reactivity between the partners to promote a new way of interacting (Greenberg & Goldman, 2008) and move forward in helping the couple resolve their EI. Part of the challenge is that couples have usually developed and are caught in a negative interactional cycle stemming from the EI that has to be addressed. This current cycle can be thought of as a form of protest against the loss of connection that likely predated the EI but was amplified with the EI. For example, the injured partner may constantly be questioning the offending partner and insisting on more details about why he or she behaved that way, how it happened, and so forth, which leaves the offending partner feeling frustrated and possibly withdrawing when his or her answers are met with disbelief or are endlessly challenged.

The therapist observes how partners relate to each other in-session, tracks each of their emotional reactions in the unfolding of the interactions and empathically reflects the processes that occur between them while also exploring the emotions that arise. Although some context is certainly needed to understand how the EI occurred, the therapist is mindful to limit his or her focus to asking content-based questions and give preference to observing how partners express and regulate their emotions related to the injury. This is usually linked to the activation of the couple's current cycle. For example, the injured partner may try to regulate his or her pain by "pursuing" the offending partner with persistent questioning or with criticisms or by withdrawing into his or her world, all of which elicit a complementary response from the offending partner. Conversely, the current cycle could be activated by the offending partner's attempts to regulate his or her remorse or shame for having committed the EI by pursuing the injured partner for closeness by insisting on being forgiven or blaming the injured partner for being the source of the couple's current difficulties given that he or she has not yet been able to move forward. The offending partner may beg and plead for forgiveness (i.e., a submissive position that invites the injured partner to take a one-up position and respond with indifference or with a sense of entitlement to punish the offending partner by making him or her "suffer" for the damage incurred).

It may also be the case that the offending partner's difficulties in managing his or her sense of despair and helplessness about not being able to reconnect with the injured partner may give way to him or her being critical of the injured partner's current state of unforgiveness and expressing anger and contempt, which likely leads the injured partner to be defensive or to withdraw. We have also observed offending partners using instrumental emotion (e.g., crying and expressing self-blame or even self-deprecation) to bring the injured partner closer and bypass the essential tasks required of him or her in the resolution process, which involve being responsive to the injured partner's pain. This behavior typically results in a type of role reversal where the injured partner approaches the offending partner with a caretaking attitude and offers reassurance but at the same time feels resentful that his or her pain is denied attention.

To move forward in the process of resolving the EI and prevent conflict from escalating between the partners, the therapist frames the couple's problematic functioning in terms of a cycle: a rigidly defined way of interacting in which one partner's emotional expression and behavior elicits a particular emotional reaction in the other partner, which further influences how the first partner reacts. Externalizing the couple's difficulties in this way creates distance between the partners and their problematic style of relating and thus de-escalates tensions. As noted earlier, the initial focus is on understanding the couple's current cycle, although it is appropriate to inquire about how the partners related to each other before the EI and to identify each partner's position in the pre-EI cycle. Once the injury is resolved, the focus shifts to understanding the couple's previous cycle and the conditions that favored the EI.

The therapist also attempts to understand what emotions are driving each partner's position in the current cycle. In this process, the therapist facilitates a shift between the expression of secondary emotions related to the EI and primary, vulnerable emotions that will favor a new way of relating.

When dealing with the pre-EI cycle, the therapist also explores each partner's sensitivities and vulnerabilities that contribute to the position they adopt in the couple's negative interactional cycle. Each partner's position in the cycle is identified and linked to his or her psychogenetic origins, which are typically traumatic experiences or unmet needs in early childhood or past relationships (Greenberg & Goldman, 2008). In this way, each partner's difficulties are reframed in terms of unmet needs rather than character flaws or defects, which also helps to decrease emotional reactivity.

### Stage 3: Accessing Underlying Vulnerable Feelings

Most of the therapeutic work in helping couples overcome an EI occurs at this stage (and in Stage 4), where the focus is on the revealing, experiencing, and owning emotions that are typically unacknowledged and that underlie each partner's position in the interactional cycle. In doing so, partners are also able to articulate attachment- and identity-related needs associated with the emotions they experience in the position they assume in the couple's cycle. In disclosing their unacknowledged emotions to each other, the partners take a risk and express vulnerability, which radically changes the interactional pattern between them; each comes to view the other as more approachable, there is more safety between them, and communication flows more easily (Greenberg & Goldman, 2008).

To help couples move forward in resolving their EI, the therapist first encourages the injured partner to express his or her primary emotions related to the injury—usually anger, sadness, and hurt—which is typically accompanied by a revelation of the idiosyncratic meaning the injury had for him or her. The therapist reflects an empathic understanding of the injured partner's experience while simultaneously being attentive to the reactions of the offending partner. In turning to the offending partner and asking what it is like for him or her to hear about the injured partner's experience, the therapist hopes that he or she will be accepting of and responsive to the injured partner's pain and ideally be able to express nondefensive responsibility for the injury. If this is not the case, further exploration is needed to understand his or her difficulties in being able to accept responsibility for the EI and be responsive to the injured partner. Over the course of therapy, the focus shifts to having the offending partner access more vulnerable emotions. It is particularly important to eventually have the offending partner express deep remorse (i.e., shame or empathic distress) and offer a heartfelt apology because this is critical to promoting forgiveness.

Nevertheless, difficulties may arise with one or both partners in accessing and expressing emotions, which require the therapist to shift to doing more individual work with one partner (in the presence of the other) to explore these blocks to accessing emotion (e.g., a self-interruptive tendency; Greenberg & Goldman, 2008).

### Stage 4: Restructuring the Negative Interaction and the Self

To restructure the couple's interactions, it is imperative that partners be able not only to express their primary vulnerable emotions and related needs to each other but also to respond to their partner's vulnerability with acceptance and validation (Greenberg & Goldman, 2008). For example, on witnessing the offending partner's expression of shame or empathic distress, the injured partner is likely to experience a shift in his or her view of the offending partner and a sense of openness and acceptance to this vulnerability (Woldarsky Meneses & Greenberg, 2014). This sequence is a prelude to forgiveness. Similarly, when the injured partner does express forgiveness in-session, it is important to ensure that the offending partner receives this gift with an accepting and grateful attitude. The restructuring process unfolds at a deeper level once each partner can hear what the other has experienced and needs because this impacts the emotional and behavioral patterns between them (Greenberg & Goldman, 2008). Thus, the couple is no longer defined by the EI, nor are they bound by their postinjury cycle, and the therapeutic work can shift to exploring what was going on between them before the injury occurred, understanding what their positions in the cycle were, as well as their underlying emotions, and discussing how it was that they could not express their primary emotions and needs to one another.

If at any point during therapy the therapist observes that one partner is having difficulty responding to the other partner's vulnerability, these difficulties must be acknowledged and the emotional blocks explored. For couples that have not entered therapy with the goal of resolving an EI, it is often at this stage that an EI is revealed and becomes a focus for treatment because the injured partner's unresolved anger and pain regarding the injury interfere with any form of empathic or accepting stance toward his or her partner.

### Stage 5: Consolidation and Integration

The task of the therapist during this final stage of therapy is to help partners reflect on their process of change in working through the resolution of the injury. Partners have to consolidate their understanding of how their previous way of functioning favored the conditions that gave way to the EI to prevent their relationship from degrading again and to be at risk of injuring each other. Typically, the couple articulates the changes and gains made during their time in therapy in the narrative they develop, which usually involves reference to how they previously functioned, the difficulties that came with this way of relating, and contrasting this to their renewed connection and relationship.

This involves addressing the pre-EI cycle by identifying each partner's position, the emotions that were underlying their positions, and the ones they expressed. It is also important to help partners articulate their understanding of their own and their partner's vulnerabilities and how they can respond when they are aware that these vulnerabilities have been activated (Greenberg & Goldman, 2008). This stage also involves discussing relapse prevention, where the therapist enquires about moments when the cycle would previously have been activated and helps them understand how they prevented this from happening (i.e., how they avoided reverting to their typical positions).

## CONCLUSION

Emotion is a central force in intimate relationships. Our work in EFT-C involves understanding how each partner's emotional experience contributes to the couple's negative interactional cycle. We aim to have partners access and express their underlying vulnerable primary emotions and needs to each other and have them be responsive to what the other reveals. In this chapter, we outlined the theoretical framework of this approach as well as the stages of treatment, highlighting the particularities of working with couples wanting to resolve an EI where the work is both on restructuring the current negative cycle, as well as addressing the cycle that predated the EI and gave rise to it. Helping couples resolve an EI requires that the injured partner express the primary emotions related to the injury and the offending partner be responsive to the expressed anger, sadness, or pain and take nondefensive responsibility for the EI. The therapist works to help the offending partner express deep remorse (i.e., shame or empathic distress) and offer a heartfelt apology, which are critical to promoting forgiveness.

## APPENDIX 5.1: HOMEWORK ASSIGNMENTS

### Instructions to Therapists for Homework

At Session 6, or if it seems suitable at another time, please implement the following homework assignment with your couple. These handouts should be stapled together:

1. Forgiveness Usually Involves
2. The Bond That Still Holds You
3. If Your Partner Feels Hurt by You or if You Feel Hurt by Your Partner

Note that if it is appropriate, both partners can write both letters to each other, but it might be a good idea for the therapist to go over them quickly with the couple to make sure that we at least have a letter from the injurer ("If Your Partner Feels Hurt by You") and that we also have a letter from the injured ("If You Feel Hurt by Your Partner"). Therapists should help the couple decide who is going to write which letter.

Ask partners to give these letters to each other to read before the next session, but ask them not to discuss the letters in any detail with each other. Instead, ask them to bring the letters to the next session where they will discuss how they felt about the letters with the therapist. Ask them to make a copy for the therapist to keep on file. Make sure you address these letters in the following session with your clients.

### Handout 1: Forgiveness Usually Involves

Please read this handout and think about how it relates to you and your partner.

***Forgiveness Usually Involves***

- holding the other accountable for a wrong done;
- acknowledging one's role in the unfolding of events that contributed to the injury or to the feelings you have about the injury;
- giving up one's sense of entitlement to hold a grudge or seek revenge; and
- making an effort to bring an end to feelings of anger, resentment, and the desire for revenge.

Taken together, this process enables the forgiver to release the offender from responsibility for "fixing" the painful effects of the injury.

***Forgiveness Is Not***

- excusing, condoning, or pardoning;
- forgetting; or
- reconciling.

### Handout 2: The Bond That Still Holds You

Following an emotional injury, we are likely to ask the question "Why did he or she do that to me?" This question most often brings unsatisfactory answers because as human beings we don't clearly know why we do or we don't do things, and we often find it impossible to fully understand what motivates others to behave the way they do. In turn, unanswered questions of this sort create frustration, which compels us to ask the same question again. Ultimately, we may find ourselves caught in a vicious circle. Perhaps we are asking the wrong question.

Rather than looking at what caused the other's behavior, it may be more helpful to examine our own difficulty letting go. Obviously, we have no control over another person's motivation, but we can have some control over our own. Therefore, a more productive question may be, Why can't I let go? Other ways of asking this same question would be the following:

- What keeps the painful feelings (e.g., hurt, anger, sadness) in place?
- What purpose does or do the painful feeling or feelings serve?
- What terrible thing might happen if I let go of the painful feeling (or feelings)?

Possible answers may be that the bond between the other and ourselves would be eliminated, and this may be difficult to contemplate because something is better than nothing. Perhaps we would have to give ourselves what we expected from the other or find someone else to fill that need, and we may not know how to go about doing this. Alternatively, we may finally feel the full depth of our wound, and that prospect is frightening.

There may be many reasons why we are reluctant to move toward letting go. Please reflect on the previous questions and journal about your thoughts. Given the uniqueness of our particular experience, there are no right or wrong answers. Your task is to discover the reasons that best reflect your experience.

## Handout 3: If You Feel Hurt by Your Partner or If Your Partner Feels Hurt by You

Complete the following letter-writing assignment. When you have both completed your letters, give them to your partner to read in private. Do not discuss the letters. Instead, bring them to the session to discuss with your therapist. In addition, please make an extra copy to give to your therapist.

### *If Your Partner Feels Hurt by You*

If your partner feels injured by you, write a letter of apology to your partner for the hurt you have caused. Please include the following three components:

- *Regret*. Express what you regret, and specify your understanding of how you have hurt your partner.
- *Responsibility*. Take ownership of your role in the injury by specifying what you are taking responsibility for.
- *Remedy*. Express what you will do now to help your partner heal from the hurt.

### *If You Feel Hurt by Your Partner*

If you feel hurt by your partner, please write a letter to your partner indicating where you are in the process of resolving, forgiving, and/or letting go of the hurt or anger toward your partner.

- Express what you don't forgive or what you are not able to let go of and why it is difficult for you to resolve the injury.
- Express what you presently need from your partner to help you let go of the hurt and anger and/or to forgive.
- If you have let go of hurt and anger or forgiven your partner, say what you have done and whether you are able to reconcile.

# 6

# Emotion-Focused Therapy and Forgiveness or Reconciliation for Couples

Many therapists struggle with helping couples overcome the damage and pain in the aftermath of an emotional injury (EI) and in aiding them in rebuilding closeness and trust. The resolution of an EI can occur through different processes (as noted in Chapter 1), including through forgiveness. The aim of this chapter is to discuss forgiveness in the context of intimate relationships from a theoretical perspective. We discuss how an EI disrupts the three basic affective and motivational systems proposed, by emotion-focused therapy (EFT), to be at the heart of intimate relationships (i.e., the systems of attachment and contact comfort, dominance and territoriality, and warmth and liking; Greenberg & Goldman, 2008). We also outline the emotional processes involved in forgiveness in couples therapy and discuss the differences between forgiveness and reconciliation in some detail. In addition, we summarize the findings of a qualitative study on the experience of forgiveness in couples therapy (Sharma, 2013), which helps ground theory in injured clients self-reports.

## WORKING WITH EMOTIONAL INJURIES AND FORGIVENESS IN COUPLES THERAPY

Damaging or threatening to damage the intimate relational bond one has with one's partner is destructive and often discussed in the literature as a traumatic

http://dx.doi.org/10.1037/0000144-007
*Forgiveness and Letting Go in Emotion-Focused Therapy*, by L. S. Greenberg and C. Woldarsky Meneses

experience (Glass 2002; Gordon, Baucom, & Snyder, 2004; Scuka, 2015). These experiences may precipitate a loss of basic trust both in a partner's reliability and ability to provide support. Some couples successfully resolve these incidents; for others, certain incidents come to represent an EI (Greenberg, Warwar, & Malcolm, 2010) whereby one partner feels that the other has violated some fundamental aspect of the relational bond on which the partner was depending. As discussed in Chapter 1, enduring injuries result from a rupture in the fundamental sense of attachment security or validation of identity in the relationship that can occur from the shattering of a sacred value. The EI then becomes a reference point for the couple because it marks their narrative and often taints the relationship such that every conflict is (at least for one partner) reminiscent of the pain related to this injury.

EIs can occur through a conscious, deliberate act such as infidelity or financial deceit or through abandonment at a time of great need. It may take the form of invalidation, such as when a husband invalidates his wife by criticizing her or is disparaging of her success or accomplishments in front of family or friends. Alternatively, one partner may seriously injure his or her spouse without awareness of the extent of the damage that this behavior could inflict on the other. This occurs, for example, when a husband is inattentive to his wife's needs during or after childbirth or at another moment of critical need (e.g., illness of a parent) or when a husband believes he is being supportive by accompanying his spouse to abort a pregnancy only to learn later that her real desire was for him to stop her from having the abortion or when a wife later learns that her husband was not a virgin when he had led her to believe he was. Essentially, any act can be damaging and be seen as a violation of trust depending on how it is construed by the couple, and therapists are required to be sensitive to the personal meaning attributed to the incident and its consequences for the couple's functioning. These incidents often crystalize an underlying theme in the relationship such as "I can't trust that I can rely on my partner" or "I feel so criticized or taken for granted and can't trust that I feel valued." The incident is a singular, concrete event, but the felt meaning is not always a result of the isolated experience. Rather, it is a crystallization of an unsatisfying aspect of the relationship.

In addition, EIs can be categorized according to the primary dimension they affect: attachment (related to closeness, safety, and responsiveness) or identity (related to self-esteem, validation, and respect). An *attachment injury* has been characterized as a perceived abandonment, betrayal, or breach of trust in a critical moment of need (Johnson, Makinen, & Millikin, 2001). An *identity injury* has been characterized as involving invalidation or diminishment of self-esteem resulting from a partner's lack of recognition, criticism, or insult (Greenberg & Goldman, 2008). We consider all injuries that occur within the context of an intimate relationship to be both emotional, in that the injured partners describe intense, lingering, unresolved feelings of hurt or anger and betrayal, as well as interpersonal, given that they occur in the context of an ongoing relationship that involved a shared sense of commitment to one another.

## IMPACT OF EMOTIONAL INJURIES

For couples that participated in the York Emotional Injury Project (Greenberg et al., 2010), incidents that constituted injuries were such things as a husband being inattentive to a wife's needs during or after childbirth, one partner not supporting the other with a dying parent, a wife criticizing her husband in front of his family for being unable to provide for her, one partner ignoring or disparaging a major success of the other, or in front of other people, a partner insulting the other partner's sexual prowess. Betrayal of marital vows of fidelity with affairs, whether real or virtual, was a special type of injury that resulted in a partner feeling that the other had violated a fundamental aspect of the relational bond on which the partner could depend. Unresolved emotional wounds of this nature for the injured person led to a loss of basic trust in both a partner's reliability and supportiveness. Although some couples successfully resolve these incidents, for others the incidents remain as EIs that affect the foundation of the relationship for years.

The experience of having been betrayed by one's intimate partner is profoundly destabilizing and is in many ways traumatic (Glass, 2002; Gordon et al., 2008). In recent years, the term *postinfidelity stress disorder* (Ortman, 2005) has emerged in the popular psychology literature to capture the suffering and distress that results from an interpersonal betrayal. As described in Chapter 1, an EI shatters assumptions and expectations of one's partner and the relationship, destroying the safety, security, and predictability that seemed inherent to the relationship. Typically, the injured person is consumed by the need to comprehend why the injury occurred, insisting on knowing the details related to the injury with the hopes that this will soothe the pain of having been betrayed, or provide a narrative or a framework of sorts that will make the injury easier to assimilate. It is a disorienting experience that requires the injured partner to accept and manage an array of intense emotions—including anger, rage, hurt, fear, shame, and sadness—and to accept that one's beloved did the unacceptable. Not surprisingly, Atkins, Marín, Lo, Klann, and Hahlweg (2010) found that couples seeking therapy because of infidelity reported significantly more symptoms of depression and greater levels of distress than couples that consulted for other reasons.

EIs disrupt intrapsychic and interpersonal functioning. On an individual level, each person is left struggling with what it means to have been betrayed ("I was so foolish, so stupid, so naive to have trusted my partner! How could I not have seen this coming?") or to have betrayed ("How could I have done this? How could I be so selfish and only think of my needs instead of how this could destroy my partner?") and managing the mix of emotions that emerge in the aftermath of an EI. This interferes with the three motivational systems of attachment, identity, and attraction or liking that act as the organizing forces in intimate relationships (Greenberg & Goldman, 2008).

From the attachment perspective, the sense of security and safety in the relationship is shaken and leads the injured partner to feel anxiety and question to what extent he or she can trust and count on the other partner. Usually, on disclosure of the injury, the injured partner goes into "fight, flight, or freeze" mode (Perel, 2017), which is incompatible with closeness. Even if there is some receptivity to being approached, even being held and touched by the offending partner—usually in moments of high distress when the injured partner seeks reassurance and closeness—there is a pervasive sense that something significant has changed between them and that it is not safe to allow the other partner to get as close as they had preinjury. For many, the experience of having been betrayed by their intimate partner is so bewildering that it leaves them with the sense that they do not know who their partner is; they thought they knew him or her, but the shock of discovering the injury strips them of the sense of safety and predictability in the relationship.

A betrayal brings with it a loss of closeness, safety, and trust and increased conflict in the couple, and it is accompanied by an array of emotions including anger, fear, hopelessness, and sadness at the loss of unity and shared identity (Glass, 2002; Negash, Cui, Fincham, & Pasley, 2014; Scuka, 2015). Although we have encountered some couples that report a resurgence of passion following the discovery of an affair, the need for greater emotional (and at times, physical) distance from the offending partner is commonplace. This may take the form of withdrawing from sexual contact with the offending partner or feeling unable to be affectionate and loving toward the offending partner, including through the use of verbal terms of endearment. Both partners must manage the pain of feeling lonely and disconnected from the other, which may be especially difficult for the injuring partner who is required to respect the injured partner's need for distance, even if it seems disproportionate and even if there may be periodic moments of closeness. In the process of resolving the injury and working through all the emotions related to it, reconnection and closeness are once again possible and usually become dominant features of the postinjury relationship, even if reestablishing trust remains an ongoing process.

The identity domain also can be greatly disturbed in the wake of an EI. Having been invalidated or betrayed by one's partner is a disempowering experience that has a negative impact on the injured partner's self-esteem because it seems to communicate "you're not that special." There is a sense of having been humiliated or mocked and devalued that is damaging to a person's sense of self and can lead to shame and/or rage. There is something about having been betrayed that leaves individuals questioning what this says about them and how much or how little their partner respects or esteems them given that they did what they did. "I felt discarded when you did that," said one of our research participants to her husband about his multiple online exchanges with other women, "discarded like a piece of trash that you threw out your car window as you drove along."

By virtue of having injured, the injuring partner is seen through a new set of eyes and questions arise about who he or she really is. This can be disconcerting and also sad because it implies assimilating a new "version" of the partner one thought one knew and distancing from the previously cherished, preinjury version of the partner. There is a sense of grieving what one understood the relationship to be and to represent (Dean, 2011). In discussing what forgiveness implies, Myriam, another research participant in our study, elaborated on how her understanding of her husband changed after she discovered he had been unfaithful to her: "You know, he can be almost selfless at times . . . and he had a certain—almost a moral—code that he lived by that I really admired and that was completely shattered! Because if he really had been this person, this wouldn't have happened the way it happened. So, you know, it means sort of letting go of this big part of him that I really sort of admired and I was very attached to . . . that really wasn't him."

Given the loss of safety, closeness, and trust in the relationship that accompanies having been betrayed, it follows that feelings of being attractive and/or of attraction and liking of the other will be blocked. Negative emotions, including anger, disgust, sadness, and shame, overshadow positive emotions and interfere with the pleasure of being in the company of one's partner. The injured partners may compare themselves with the people with whom their partners have betrayed them and feel not as attractive and somehow inferior. Even when partners know that they love each other, once betrayed it is difficult for tender feelings to be expressed freely between them because the injured partner's wound is too raw and open to appreciate and reciprocate gestures of kindness and affection. However, once the couple begins working on healing the injury, these feelings of attraction and liking resurface rather spontaneously.

In sum, an EI shakes the foundation of the relationship; it threatens security and identity and rattles both partners' understanding of the relationship, of who they are, and who they understood their partner to be. In the words of Perel (2017), infidelity "not only hijacks a couple's hopes and plans but also draws a question mark over their history: If we can't look back with certainty and we can't know what will happen tomorrow, where does that leave us?" (p. 64). All the things that were once familiar in the relationship and each other perish, only to be reconquered as the couple resolves their injury.

## EMOTIONAL PROCESSES INVOLVED IN INTERPERSONAL FORGIVENESS

Interpersonal forgiveness is a profound experience that involves a series of emotional changes and a radical shift in cognitions related to the injurer and the injury. In this section, we present an overview of the major emotional processes related to forgiveness and outline the roles of anger and sadness, empathy, and remorse. We close this section with a discussion of reconciliation.

## Anger, Sadness, and Pain in Forgiveness

Being injured by one's partner brings with it a mix of emotions that are often difficult to bear and that have to shift in the process of resolution. Emotional change is not a linear process but more a process of going two steps forward and one step back because certain emotions resurface in working toward achieving forgiveness.

After the shock and emotional numbness that come with the occurrence of the injury, anger (and perhaps even rage) seems to be the most common reaction. Although its intensity may seem overwhelming, anger is adaptive in that it is an appropriate response to having had one's expectations violated and the integrity of the relationship shattered. From the reports of one of our couples, it appears that some therapists in the community actively discourage the injured partner from expressing anger in working on the injury of an affair. The couple stated that in their first therapy after the affair they were told that expressing anger was not helpful in trying to deal with the injury. In their second therapy, 1 year following the affair, a different therapist repeated the same message. This exacerbated the wife's feelings of powerlessness and victimization about her husband's affair.

In our view, the type of anger that needs expression is empowered, assertive anger, not blaming, destructive anger. This type of anger communicates boundaries and demands respect. Intrinsically related to anger at being injured is sadness, the feeling of loss that comes with realizing one has lost the trust, safety, and security that were inherent to the relationship, as well as the loss of positive regard for one's partner. Both anger and sadness thus need to be expressed.

There is also a general sense of hurting, aching, and being in pain—of something having been broken or shattered. Other emotions may also arise, including shame, fear, and loneliness. All these feelings are appropriate responses to having been injured, even though they may feel uncomfortable. In the spirit of EFT, we take an accepting attitude toward these emotions because we believe that the only way out of a given emotion is through it (Greenberg, 2002). We facilitate emotional awareness (and regulation) to move toward emotional transformation, which for couples requires the expression of vulnerability before a remorseful and responsive other.

Lawler and her colleagues (2005) found that individuals who forgive tend to be more in touch with painful feelings than those who do not forgive. Personal accounts of forgiveness concur with this empirical finding and highlight that releasing negative feelings is one of the key experiences associated with forgiveness, as reported by interviewees in studies by Sharma (2013) and DeCourville, Belicki, and Green (2008). For example, one interviewee in

Sharma's study elaborated on the importance of working through her feelings of anger in therapy:

> I can't believe how angry I was. I knew that I was angry when I came in to therapy, but I didn't realize to what degree . . . I didn't feel like I was being heard by him—he knew the words but I don't think he really heard what I had to say and so with therapist I feel what she was able to do was have him hear me and really get beyond me being angry. (p. 104)

## Empathy and Forgiveness

Empathy, as we have seen, is recognized in the literature as an important element related to forgiveness (McCullough, Rachal, Sandage, & Worthington, 1997; McCullough, Worthington, & Rachal, 1997) that is substantiated by empirical research (Burnette, Davis, Green, Worthington, & Bradfield, 2009; Paleari, Regalia, & Fincham, 2009). However, there are important differences in the role that empathy plays in individual and couples therapy, which are briefly outlined in this section.

As discussed in Chapter 3, therapeutic work in individual EFT involves the use of the empty-chair dialogue, which is an effective means of helping clients in their efforts to resolve past EIs with significant others that cause current distress. It involves bringing the injurer and injury alive so that the client is engaged in an imaginal confrontation and dialogue with the injurer rather than a cognitive discussion with the therapist about what happened. In so doing, the client is helped to move inner representations of self and other into a transitional space in conscious awareness where the representations can be examined, explored, and resolved. There is compelling evidence in successful forgiveness-oriented EFT couples therapy for the need for reciprocal empathy (Woldarsky Meneses & Greenberg, 2011; see also Chapter 8, this volume). EIs disrupt safety because they represent a shattering of personal and relational expectations that were once held dear by both partners. These injuries also interfere with mutual emotion regulation, and an EFT couples therapist must be able to help couples manage their distress and anger so they can engage in self-disclosure about the underlying vulnerabilities that have been activated in the wake of the pain of the injury. Mutual empathy is required if either person is to risk asking for what they need from their partner and, more generally, to move the forgiveness process forward. Empathy is necessary on the offending partner's part to compassionately and nondefensively respond to the injured partner's pain and distress.

However, this degree of emotional responsiveness to the injured partner's pain can only emerge if the offending partner can take responsibility for the damage he or she caused. This dialectical relationship between the two *R*s of responsibility and responsiveness means that as the offender takes nondefensive responsibility for his or her actions, he or she is now able to be responsive to the other's pain, and being responsive to the partner's pain opens the door to having him or her assume responsibility for the harm done

(W. M. Malcolm, personal communication, 2006). This can be painful and often evokes feelings of deep remorse or shame in the offending partner, which is crucial for the injured partner to see because this is what will generate empathy toward the injurer, help to rebuild trust, and move the forgiveness process forward. Furthermore, the hurt person must be willing to accept the deep remorse their partner feels in facing their hurtfulness for the harm they have done to facilitate healing between them. Our analyses on the process of couple's forgiveness in EFT couples therapy (Woldarsky Meneses & Greenberg, 2014) revealed that there are varying degrees of expressed empathy and that at the most basic level it is an accepting attitude toward the offending partner's suffering (i.e., recognition of the pain vs. denial or rejection of it) that signals that there is an emotional opening from which forgiveness can blossom. Indeed, the empirical findings confirmed that an accepting response of the offending partner's shame promoted forgiveness at the end of therapy.

Worthington (1998a, 1998b) proposed an empathy–humility–commitment model of forgiveness in which forgiveness begins with empathy toward the offender. Research by McCullough and his colleagues (McCullough & Worthington, 1995; McCullough, Worthington, & Rachal, 1997) illustrated the role that empathy plays in mediating forgiveness, finding that those who forgive their offenders tend to experience more empathy toward them than nonforgivers. Enright and Fitzgibbons (2015) highlighted the importance of empathy in helping people move toward forgiveness but warn therapists that promoting empathy too early can lead to enmeshment or enabling. They proposed that the work of reframing and promoting empathy not be done during the first stage of therapy. For Worthington (1998a, 1998b), empathy is insufficient for forgiveness; he argued that injured individuals that must be able to respond to their offenders with a sense of humility, which acknowledges the fallibility of humans, rather than rage. The final step of forgiveness proposed in this model is commitment, which involves acting in a manner that conveys the victim's commitment to forgiveness (e.g., acknowledging forgiveness in front of a therapist).

McCullough, Worthington, and Rachal (1997) also theorized that empathy on the part of the offending party evokes feelings of guilt and distress over harm done, whereas empathy on the part of the injured person evokes a caring response to the offender's distress in the face of harm done and facilitates the desire to repair the relationship. The empirical analyses of couples who reached forgiveness in the York Emotional Injury Project (Woldarsky Meneses, 2006; Woldarsky Meneses & Greenberg, 2011, 2014) also highlighted that mutual empathy is important to promote forgiveness because it provides a soothing (validating) function for both the injured and the offending partner that aids in emotional regulation and provides the resources and stability to move toward reestablishing the couple's connection. We agree with Hill's (2010) formulation of forgiveness as a complex psychological and relational process that is not merely an act of will but rather a discovery that occurs via empathy.

## Role of Remorse in Forgiveness

In addition to empathy, an expression of remorse is important for forgiveness. The offender's remorse indicates that he or she has a thorough understanding of the harm he or she has inflicted on the injured partner and takes responsibility for it, which in turn makes it possible for the partner to forgive and move into the work of restoring trust in the relationship. Our research (Woldarsky Meneses & Greenberg, 2011, 2014) has suggested that there are two kinds of remorse and that both are integral to repairing an ongoing intimate relationship: other-directed and self-directed.

### Other-Directed Remorse

*Other-directed remorse* refers to the regret and sorrow one feels for the other person's suffering that come from understanding and appreciating the consequences of one's choices and actions. As such, it is an affirmation of the other person's basic worth and right to be seen and treated as a subject rather than an object. It is also an acknowledgment of the damage that has been done to the relationship the offender had with the other person before he or she hurt them. Other-directed remorse gives rise to a deep desire to make amends for the harm done and to participate in the transformative process of repairing the relationship, so the same thing does not happen again. When a partner sees that the other partner can feel and stay with the remorse he or she feels about what he or she has done to the partner and their relationship, he or she knows that that partner is again capable of loving well and of being careful in the way he or she treats the partner and their relationship.

### Self-Directed Remorse

This type of remorse refers to the regret and sorrow felt for the damage a partner has done to his or her self-respect and worth as a person in meaningful relationships. It may involve shame (or "guilt before oneself"; Murphy, 1999) or empathic distress (see Chapter 7, this volume, for further discussion) that, if adaptive and reasonably well regulated, will evoke empathy from the hurt partner and invite him or her to soften in his or her stance toward the offending partner, thus opening the way for repair of the loving bond they used to enjoy without reservation. Self-directed remorse gives rise to a deep desire to participate in the transformative process of being "repaired" so that the offending partner becomes a person who would not and, in some real way, could not act this way again. Seeing this in the offending partner, the other partner is doubly assured that he or she is again capable of loving well or being careful in the way he or she brings him- or herself to relationships that are of crucial importance to his or her well-being and sense of self as a person capable of loving well.

Our work attests to the importance of expressing self-focused remorse (operationalized as shame) in facilitating forgiveness (Woldarsky Meneses & Greenberg, 2014; see also Chapter 7, this volume). Shame as a response to violating sacred vows or inherent expectations of an intimate relationship is adaptive because it signals to the injured partner that the offender is suffering on a personal level because of what he or she has done. It is the expression of deep remorse that allows the injured partner to reconsider approaching (trusting) the offender versus distancing from him or her. Shame, when expressed in relation to the injury committed (i.e., not as a global expression of worthlessness or as an act of self-flagellation with the intention of pulling for comfort or reassurance) is transformative for couples attempting to resolve an EI. Self-reports echo this empirical finding. For example, one of the women in Sharma's (2013) study stated that a pivotal moment in therapy was witnessing her husband express shame about the injury:

> Although he had kind of apologized in the past and said sorry for his actions, I really hadn't seen him admit shame and full remorse, so to be able to see that without the defenses and justification and the reasons why, which you know, whenever I heard that made me retreat, and so to see it without any of that, it was easier to be able to forgive the actions. (p. 111)

Thus, forgiving is a highly emotional process in which anger, sadness, empathy, and remorse all play an important role. A therapy that helps people deal with these and other emotions targets some of the important components of the forgiveness process.

## Forgiveness and Reconciliation

People often reach for forgiveness when they want to repair a break in an intimate relational bond caused by the pain of an EI. Similarly, not being able or willing to forgive is often part of what prevents a couple from restoring trust and recovering from a significant EI. Because they are often intertwined in everyday life, we tend to use the words *forgiveness* and *reconciliation* interchangeably. It should be noted, however, that these are two distinct processes. The crucial difference is that forgiveness is something that happens within a person and is a bodily felt experience, whereas reconciliation takes place between people and is a relational experience. It is entirely possible to forgive but not reconcile, and vice versa.

One of the legitimate concerns people have in the wake of being emotionally injured by someone they thought they could trust is the fear that, if the relationship is reentered unchanged, the same thing could happen again. Seeing forgiveness and reconciliation as separate but often interacting processes is particularly important in individual psychotherapy, where it would be difficult, and in many cases inappropriate, to attempt to bring about reconciliation in the absence of all parties involved. It is also inappropriate to promote reconciliation when there is current on-going violence or other kinds of abuse within the relationship that brought an individual or couple to therapy. It is possible, however, to facilitate the psychotherapeutic process of forgiveness even in those instances when reconciliation is not appropriate or possible.

Some writers and clinicians insist that reconciliation or restoration of relationship is essential if we are to consider forgiveness to have happened in its entirety. Worthington's (2006) REACH program is designed to help couples forgive and includes reconciliation as the final step. Pattison (1965) went so far as to define forgiveness as the completed act of reconciliation of the guilty one with the offended one. Similarly, Augsburger (2000) stated that reconciliation is the proof that forgiveness is genuine. Others (e.g., Downie, 1965) have taken a more tempered position and acknowledge that although forgiveness is the vehicle to restoring a severed relationship, reconciliation can only be accomplished in so far as the offender participates. This is certainly consistent with our view of reconciliation.

In contrast to those who see reconciliation as a return to the relationship that existed before the hurtfulness (e.g., Berecz, 2001), our understanding of reconciliation is much closer to Virginia Holeman's (2004). She defined reconciliation as "the active commitment to the restoration of love and trustworthiness by both injured party and transgressor *so that their relationship may be transformed*" (p. 12, emphasis added). We see reconciliation as a process of reconnection that involves the reconstruction of the relationship and a "reclaiming of the we" (W. M. Malcolm, personal communication, 2006). This can only occur when both partners have a sense of closure around the EI, which gives them a sense of having transcended not simply survived the EI. Participants in Sharma's (2013) study who were able to "close the chapter on the EI" described a marked shift from feeling isolated to feeling a sense of union and partnership, apparent in the day-to-day sharing of household duties and in the planning of future-oriented activities, which prevailed even during times of conflict.

## THE PHENOMENOLOGY OF FORGIVENESS

To aid in developing an experientially grounded understanding of what constitutes forgiving and not being able to forgive for women who had undergone an EI in their intimate relationships, a qualitative study was conducted based on interviews with nine women (Sharma, 2013). These interviews were subjected to a modified grounded theory analysis to provide a rich understanding of the participants' narratives that remained closely connected to their experience. Six of the women participated in the York Emotional Injury Project, and three were community members. EIs included partner's infidelity, sudden abandonment and drug abuse kept secret, and financial deceit. The participants described the process of forgiveness as involving a number of different elements. These were organized into three main categories: letting go, nondefensive stance, and empowered identity (Sharma, 2007, 2013). According to this model, forgiveness occurs through three interrelated processes, which involve the letting go of negative emotion, an increased openness to the woman's experience and that of the partner (i.e., an appreciation of the offending partner's responsiveness and vulnerability), and a shift in identity in relation to the other partner based on revived agency through self-assertion.

In this section, we summarize the experience of forgiveness based on this qualitative study that provides an elaborate understanding of these nine women's narratives, and we discuss how their experience corresponds with theoretical assumptions discussed earlier about forgiveness in intimate relationships.

## Letting Go

The women reported that forgiving involves, in part, letting go of negative emotions by taking a self-reflective stance. The interviewees indicated that they did this by accessing the painful emotions associated with anger and exploring the meaning of this emotional experience, rather than being emotionally avoidant or reactive. Several participants reported that communicating the softer emotions to the offending partner, such as sadness about the relationship and longing for their partner, helped them move forward. This emotional openness is a stark contrast to the guardedness of unforgiveness, which involved a self-protective stance in the face of a perceived lack of safety.

In their pretherapy interviews, all the women reported feeling consumed by the emotions, images, and memories of the EI. They described a vivid sensation of being weighed down by emotional pain and aspired to reach a place of forgiveness in the hope that it would lighten their emotional load. They described the EI as occupying a large amount of space in their lives and as being a continuing source of negativity, with physical and emotional repercussions for them. These individuals expressed a wish for the emotions to feel less raw so that they could move forward in their lives. Being consumed by anger and/or hurt for such a length of time was experienced as exhausting and overwhelming. As one participant put it, "The worst is constantly getting upset—I'm tired of this [crying]. I'm tired of it having it consume me. After 2 years I thought it would be over" (Sharma, 2013, p. 74).

Of all the negative emotions interviewees identified, anger toward the offender was noted as being particularly potent and difficult. Whether they expressed the anger directly or experienced rage in silence, the women reported being angry about waiting in vain for the offending partner to accept responsibility for the EI. Some of them described feeling outraged about not seeing changes in the offending partner that reflected remorse or culpability. Those who were in therapy reported that making contact with their anger, expressing it, and accepting it helped to diminish its intensity.

In addition, the participants identified feelings of shame and inadequacy at having been deceived by their partners, as well as embarrassment regarding how others perceived their decision to remain with their partner when they were in a state of unforgiveness. One participant elaborated on her ambivalence about the meaning of forgiveness, questioning whether this meant accepting having been humiliated by her husband, who had an affair that lasted years without her knowing. Overcoming feelings of personal shame related to the EI seems to involve the ability to forgive oneself and relinquish anger directed at oneself for having been "fooled" without taking the blame or responsibility for the actions of the offender. This is supported by findings in another study in which women who had resolved experiences of complex trauma reported less self-blame and higher self-esteem (Chagigiorgis & Paivio, 2008), suggesting that an important component of healing from a traumatic wound inflicted by another person is self-forgiveness.

These qualitative reports of the importance of letting go of negative emotions as part of the forgiveness process are also widely supported by a number of quantitative research studies that showed a negative relationship between anger and forgiveness (Huang & Enright, 2000; Kaplan, 1992; McCullough et al., 1998; Weiner, Graham, Peter, & Zmuidinas, 1991). In addition, Barber, Maltby, and Macaskill (2005) studied different aspects of anger in relation to a transgression and found that holding onto an angry memory interferes with self-forgiveness and holding onto thoughts of revenge is a significant barrier to interpersonal forgiveness.

### Nondefensive Stance

Interviewees also described experiencing a shift in the way they understood themselves, as well as their perceptions of and attitude toward the offending partner. This came with a movement away from judging and blaming toward a more empathic stance of wanting to understand. This shift in understanding was prompted by witnessing the offending partner's vulnerability, particularly shame. Participants reported that seeing their partner's shame conveyed that the partner finally understood the profound impact of his behavior on the injured partner, and seeing him do this in an authentic, "surrendering" manner with heartfelt emotion made him seem "more human" and trustworthy. The women who had the opportunity to witness their partner's heartfelt vulnerability described how their anger diffused and how "softer" emotions such as sympathy and empathy emerged when they saw that their partners were also suffering. The injured partner's shift toward a nondefensive stance was promoted by the offender demonstrating emotional attunement toward the injured partner's painful emotional experience (communicated in his expression of shame). This invited the injured partner to move away from a hostile, blaming stance and toward empathy, thereby opening the door to forgiveness.

The link between shame and forgiveness has also been documented in the restorative justice literature. Two styles of shame management have been empirically identified within the context of restorative justice research: *shame acknowledgment,* which involves recognizing that one's behavior is wrong and expressing remorse for it; and *shame displacement,* when the offender blames others for the wrongful act and expresses anger (see Ahmed, 2001; Braithwaite, Ahmed, Morrison, & Reinhart, 2003). Ahmed and Braithwaite (2006) tested the link between adolescents' shame management style regarding bullying others at school, perceived parental response to the adolescent's bullying behavior (i.e., a forgiving and reconciliatory stance toward the adolescent), and propensity to continue bullying others. They found that adolescents' shame acknowledgment influenced how forgiving and reconciliatory they perceived their parents to be, which in turn was linked to bullying at school. Consistent with previous research (Ahmed, 2001; Ahmed & Braithwaite, 2004; Bessant & Watts, 1995; Braithwaite et al., 2003), Ahmed and Braithwaite found that shame acknowledgment predicted less bullying, whereas shame displacement predicted more. They also tested a separate model and demonstrated that parental forgiveness decreases significantly when adolescents engage in shame displacement.

Sharma's (2013) observations are also consistent with process research conducted by Greenberg and colleagues (Greenberg, James, & Conry, 1988; Johnson & Greenberg, 1985) showing that when one partner expresses genuine vulnerability, the other partner "softens" in his or her position and that this transforms their interactional dynamic (McKinnon & Greenberg, 2017). In exploring forgiveness in individual therapy, Malcolm, Warwar, and Greenberg (2005) found that a key change event associated with forgiveness was the client's perception that the imagined other was genuinely apologetic in his or her acceptance of responsibility. Similarly, Gottman's (2011) observational research suggested that couples must enhance their receptivity to one another after an EI to heal from it. This requires the partners discussing their feelings and relating their subjective reality of the EI without blaming each other and the offender expressing genuine remorse that the injured partner can accept. Earlier work by Gottman (1994) also highlighted that validation plays an enormous role in conflict de-escalation and relationship satisfaction.

The relationship between empathy and forgiveness is supported by a large body of social psychological research (e.g., Baumeister, Stillwell, & Heatherton, 1994; Fincham, Paleari, & Regalia, 2002; McCullough, Worthington, & Rachal, 1997; Paleari, Regalia, & Fincham, 2005; Zeichmeister & Romero, 2002). There is also evidence indicating that the experience of forgiving is associated with the renewal of affection and warmth. For example, Makinen (2004; Makinen & Johnson, 2006) conducted a task analytic study of 24 couples wanting to resolve an "attachment injury" (i.e., any perceived abandonment, betrayal, or breach of trust in a critical moment of need of support) and found that couples that resolved the injury at the end of their therapy were more affiliative in their interactions than were those who were unable to move forward from the injury.

### Empowered Identity

Sharma's (2013) qualitative analyses revealed a third main category, *empowered identity,* that reflects the changes in the injured partner's sense of identity following the forgiveness process. Her participants indicated that in the experience of forgiving, the injured partner's sense of identity, previously associated with a sense of diminishment, underwent a transformation out of which a highly agentic, empowered self emerged. Forgiving was described as an empowering process characterized by decreased self-blame for the EI and heightened awareness of one's responsibilities and choices in the relationship. One participant stated that permitting herself to consider leaving her husband was an acknowledgment of the limits of her control over her husband and that thinking about her options was a novel experience because she had spent most of her marriage catering to her husband's needs:

> I gave myself permission that if he wasn't working on things, that I had put in all that I could put in and that I had been doing what I needed to do, and if he was incapable of fulfilling his end of the bargain, I gave myself permission that it was OK to walk away. And I think through that permission, it has also allowed me to examine how to stay together without feeling like we have to stay together. Probably it empowered me. (Sharma, 2013, p. 123)

Several women who forgave described forgiveness as a choice they had made at a critical juncture in the relationship after the EI. They reported being faced with the decision to let go of the pain and the anger or to permit it to continue festering inside themselves. They realized that in making this decision, they had the power to determine the future of the relationship. For one participant, this critical moment occurred in therapy when her therapist confronted her with the question. She suddenly realized that hanging onto the anger and the hurt would probably be toxic for the marriage: "Eventually he would be tired of paying for this crime [*laughing*], so to speak, so I had to make a choice then so I decided that it was time to put it in the past" (p. 125).

Forgiveness seems to have enhanced the injured partner's self-esteem by reconnecting them with their sense of agency—by choosing to forgive they were no longer condemned to being victims. Experimental research by Wenzel and Okimoto (2010) showed that the act of forgiveness returns status and power to the victim because it involves determining a course of action; there is a feeling of being in control and having self-efficacy in choosing to forgive. They further suggested that the act of forgiving repairs the status and power imbalance caused by the transgression and also restores a sense of justice.

## CONCLUSION

This chapter has outlined the major emotional processes involved in forgiving an intimate partner, including expressing and experiencing sadness, anger, and pain to be able to access empathy. We conceive of forgiveness in couples as involving the mutual revealing of and responding to emotional vulnerabilities, where the injured partner moves from expressing anger to revealing the deep hurt and sadness that resulted from the EI, and the offending partner is able to express self-oriented remorse and shame in a genuine way. Sharma's (2013) qualitative analysis of the forgiveness process, summarized in this chapter and complemented with empirical research, suggested that forgiveness involves three interrelated processes of letting go (of negative emotion and the meaning attributed to the injury), taking a nondefensive stance, and experiencing a renewed sense of agency and empowered identity. In Chapter 7, we present an empirically based model developed from actual processes observed in-session.

# 7

# A Model of the Process of Forgiving in Couples Therapy

Although it is not always clear why we hurt the ones we love, the reality of human nature is that we sometimes do. The need to resolve an emotional injury (EI) is, for some couples, evident and often is identified as a goal for therapy. For other couples, this goal emerges over the course of therapy, representing a major block that has impeded progress. Once a couple embarks on the path toward resolution of an injury, the question of how the resolution process unfolds and, particularly, the therapeutic tasks that promote forgiveness become a central concern.

This chapter outlines our empirically based model of the forgiveness process (Woldarsky Meneses & Greenberg, 2011) and describes the therapeutic tasks that are important in promoting interpersonal forgiveness. These tasks are embedded in the global work of emotion-focused therapy for couples (EFT-C) that unfolds in five stages as outlined in Chapter 5 of this volume (see also Greenberg & Goldman, 2008) and include de-escalating, blaming, and retaliation by identifying the negative interactional cycle the couple habitually gets caught in, as well as helping the couple become aware of the underlying sensitivities each partner brings to the relationship that make them vulnerable to the hurtfulness of either criticism, attack, or withdrawal by their partner. In addition, in this chapter we address the common difficulties therapists encounter when clients find it difficult to engage in the work because of poor emotion regulation or habitually blocked awareness and reluctance to express vulnerability-related ("soft") emotions such as sadness, fear, and shame.

http://dx.doi.org/10.1037/0000144-008
*Forgiveness and Letting Go in Emotion-Focused Therapy*, by L. S. Greenberg and C. Woldarsky Meneses

## EFFECTS OF FORGIVENESS IN COUPLE THERAPY

Over the past 10 years, my colleagues and I (LSG) at York University have developed an approach to working with couples who wish to resolve an EI through the process of forgiveness. The treatment was designed for couples who were stuck in a state of "chronic unforgiveness," in the sense that the injury was required to have occurred at least 2 years before the start of therapy (to ensure that the natural process of recovering from hurts had already been given time to unfold without outside interference and that the injured person was not in the midst of coping with the immediate aftermath of the injury). Injuries involved abandonment, betrayals, humiliations, or violations by intimate partners. Couples received 10 to 12 sessions of treatment distributed over approximately 12 weeks where forgiveness was explored but was not the objective of therapy. As with individual therapy, our team emphasized a nonauthoritarian approach to working with forgiveness in helping couples overcome an EI.

An initial study compared treatment with a no-treatment wait-list period in which couples served as their own controls (Greenberg, Warwar, & Malcolm, 2010). The wait-list comparison period was also approximately 10 to 12 weeks per couple. The results of this study indicated that couples who received the EFT-C treatment showed significantly more improvement on all measures of change from the beginning to the end of treatment than was observed over the wait-list period. Partners reported being significantly more forgiving and trusting after treatment, having greater marital satisfaction, and experiencing positive changes and reductions in distress on key target complaints and global symptoms. In addition, this study demonstrated the effectiveness of EFT-C in promoting forgiveness in couples therapy.

Subsequent studies conducted by our research team focused on understanding the process of interpersonal forgiveness to explore how forgiveness unfolds in EFT-C (Woldarsky Meneses & Greenberg, 2011, 2014) and exploring the phenomenology of forgiving (Sharma, 2013). The former research study is presented in-depth in this chapter, whereas the latter study was described in Chapter 6.

## PROCESS MODELS OF FORGIVENESS IN EMOTION-FOCUSED THERAPY FOR COUPLES

Both Johnson and Greenberg's research groups have independently conducted intensive research studies aimed at understanding how forgiveness unfolds in EFT-C. Johnson and her colleagues developed the attachment injury resolution model (AIRM; Makinen & Johnson, 2006; Millikin, 2000) from clinical observations of three couples who received 15 sessions of EFT-C and resolved their attachment injury. This model proposed that resolution of an attachment injury involves four overarching phases: affect differentiation, reengagement, forgiveness, and reconciliation. The actual steps of the process were then conceptualized through the lens of EFT-C and attachment theory (Greenberg & Johnson, 1988; Johnson, 2004). In line with previous process studies looking at the characteristics of positive outcomes in EFT-C (Greenberg, Ford, Alden, & Johnson, 1993; Johnson & Greenberg, 1988), the results of follow-up studies on the AIRM indicated that couples that resolved their injuries attained deeper levels of experiencing and shifted from a hostile to an affiliative stance (Makinen, 2004; Naaman, Pappas, Makinen, Zuccarini, & Johnson, 2005). These observations are not unique to forgiveness cases; they characterize successful outcome cases in EFT-C in general. Although the AIRM represents an important starting point for studying forgiveness in EFT-C, it did not differentiate the unique aspects needed for promoting resolution of an attachment injury.

To identify the moment-by-moment processes that emerge en route to resolving an EI through forgiveness we used a data-driven methodology called *task analysis* (Greenberg, 2007). This work involved intensive examination of video and audiotapes of therapy sessions that were part of the York Emotional Injury Project (Greenberg et al., 2010). Specifically, four couples that reached forgiveness were observed, and their processes were then compared with the processes observed in two couples that did not forgive at the end of therapy. A model of forgiveness was subsequently built based on categories that were common to all the resolved couples but absent in couples who were unable to forgive (Woldarsky Meneses & Greenberg, 2011).

The sequence we identified as being exclusive to couples that resolved their injury at the end of therapy, as shown in Figure 7.1, began with the offending partner first assuming responsibility for the EI, then expressing either shame or empathic distress or offering an apology (these were interchangeable) and, finally, accepting forgiveness. The injured partner revealed a shift in the view of the other at some point in the process, sometimes following the offender's acceptance of responsibility and, at other times, following the offender's expression of shame and/or the apology.

We conducted a follow-up study (the validation phase of the task analysis) to assess the individual impact on the outcome of specific processes that we found to be unique to couples that forgave (Woldarsky Meneses, 2011; Woldarsky Meneses & Greenberg, 2014). Working from 205 videotaped segments from 33 couple's therapies and using hierarchical regression models, we examined the impact on the outcome of the "offender's expression of shame" and the injured partner's "accepting response to the shame," followed by an "in-session expression of forgiveness." The strongest independent predictor of forgiveness at the end of therapy was the offending partner's expression of shame (accounting for 33% of the variance on the Enright Forgiveness Inventory; Enright, Rique, & Coyle, 2000). Testing the sequence of the three processes of interest together we could account for nearly 50% of the variance on the Enright Forgiveness Inventory. This finding supports the adaptive function of shame (self-focused regret) in resolving injuries; its expression suggests

**FIGURE 7.1. Model of the Resolution of Couples' Emotional Injuries**

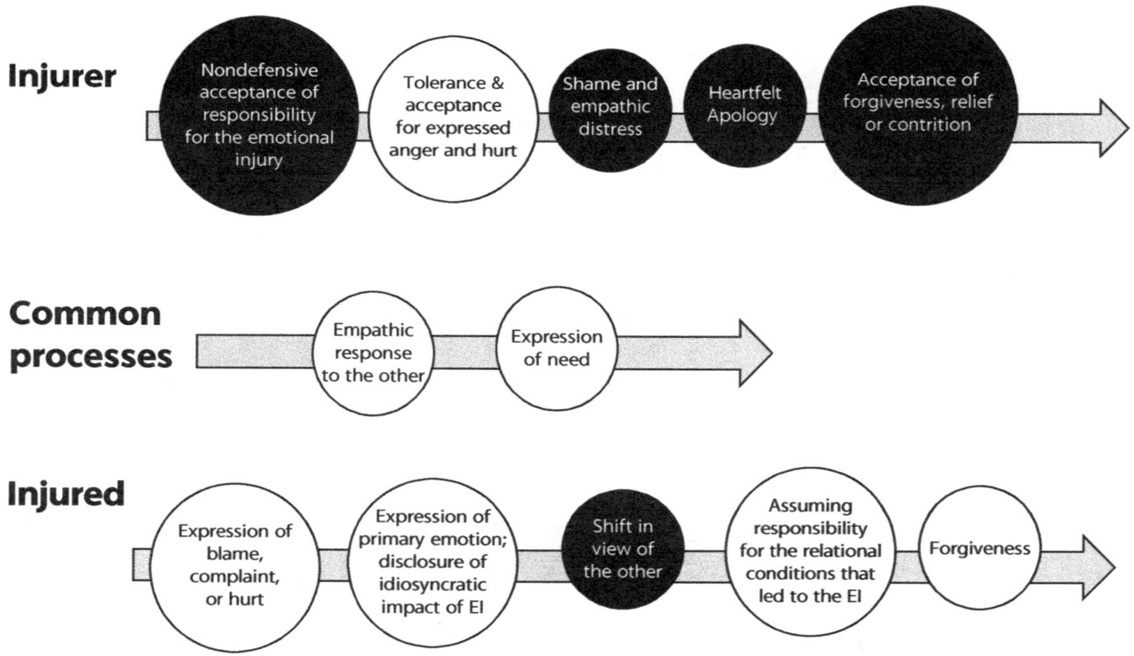


Black circles represent crucial steps in the forgiveness process. EI = emotional injury.

that the offender is suffering as a result of his or her behavior and elicits an accepting (rather than rejecting) stance from the injured partner. Specifically, it seems that the offender's expression of shame touches the injured partner so deeply that it reorganizes the injured partner's disposition toward the offender, inviting empathy and paving the way to forgiveness.

## FACILITATING FORGIVENESS IN EMOTION-FOCUSED THERAPY FOR COUPLES

In this section, we describe the specific therapeutic tasks that promote forgiveness (Woldarsky Meneses & Greenberg, 2011, 2014), shown in Figure 7.1, and how to help facilitate them. These processes do not always occur in the sequential order in which they are outlined; the process of change is dynamic and circular, moving forward and backward in real time but eventually moving forward to forgiveness, as shown in the model.

### Moving Out of Unforgiveness

Independent of therapeutic outcome, all the couples we studied (Woldarsky Meneses, 2006; Woldarsky Meneses & Greenberg, 2011) began with the injured partner expressing blame, complaint, or hurt in a reactive manner, characteristic of secondary emotion, which is a reaction to more primary underlying emotions (Greenberg, 2002). As discussed in Chapter 1, a person in a state of unforgiveness experiences distress that involves ruminating about the injury and feeling hostile toward the injurer. This is met by a defensive stance from the offending partner, who typically attempts to minimize the severity of the EI and avoids taking responsibility for it. Thus, the injured partner's reactive anger in combination with the offending partner's reactive or defensive position represents the marker (i.e., starting point) for the task of forgiveness because it signals that the couple is in conflict and that the injury is indeed unresolved.

The injured partner initially expresses a complaint, blame, or hurt and, over time with the help of the therapist, comes to differentiate these emotions to access the underlying primary emotion linked to having been injured by the other partner. The therapist can promote this shift by first validating the secondary emotion and then making an empathic conjecture about the pain that he or she must have felt and finally asking what this meant for the injured partner (e.g., "I can see you're really angry about this, and yet I imagine it must have also been so difficult to bear. What was the worst part of having been injured by your spouse? What did it mean to you?"). In focusing on the primary emotion, the idiosyncratic meaning is revealed and suddenly provides new depth to the experience of the injury. Even if two people experience the same injury, the personal meaning they attribute to it is determined by their individual context and makeup.

For example, many women participated in the York Emotional Injury Project because their husbands had engaged in extramarital affairs, yet each experienced different emotions related to this and, at the core, each ascribed different meanings to the affairs. One participant, Sandra, arrived at expressing intense anger at the timing of the affair (i.e., when they were trying to get pregnant), which she expressed in Session 4:

> It's the time, it's, it's what you did . . . we could have said, "You're unhappy with our relationship, we've got to work on it, or else you're just, you're unhappy enough, and you're leaving." You know, then I think, "Okay, I would've, you know (sighs), I would have maybe (sighs), and I feel at least (sighs, crying) if you had, before we—I—got pregnant (sighs), I would—we could—have worked out and decided whether we could stay together, or at least it would have ended, and I would have had a chance with somebody else." I just feel that (crying) I'm here! And I don't, I'm, I'm here with you, and I'm working on it, but I still, I can't. . . . I'm in a relationship with someone I can't really depend on, and it's very hard for me. I feel angry! [The therapist responds, "Right, right"] And you know, and hurt! That, you know, I'm in this place, like I'm so angry that, you know, I didn't have a chance, maybe to have the life that I wanted.

Before this point, Sandra had only ever expressed blame to her husband. She would say this with a tone of complaint, a whining hopelessness that nothing could change their situation, and would repeat that her husband was irresponsible and careless. For her, the idiosyncratic impact of her husband's affair was that she was robbed of the choice to live the type of family life she wanted. She was both indignant about the injustice of this and also hurt that her husband was not more considerate of this.

Another woman, Anne, initially blamed and shamed her husband, Martin, for having been unfaithful to her. She finally shifted from this stance and revealed the impact of the injury after her husband expressed shame and offered a heartfelt apology. That is, she risked being vulnerable only once she had seen her husband's vulnerability, which signaled that her husband had also suffered and could, therefore, be trusted again. Anne disclosed the impact of the affair during a discussion of the couple's interactional cycle and her tendency to critically attack her husband rather than express any vulnerable emotions underlying her position in the cycle. This occurred in the ninth session, from which the following excerpt is taken.

**ANNE:** I think for me—it's kind of, ah, my whole life has proven to me so far that, that, nobody looks after that part of me. Nobody has ever looked after that part of me. [*Therapist:* Mm-hmm.] Nobody's ever—you know, I've been very alone in terms of protecting that part of me [*Therapist:* Mm-hmm], so the idea of having that part rethreatened with something that's going on and not put up any kind of pro-, it's almost—in a way, um, me also betraying me.

**THERAPIST:** Because you've always needed to protect that little girl who got abused because nobody else would listen, nobody else would be there for her.

**ANNE:** (Crying)

**THERAPIST:** Tell us what that's like. Can you do that?

**ANNE:** (Crying) I just feel that's the part that it just, can cry forever [*Therapist:* Mm-hmm] there's no end to that (crying) because how do you ever have an end to that? It's scary because part of what was so painful about the affair (crying) was that, in a way does that mean that I can't trust Martin either? [*Therapist:* Mm-hmm.] Do you know what I mean? [*Therapist:* Mm-hmm.] It's like, what does that mean now? Every single person who's ever been important in my life has betrayed that [*Therapist:* Little girl]. Yeah, so it's really scary (crying).

At the core of Anne's experience of Martin's affair was a deep fear: What if people are not trustworthy? What if every meaningful relationship ends in betrayal? The impact of the injury was unique to her life experience as an incest survivor. Anne felt betrayed by her mother, who despite being physically present and aware of the abuse, did not intervene to protect her daughter.

### Nondefensive Responsibility for the Injury

Our research findings have indicated that one of the initial steps toward facilitating forgiveness is having the offending partner take responsibility for the harm done. This was the first "step toward resolution" that was found to discriminate between couples that forgave at the end of therapy and those that did not (Woldarsky Meneses & Greenberg, 2011). To promote this step, the therapist is required to coach the offending partner to take a nondefensive stance by having him or her speak in the first person and, ideally, using an *enactment* (when partners turn to each other), have the offending partner look at the injured partner directly and have him or her elaborate on his or her understanding of the injury. The therapist may say something such as, "Can you turn to him and tell him what you understand about his pain? Let him know what was going on for you at the time." If the therapist perceives that the offending partner has difficulty truly owning the responsibility for the EI and is attempting to shift the blame onto the injured partner, it is important to intervene and shift to doing some here-and-now processing in which the focus is on exploring the offending partner's experience as he or she engages in this task.

To illustrate nondefensive acceptance of responsibility, two examples are presented, one from a couple that did not reach forgiveness at the end of therapy and the other from a couple that did. The following excerpt is taken from the first session of one of the unresolved couples where the husband habitually neglected his wife after their children were born and withdrew from her emotionally.

**HUSBAND:** Um, I stand behind the mental illness thing as far as I'm concerned, and I have the, um, paperwork to back it up.

**THERAPIST:** And what illness are we talking about?

**HUSBAND:** It's the whole depression [*Therapist:* Mm-hmm], you know. It's a disease or whatever. It's a hard thing to deal with. Well, anyway, for me, it's hard to be angry at someone for being ill! I mean they did something to hurt you, but it wasn't done that way.

**THERAPIST:** So, you're saying that she shouldn't be angry at you for what happened in the past.

**HUSBAND:** Oh, no! She has every right to be angry. If I was her, I'm sure I would feel a lot of that anger too [*Therapist:* Mm-hmm], maybe not to the level or to the degree that it went to, but it's like somebody accidentally shooting you—you still get hurt [*Therapist:* Mmm], but it wasn't intentional.

**WIFE:** So, I shouldn't feel as hurt or as angry as I do?

**THERAPIST:** Is that what you're saying?

**HUSBAND:** I'm not trying to make an excuse now, but like I said, when it was happening, I didn't, I wasn't aware of it. I had enough beating up of myself to do that, you know, I didn't know that anyone else was getting hurt in the process.

Instead of owning his role in neglecting his wife, Robert unhooked himself from the responsibility of the injury by insisting he was not an active agent because he was too ill to recognize what was happening. This became his defense or alibi, in a sense (he even has paperwork to confirm his illness), and the message to the injured partner was that she had no right to feel so angry or hurt because he had nothing to do with his role as perpetrator of the neglect.

In contrast, George took a completely different stance by fully accepting responsibility for the fact that he was adamant that his wife abort their second child. This excerpt is taken from Session 2.

**HUSBAND:** I don't like confrontation [*Therapist:* Right], so I think that in a lot of ways, I was even more cold and detached and firm because I wanted to avoid any possible, any [*Therapist:* Mm-hmm] chink in my armor would be seen as weakness [*Therapist:* Right] . . . because I was worried that if, you know, the decision changed (clears throat) . . . I was already thinking, "Okay, the next step is to start my own business." It was like, you know, we're having kids, we're buying a house, you know, I'm never going to—it just seemed like a shitty scenario.

**THERAPIST:** Yeah, was there a lot of fear around it at the time?

**HUSBAND:** Oh, sure. Yeah, I mean . . . oh, my God, you know, I could feel the plan slipping through my hand, and any plans I had for our life [*Therapist:* Mm-hmm] were attached to the idea of starting the business, and I'm sure that I was in mortal fear of that disappearing. [*Therapist:* Mm-hmm.] For sure, I remember [*Therapist:* Mm-hmm] it was like, "No, this, this just can't happen."

This excerpt illustrates the offending partner's ability to own and assume responsibility for his role in the injury. Fearing that his wife could attempt to convince him that they should have the second child and that his lifelong dream of starting his own business would vanish, George was firm and adamant that she had to have an abortion. He recognized this and provided the context for his reaction without ever making it seem like a justification of his behavior.

## EMPATHY AND SHIFT IN VIEW OF OTHER

Part of the forgiveness process involves accompanying partners as they respond to each other's expressions of vulnerability. In the majority of the cases I (CWM) studied (Woldarsky Meneses, 2006), the injured partner's expressions of vulnerability were met with an empathic response by the offending partner (including responses of physical comfort, such as offering them a tissue or holding them while they cried). Empathic responses of this nature communicate an understanding and appreciation of the injured partners' pain, which seemed to be important for the injured partner, although it was insufficient for resolution, given that this component did not distinguish the couples who forgave from those that did not.

Interestingly, our research findings revealed that the injured partner's ability to experience a shift in the way he or she viewed the offender was found to be unique to couples that forgave (Woldarsky Meneses, 2006; Woldarsky Meneses & Greenberg, 2011). In other words, this was observed exclusively in the resolved cases and typically occurred after the offender was able to take nondefensive acceptance of responsibility for the injury and provide some context or reveal some new information about his or her actions and what was going on that led him or her to make certain decisions, although it sometimes appeared following the offending partner's expression of shame, remorse, or empathic distress and a heartfelt apology.

In some of the cases we studied, the offending partners also experienced a shift in their way of viewing the injured partner. This occurred in both of the abortion cases we studied (Woldarsky Meneses, 2006; Woldarsky Meneses & Greenberg, 2011) where the husbands pressured their wives to abort their pregnancies. Interestingly, both the men saw their wives in a new way and were finally able to understand the depth of their pain once the women revealed the idiosyncratic impact of the injury. The following is an excerpt from one such couple that came to therapy wanting to resolve the difficulties that stemmed from the decision to have an abortion 13 years prior, which Shannon felt was something that her husband, George, had imposed on her. In Session 6, Shannon finally moved away from expressing secondary anger toward George and was able to express sadness and grief over her lost baby, talking about the "void" she felt in her life (idiosyncratic impact). George witnessed her vulnerability and for the first time saw the depth of her hurt. Toward the end of the session, his view of her shifted, and he no longer saw her as an "angry woman stuck in the past" but rather as a sad mother who had lost her child. This, in turn, allowed him to feel more empathic toward her and to understand his role in the injury, which was important for Shannon.

**THERAPIST:** What is it like for you to see her hurt?

(Silence for nearly 30 seconds)

**HUSBAND:** Well, I guess, uh, kind of a powerlessness. (Pause of 10 seconds) I feel like kind of confused right now. [*Therapist:* Mm-hmm.] I don't know! Shocked, almost. I mean, I guess, surprised of my own misunder-, not misunderstanding but sort of lack of, of not really getting it before and then not, not really, guess I just didn't see the sadness of it because that wasn't what was . . .

**THERAPIST:** Being presented to you necessarily?

**HUSBAND:** Yeah, yes.

**WIFE:** Well, what happened today, that made it make sense? [*Therapist:* Mm-hmm.] What did I say differently? Or maybe . . .

**HUSBAND:** Just the way that you explained that it, how it made you feel sad, and you carried the sadness with you every day, and it, it affected, you know, it was, it was this thing that you regret, feel powerless, all of those things, and it wasn't about how, I forced you to, like, the usual presentation is that, you know, I forced you into the making the decision. It was an immoral one, you've had a hard time with it, um, but mostly because

> you're angry at me for making the decision. Those things are totally different from feeling sad. Being angry and being sad are two things that to me are separate. [*Therapist:* Mm-hmm.] So, I didn't see you as sad or hurt. [*Therapist:* Mm-hmm.] So, now I see you as sad about it, and the anger is just, the ab . . . if you had been able, if we had been able to talk about it, and I hadn't, um, negated your, your, your, feelings about it, [*Wife:* Then it wouldn't have.] then it wouldn't have transferred into anger. [Wife sighs.] So, I see my role in it as different than just being the decision, [*Therapist:* Mm-hmm] being part of the decision to have the abortion is more what happened afterwards in terms of, and that, that's never been, I mean, to me it's always been, the decision that was sort of the, the biggest thing that I did to make it impossible for you to get over it, whereas now it's, it's not the decision, it's immediately afterwards how, I guess, unsympathetic I was, so, and not that I didn't feel sympathy but just, my inability to express sympathy in a way that was helpful to you at all.

## INJURED PARTNER EXPRESSES A NEED, AND THE OFFENDER RESPONDS TO THE EXPRESSED NEED

The EFT-C therapist can help move the process of forgiveness forward by asking the injured partner what he or she needs from the offending partner to heal the wound left by the EI and rebuild trust. In our research studies (Woldarsky Meneses & Greenberg, 2011, 2014), we found that all injured partners were able to engage in this process regardless of whether the couple reached forgiveness at the end of therapy. However, the offending partner's response to this expressed need was of utmost importance: It either served to reestablish safety in the relationship and allow for a negotiation of relational needs in the couple, or it reinforced the injured partner's view that the offender was indeed incapable of dealing with his or her pain. The former type of response from the offending partner would typically evolve into an expression of shame or empathic distress, processes unique to the couples that reached forgiveness.

## THE HEARTFELT APOLOGY AND SELF-FOCUSED REMORSE

Even if the offending partner has apologized in the past, it is important that he or she apologize for the injury in-session. Moreover, therapists should encourage the expression of a heartfelt apology that includes sincere regret and reflects a deep understanding of the impact of the EI and its damage to the relationship and the injured partner. Typically, the offending partner begins by expressing other-focused regret (guilt) and offering to make amends for the damage done before moving into expressing self-focused regret that communicates that the offender has in some way changed, which ensures that the injury will never be repeated.

Shame can be conceptualized as *self-focused* regret or remorse (see Chapter 6 for a full discussion), where the offender feels great disappointment not only about how damaging his or her behavior was to the injured partner (*other-focused regret*) but also about being the type of person capable of behaving in such a way. Shame can promote interpersonal forgiveness if it is an authentic expression of remorse and not used in an instrumental manner (i.e., with the intention of evoking a particular response, such as reassurance or compassion from the injured partner) or as an expression of global self-contempt that shifts the focus away from forgiveness that pulls for reassurance from the injured partner, thereby shifting the focus away from the injured partner's experience and the process of forgiveness. Our research has indicated that for shame to lead to healing, it must be a self-focused process in which the offending partner expresses deep remorse, including feelings of worthlessness because he or she has deeply wounded a loved one (Woldarsky Meneses & Greenberg, 2011, 2014).

Shame is a powerful emotion that is about a person's self-worth and sense of connection to his or her group (in this case the dyad); it "informs one that other people will not support one's actions, that one has broken a very basic social norm . . . that one has violated standards or values that one recognizes as deeply important" (Greenberg, 2002, p. 145). It is thus an adaptive emotion when it comes to having committed an EI. Witnessing the offender express shame and pain over the injury signals to the injured partner that he or she is also hurting as a result of having committed the injury and violated personal moral standards.

Related to shame, but distinct from it, is the process of *empathic distress*, which involves the offender experiencing distress by and empathizing with the pain caused to his or her partner. The offender is also hurting from the pain and damage he or she caused; however, unlike shame, empathic distress does not involve a negative evaluation of the self.

Shame and empathic distress were found to be central to the forgiveness process. The expression of one rather than the other depended on the nature of the EI. Specifically, Woldarsky Meneses (2006) observed that the husbands who had engaged in extramarital affairs that violated a sacred trust in the relationship expressed shame, whereas those involved in abortion not supported by the partners or in other injuries involving less deep a violation expressed empathic distress for the pain caused and the harm done.

## FACILITATING SHAME AND EMPATHIC DISTRESS

Rather than imposing an agenda on the session, the therapist is advised to be fully present to both partners and to the process that unfolds, listening attentively for the offending partner to express remorse, which is usually embedded in the apology. Therapists have to have the courage to be with and follow the offending partner's pain because this can be uncomfortable to bear. At the same time, they have to be mindful of not shaming the offending partner. It is helpful for the therapist to validate how difficult it is to feel these painful feelings and at the same time insist that they are important for the couple's healing. Therapists are also encouraged to slow down the process so that the offending partner connects with the feelings of self-focused remorse and expresses his or her suffering in a focused vocal quality (see the Client Vocal Quality measure; Rice & Kerr, 1986). This means that he or she speaks from the core of his or her being with a searching and discovering quality (rather than a rehearsed quality). There is a clear sense that the offender feels distressed by, experiences some form of suffering for, and empathizes with the pain caused to his or her partner. The therapist helps the offending partner to stay in contact with these vulnerable emotions and express them to the injured partner. If during this process the therapist observes the offending partner withdrawing or becoming defensive or if the expressions of shame or empathic distress have an instrumental quality to them, the therapist should intervene and explore the here-and-now experience for the offending partner, as well as the impact on the injured partner (e.g., "What is going on for you right now? I'm getting the sense that you're closing up or that this is becoming increasingly difficult. Can you say a little bit about what it's like for you now?"). Once the offending partner can identify his or her block to expressing self-focused remorse and articulate this to the injured partner (e.g., "I'm hesitating to really open up because we've been through this before, and I'm afraid that you won't take my feelings seriously"), the therapist again resumes the task of promoting the expression of shame or empathic distress (e.g., "Can you try telling her in a way that she can see how much pain you're carrying inside? Maybe look at her and tell her in a way that she can see it is real").

The difference between shame and empathic distress can be seen in the following two excerpts. The first excerpt is from the fifth session with a couple whose presenting injury was the husband's extramarital affair.

**HUSBAND:** (Clears throat) Well, I'm actually very ashamed of those things. I guess this is something I have to carry around for the rest of my life.

**THERAPIST:** And I think the shame is really important, even though it's not an easy feeling. I guess it's like recognition that what you did then is not what you would do now?

**HUSBAND:** I still can't believe I did it because I had, you know, I always thought of myself as a very moral person [*Therapist:* Mm-hmm] and religious and, uh, you know, I carried around these values with me, and I betrayed my own values, so I betrayed myself [*Therapist:* Mm-hmm, mm-hm] and, uh, I have to live with that.

**THERAPIST:** And that's a painful thing to live with.

**HUSBAND:** Right. I let myself down, and I let her down. (Clears throat) It makes me reevaluate what my value-system is, and a value is, is a value, you don't, you can't [*Therapist:* Mm-hmm] change it. So, I can't say one thing and then be hypocritical by doing another.

Although shame involves questioning one's sense of self and trying to understand how one could behave in a certain manner, empathic distress involves experiencing the pain that comes with recognizing one has deeply wounded another person. This process is illustrated in the following excerpt, taken from the sixth session of another resolved couple. Here, the offending partner, George, came to appreciate the deep hurt he caused his wife, Shannon, who earlier in the session wept as she revealed the idiosyncratic impact of having aborted their second child.

**HUSBAND:** I've always thought there was nothing I could do [*Therapist:* Right], but now I suddenly realize that all I had to do was not say things like, "Oh, it's for the best"—all of the things that I guess made me feel better about the decision. [*Therapist:* Mm-hmm.] I'm just realizing that all of this made you feel like you couldn't even talk to me about it. I guess I'm just shocked at how I [*Therapist:* Mm-hmm] completely missed the boat on that.

**WIFE:** And I feel badly, like I can see that you really feel badly.

**HUSBAND:** Well, yeah, because I'm finally seeing that you carried the sadness with you every day. It was this thing that you regret, feel powerless, all of those things you said, and it wasn't about how I forced you to do it, it was afterwards how, I guess, unsympathetic I was—not that I didn't feel sympathy but just my inability to express sympathy in a way that was helpful to you. (Sighs) It's such a small thing, I mean, I can't take away all of the [*Therapist:* Mm-hmm] pain and the sadness [*Therapist:* Mm-hmm], but if all I had to do was validate her feelings, then it seems—I don't want to use the word *selfish*—it was ignorance, I guess.

## ACCEPTING THE OFFENDING PARTNER'S SHAME OR EMPATHIC DISTRESS

Empathy plays an important role in the process of interpersonal forgiveness (see Chapter 6, this volume). Given that empathy is a charged concept that is often associated with a therapist's ability to convey a deep understanding of a client's experience, we used the term *acceptance* instead in our research to refer to an affiliative stance characterized by a degree of openness (letting down one's guard) and a willingness to momentarily enter the world of the other rather than refusing to consider what he or she is experiencing. We found that an *accepting response* to the offending partner's shame promoted forgiveness at the end of therapy (Woldarsky Meneses & Greenberg, 2014). We consider an accepting response to signal welcoming rather than rejection of the offending partner, and we encourage therapists to be aware that the response to the offending partner's vulnerability (in the form of self-focused remorse) is important in promoting forgiveness. Therapists are encouraged to observe how the injured partner responds to the offending partner's expression of remorse and explore what may be getting in the way of offering an accepting response when one does not emerge (e.g., "I can see it's difficult for you to accept his apology and feelings of shame. What is going on for you right now? Can you turn to him and tell him that you're having a hard time taking this in?"). It may be that the offending partner is fearful of being hurt again and will not risk offering any remark that could invite reconnection or that he or she continues to feel misunderstood or angry, and it has to be acknowledged and explored in-session.

## INJURED PARTNER ASSUMES RESPONSIBILITY FOR THE PRE-EMOTIONAL INJURY CONDITIONS

Once the offending partner expresses self-focused remorse and the injured partner offers an accepting response in return, it sometimes occurs that the injured partner returns to discussing the context in which the EI occurred and can assume some responsibility for his or her role in the precipitating conditions that gave way to the injury. Although we did not find that this particular step increased the probability of the couple reaching forgiveness at the end of therapy, if it does occur, the therapist's task is to help both partners recognize that the injury evolved within the coconstruction of the relationship and that both have some degree of responsibility even if it was ultimately the offending partner's behavior that resulted in the EI. Usually, this emerges later in therapy once the couple has restructured the negative interactional cycle and in light of discussions about the couple's functioning before the injury, including their negative interactional cycle preinjury.

## INTERPERSONAL FORGIVENESS AND BEYOND

In our view, forgiveness is a transformative process in which anger, hurt, and the urge to seek revenge are resolved and give way to compassion. In the context of our research in the York Emotional Injury Project, we measured forgiveness as an in-session statement of having forgiven, which marked the endpoint of the task analysis (Woldarsky Meneses & Greenberg, 2011). Although we also used formal outcome measures of forgiveness posttherapy, we felt that a formal statement of forgiveness was necessary to mark an endpoint of the therapeutic process. We observed that once the injured partner expresses forgiveness, the offending partner responds with genuine acceptance, relief, and at times, gratitude. If this is not the case and the offending partner rejects the injured partner's forgiveness, more work is needed to explore his or her hesitation in accepting this precious gift.

One important caveat in forgiving is that it does not imply forgetting. For some couples, arriving at forgiveness invites the opportunity to reflect on the conditions that gave way to injury, including their pre–EI relational dynamics. In reflecting on her experience of forgiving, one injured partner in our research study acknowledged both her role in the precipitating conditions that led to the injury (while continuing to hold her husband accountable for his behavior) and also elaborated on the sense of loss that accompanied seeing her husband in a different light:

> It just made me realize that there were problems in the, in the relationship that I knew were there, but he didn't talk about them, and I let him not talk about them. I mean, I saw him unhappy, and I often thought that he would leave me, not that he would have an affair. And then, for me, this has meant letting go of a part of him that I once saw. You know, because he really goes out of his way to help people at times; he can be very selfless, and I remember thinking that he had a certain, almost a moral, code that he lived by that I really admired. And that was completely shattered. So, in a way, this has also been about letting go of this big part of him that I was attached to and somehow understanding him differently. I understand how it could've been for him, not that I was okay with what happened, but I can see how it was for him. . . . So, I'm forgiving in many ways, and the pain is starting to go away and get left in the background. I don't think I'll ever trust him the same way again. I think as time goes on I'll trust him more and more. But it feels like we really are back at the core issues, so I think in some ways, this has really helped get past focusing on the symptom versus the problem, and it feels hopeful. It feels more real.

Couples who reach forgiveness have a sense of having transcended, not just survived, the EI, which is a profound experience that impacts their joint identity as a couple (i.e., "we-ness"). This is typically embedded in the couple's narrative that emerges with forgiveness and evolves as the couple reconciles and focuses on rebuilding their relationship (see Woldarsky Meneses & Greenberg, 2015, for further discussion).

In the context of couple's work, reconciliation represents an important goal that typically arises following forgiveness (see Chapter 6 for a more detailed discussion). In our view, reconciliation involves reconnecting and reconstructing the relationship and, in the words of W. M. Malcolm (personal communication, 2006), "reclaiming the we." Reconciliation can also be understood as a reaffirmation of the commitment to the couple that carries with it the recognition that the relationship will never be the same as before the EI.

Postforgiveness work involves validating and at times encouraging couples to reflect on their healing process to access and explore their relational narrative. This is an important aspect of the consolidation phase of couple therapy because, as in individual therapy, successful change involves the client's ability to articulate, elaborate, and transform his or her narrative (Angus & Greenberg, 2011; see also Chapter 2, this volume). The therapist's role at this stage includes being receptive to the couple's discussion of their progress, their way of "storying" their experience of forgiveness, and facilitating deeper reflection by asking questions such as, What has changed since the beginning of our work together on an individual level and as a couple? What were some of the "turning points" in the process?

Typically, couples use metaphors to describe their journey together and the experience of having transcended the injury. Idiosyncratic metaphors for the couple's healing arise and become part of a shared narrative that reflects a new sense of "we-ness" (Fergus & Reid, 2001). For example, one couple in our study reported that forgiveness helped breathe life into their relationship that brought with it more freedom and flexibility in their interactions, which had been previously crystallized by the EI:

> It was like we were frozen in time, and everything seemed to revolve around the event, all the fights and all the discussions, but in forgiving it feels as though we are thawing and coming back to life, back to being who we were before the event.

At this stage, couples report a greater sense of connection, an increased intimacy, and a resurfacing of positive emotions linked to the dimension of liking and attraction (Greenberg & Goldman, 2008). Couples may even engage in a symbolic act to mark their reengagement to one another, which therapists can explore with them (e.g., at the end of therapy, one couple in our study expressed an interest in having a second child, whereas another couple decided it was finally time to realize their dream of moving to the countryside). It is this sense of going beyond the injury that now defines the couple's narrative and offers a structure for the experience lived.

Additional work during this consolidation phase of treatment involves helping the couple return to examining the core cycle, to discuss how it has been restructured (or what changes would need to happen to restructure it), and to also validate the couple's new way of interacting. It is helpful to highlight what their previous positions in the cycle were, remind them of what prevented them from being able to express their primary vulnerable emotions and needs to one another and also discuss or negotiate existing relationship stressors or issues.

## BLOCKS ON THE PATH TO FORGIVENESS FOR COUPLES

It is also useful for therapists to be aware of processes that can interfere with forgiveness. In the initial phase of our task analytic work on forgiveness (Woldarsky Meneses & Greenberg, 2011), we closely analyzed the processes of couples that did not resolve their EIs and found that the offending partners of these couples were unresponsive toward the injured partners' pain. This went hand-in-hand with marked difficulties assuming responsibility for the EI and highlights the relationship between responsiveness and responsibility: One cannot occur without the other in the context of forgiveness.

Moreover, we found that the lack of responsiveness we observed among the offending partners of unresolved couples took two forms, which we called *pressure to forgive* (involving a shift of blame onto the injured partner for not having yet forgiven or being willing to forgive and move forward) and *competition of hurts* (where the offending partner prioritizes his suffering and blames the injured partner for not being responsive to him or her). These tendencies are major obstacles to forgiveness.

Therapists are also advised to be attentive to the hopelessness and dominance exhibited by the offending partner. In one couple studied, the offending partner would express instrumental hopelessness at critical moments that served as a means of avoiding responsibility (e.g., "Yeah, that stuff happened, but what's the point of me telling you how sorry I am again? I've been saying it for years, and nothing's changed") and consequently from being responsive to his partner's pain (e.g., "You know, every time you start talking about the pain you carry inside, I sit here and I think what's the point of this? I can't do anything about it. Haven't we been here already? I just don't know see how this time it will be different"). Similarly, the offending partner's nonverbal gestures (including sighing, eye rolling, fidgeting, as well as interrupting the injured partner and/or abruptly switching the topic) served to dominate the in-session discussions and prevented the injured partner from fully processing his or her experience.

When working with highly invalidating offending partners, most of the work focuses initially on Stage 2 of the EFT-C model (Greenberg & Goldman, 2008), negative cycle de-escalation. The aim is to explore the offender's invalidating stance and the defensiveness implied in his or her in-session behavior, as well as to make explicit the impact this has on the injured partner (i.e., shutting down or becoming defensive and combative). Ideally, the therapist helps the offending partner move from secondary anger to accessing the primary emotion that underlies his or her behavior (i.e., fear or shame) and to be able to express his or her primary emotion to the injured partner. Work is also needed to explore the blocks that prevent the offending partner from being able to respond empathically. Nevertheless, the offending partner's difficulties may reflect deeply entrenched characterological issues (e.g., narcissistic features) that prevent him or her from being empathic and indicate a strong need for individual therapeutic work before returning to couple's work. Other challenging issues are discussed next.

### Working With Multiple Injuries

Sometimes couples may seek therapy because they have experienced a series of EIs in their relationship, and both partners have been the injurer and the injured one. In these cases, it is helpful to understand the couple's narrative about their evolution as a couple and their injuries to identify a core injury on which all other injuries revolve. This means working with the injury that seems to have the most emotional relevance for the couple and/or for each partner rather than following the chronology of the injuries. The therapist can validate that all of the injuries have been damaging but that for the sake of organizing the therapeutic work, you will initially focus on one injury. The therapy unfolds in the process we have described in this chapter; however, "multiple rounds" will be necessary to address additional injuries and for each partner to have a chance to be in the role of the injured one.

### Difficulties De-Escalating Conflict

In cases in which partners are highly reactive and seem to be in constant conflict, the therapist has to be more active than usual to prevent them from escalating further and also to maintain control in the session. The core skill to use in such cases is validation to contain them. The therapist is advised to quickly move to name their cycle (which at this stage is likely "attack or defend") and insist on there being important emotions underneath their aggressive behavior and that these have to be accessed to change the couple's destructive way of relating to each other. We suggest therapists say something such as,

> I'm going to stop you now and ask that you each take a deep breath because this exchange does not seem productive. I can see you're both desperately wanting the other to see how hurt or frustrated you are. My sense is that you're both suffering, and I want to help you resolve this. I think that your intensity is an indicator of how important this relationship is to you both. But I need for us to slow down and to respect the other's position and turn to talk. I know that you, [injured partner], are indignant about what she did and that you, [offending partner], are frustrated that nothing you say about what was going on for you at that time seems to be getting through to him, and we will get to exploring all of this, but I need to ask both of you to slow down. I can see that this is really hard and that you each take what the other says as an attack and so you defend yourself by attacking back. We need to move past this so that we can understand what is going on. Maybe let me start by asking each of you what seems to be the most painful aspect of working through this injury.

Using empathic conjectures, the therapist can arrive at articulating an understanding of each partner's underlying position that will help define their cycle and hopefully give way to a less hostile mode of working in therapy (see Greenberg & Goldman, 2008, for further details on Stage 2 work).

In addition, it may be useful to be direct and confrontational with a highly reactive couple if de-escalation is a challenge and explore their motivation to change. It may be useful to explore what they gain by remaining stuck in this gridlock and, conversely, ask what they risk losing if they give up this style of relating. An individual session with each partner would also be appropriate to explore these questions and understand each partner's position because safety (and the lack thereof) may be what is preventing them from taking a more vulnerable stance. It may also be that the injured partner is ambivalent about resolving the conflict because this implies accepting a shift in the power dynamic and no longer being in the "one-up" position in terms of having the "right" to use the injury as a way of gaining leverage over the offending partner in everyday life.

### Highly Dominant Partner

There are different manifestations of dominance in couples therapy and different degrees of dominant behavior. We make the distinction between *soft* dominance and *hard* dominance, where the former refers to a stance that is more "malleable," and the latter refers to a character trait that is deeply entrenched. Usually, shame underlies the dominant partner's position where the profound sense of inferiority leaves the person feeling that his or her self is at stake if he or she is not in the "one-up" position, which often results in partners engaging in "influence" cycles (Greenberg & Goldman, 2008).

The dominant partner takes the position of being the "expert" on the other and the relationship and feels entitled to "define reality" without concern for the subjective experience of the other partner or the therapist. This may be evident in the dominant partner's tendency to speak for the other partner, to interrupt to "correct" what is being stated, or to use nonverbal gestures such as eye-rolling, sighing loudly, laughing inappropriately, or expressing sadness or anger in an instrumental way so as to draw attention to him- or herself and "hijack" the interaction. The dominant partner's style of defining reality may be irreverent, disrespectful, or even benevolent and warm (condescending). In moments when the dominant partner exhibits any form of dominant behavior, we advise therapists to stop the interaction and name what they observed to engage the partners in moment-by-moment processing. For example, the therapist may observe that as the nondominant partner is speaking, the other partner fidgets in his or her seat looking disapproving and finally interrupts to dismiss what the other partner says by saying, "Your problem is that you're insecurely attached," and then turns to the therapist to elaborate on the other's family of origin. The therapist should say something such as,

> I see you want me to hear about his background, but I want to go back to a second ago when he was talking, and you interrupted him abruptly. Did you notice that? This happens regularly, and I'm curious about what was going on for you as he was talking. Can we do that?

The aim is for the therapist to identify the emotion underlying the dominant behavior and also have the dominant partner see the impact of his or her behavior on their partner and their interaction.

In the scenario we outlined previously, the therapist helped the dominant partner identify his or her emotional experience by going back to the moment just before he or she interrupted the other: "So, I saw you fidgeting in your seat. Do you remember doing that? It seemed like you were uncomfortable. What was going on inside for you?" If the dominant partner is having difficulty with this task, the therapist should use empathic conjectures to help him or her identify what was underlying the dominant behavior: "I wonder if you were fidgeting around feeling [*in a tentative voice*] annoyed or maybe blamed? Like there was something in what she was saying that made you feel like a bad person?" Once the emotion underlying the dominant behavior has been named, it is important to explore its impact on the other partner and link this to the couple's interactional cycle. The therapist will eventually help the dominant partner access and express his or her underlying shame and follow the therapeutic process outlined by Greenberg and Goldman (2008).

In the case of hard dominance, the therapist is required to be more confronting with dominant partners because they may not even be able to accept their underlying shame, let alone express it to their partner. The therapist is encouraged to be explicit in stating what he or she observes, the impact of the behavior on the other partner, and the potential risks for the dominant partner if he or she does not soften his or her stance (e.g., "Again, you're dismissing what she's saying by joking around. It's invalidating, and she feels totally disempowered. She will likely be cold toward you and reject your attempts at closeness, and then you'll say she's not fun and call her frigid, and she'll be left feeling hurt, and you'll be left feeling lonely and unhappy. Do you want to be right, or do you want to be happy?"). We also recommend exploring the dominant partner's motivation for resolving the injury; this will rebalance the power dynamic and may represent a threat or risk to the dominant partner's position.

### Extreme (Nonproductive) Remorse

Sometimes an offending partner may be so remorseful about what he or she did that expressions of guilt and/or shame are overwhelmingly present. We have previously discussed the qualities of self-oriented remorse (i.e., shame or empathic distress) that we observed to be important to the forgiveness process (see Chapter 6)—namely, that it be about the injury or the self with regard to the injury. We observed that global expressions of worthlessness ("I'm a terrible person" vs. "I was terrible to have hurt you the way I did") or statements of self-flagellation ("And I don't deserve to live") divert the forgiveness process and shift the focus entirely onto the offending partner; the injured partner is required to comfort and reassure him or her. We consider these to be desperate attempts to resolve the injury without actually doing the emotional work required to soothe the pain of the injured partner, which entails "sitting in" the shame or empathic distress and responding to the injured partner from there rather than "drowning" in it and pulling the injured partner in to rescue him or her. In other words, we consider expressions of extreme remorse to be unproductive in terms of how the emotion is processed by the offending partner (Auszra, Greenberg, & Herrmann, 2013).

In a situation in which the offending partner is expressing extreme or unproductive remorse, we urge the therapist to intervene by "containing" the offender (i.e., validate that this is painful) and exploring the impact on the injured partner to highlight that this expression is not helping the injured partner move forward. Regardless of whether the injured partner shifts into a reassuring and comforting stance or remains cold and distant toward the offender's remorse, the therapist should explore what is happening inside for him or her and use this as a teaching moment to explain that, ironically, in expressing so much remorse, the experience of the injured partner is getting lost. Then the therapist's focus should shift back to the offender to help him or her express remorse in a way that will be more productive to the couple's healing process by coaching him or her to respond more appropriately to the injured partner's pain and eventually get to expressing self-directed remorse in a productive manner (i.e., by keeping the injured partner's experience present and expressing remorse in a proportionate way).

## CONCLUSION

Forgiveness is a transformative process that can be facilitated in couples therapy. Essentially, this requires that the therapist be able to evoke previously undisclosed vulnerability and promote responsiveness to the vulnerability expressed while also being able to guide the couple through specific forgiveness-oriented tasks. These include helping the injured partner articulate the idiosyncratic impact of the injury, encouraging the offending partner to take responsibility in a nondefensive manner, and with great finesse, facilitating the expression of self-focused remorse (shame or empathic distress) and promoting a heartfelt apology. The therapist also has to explore the injured partner's response to the offender's remorse. Consistent with the general EFT-C model (see Chapter 5), the therapist has to work with partners' blocks to responsiveness (i.e., lack of empathy for the other), as well as attend to the couple's negative interactional cycle, which keeps them stuck in a state of unforgiveness.

# 8

# Case Example of Forgiveness for Couples

In this chapter, we present the therapeutic process of Myriam and Steve, who are in therapy 3 years after Steve disclosed that he had an extramarital affair that lasted several months. They are a common-law couple in their mid-30s that have been together for over 10 years, and this is their third experience with therapy together. Steve and Myriam have a 2-year-old son, and they are considering having a second child, but the unhealed wounds of their emotional injury (EI) are interfering with this project. They are seen for 11 sessions by a therapist experienced in emotion-focused therapy.

The therapist begins the first session by exploring how the affair occurred and what the impact has been on the couple and each partner. He is validating and empathic with both of them and works with Myriam to help her express the emotions related to the injury while at the same time helping Steve tolerate and respond to these emotions. Parallel to helping the couple resolve their EI, the therapist aims to understand the couple's interpersonal dynamics to help them restructure their negative interactional cycle.

As therapy evolves, two cycles that represent difficulties in the domains of attachment (closeness) and identity (self-esteem and agency) emerge. Before the affair, Steve pursued Myriam for closeness, and Myriam withdrew because she felt depressed and uninterested in sex. Steve felt rejected and sexually unsatisfied but felt he did not say this to Myriam directly because he feared she would take this as a criticism and feel even more depressed. By midtreatment, Steve reported that he had felt pressure to be "her rock" and not let her down, so he sought his sexual needs outside the relationship. In Session 2, an additional cycle became apparent because Myriam overfunctions, feeling

http://dx.doi.org/10.1037/0000144-009
*Forgiveness and Letting Go in Emotion-Focused Therapy*, by L. S. Greenberg and C. Woldarsky Meneses

she cannot rely on Steve, whom she describes as forgetful, unfocused, and conflict avoidant. Because of her anxious style, Myriam tends to take control, and rather than delegating tasks, she takes on the "lion's share" of responsibilities, in particular, managing the household and raising their son. She describes feeling overwhelmed and unsupported, as well as resentful of Steve whose tendency is to minimize her concerns and not follow through on what he says he will do. Steve, whose tendency is to become defensive, eventually discloses that he often feels that he falls short of Myriam's expectations, that nothing he does is good enough for her, and so rather than feel inadequate, he tends to avoid taking on the tasks she proposes. This reinforces Myriam's view that she must do it all, for which she feels resentful, unsupported, and unloved, so she distances herself from Steve when he seeks closeness, which leaves him feeling rejected, so he begins to be critical in his attempts to pursue her, and the two of them go around and round in their concurrent cycles.

## DEFENSIVENESS AND DISTRESS

At the beginning of therapy, Steve and Myriam are both highly defensive. The therapist's task at this stage is to help them differentiate the emotions underlying their distress (i.e., help them articulate what is at the core of their pain) so that they may each express a primary, vulnerable emotion that will invite responsiveness instead of defensiveness. The following is an excerpt from this couple's first session in which they discuss the context of the affair and its effects on their functioning. Myriam expresses anger and hurt at having been betrayed, and toward the end of the session, she reveals the idiosyncratic impact of having been betrayed: losing the opportunity to have a choice about whether to stay together.

**MYRIAM:** I wasn't pregnant at the time when the affair started, so I have a lot of anger around that I really feel like, um, you know, (sighs deeply) there was a point at which, we, we may have not gone down this road together, and I would have had an opportunity to have a choice in some ways, like I feel like, you know, I love him, but there's times when I think, you know, I'm, I'm here partly because I want (sighs), I want a family, and I want a family to work, and we have a child together [*Therapist:* Mm-hmm], and I'm not going to deny that that's not part of it [*Therapist:* Uh-huh], you know, and I sort of feel like, you know, I would have at least, I might've chosen to stick with him and work it out or not, but I wasn't given that choice.

**THERAPIST:** So what's burning is this issue that he was having an affair before we got pregnant.

**MYRIAM:** Right.

**THERAPIST:** And somehow he lied, and you found out about it later—it's that it was going on at the time it went on [*Myriam:* Right] that's the most upsetting to you. [*Myriam:* Right.] I understand.

**MYRIAM:** Right. Yeah, part of it, I mean, it was just really, really selfish to not think at all about me. At all! (laughs slightly) About me or our child! Um, like just really reckless and irresponsible, um, he was having unprotected sex so, there's the health implications as well, [*Therapist:* Mm-hmm] which, I can't; you know, he says he was just oblivious . . . and he started this, you know, before things got really, really permanent, and, ah, it wasn't fair to me.

**THERAPIST:** Okay. So, in the end, when you found out, you felt betrayed and angry. [*Myriam:* Oh, yeah!] It shattered your trust.

**MYRIAM:** Oh, totally. Yeah, very angry.

**THERAPIST:** And now there's a feeling still of how could he have done it then, [*Myriam:* Mm-hmm] as well as the feeling of hurt that's s still there.

**MYRIAM:** Oh, yes.

**THERAPIST:** And how do you feel in terms of the fact that he had an affair now?

**MYRIAM:** I don't dwell on it daily. I'm not depressed or upset about it. [*Therapist:* Yeah, yeah, yeah.] I think the hardest thing, to be honest, is that, um, I don't feel like I can talk about my feelings about it with him. Because he doesn't want, he wants to pretend it never happened (sighs).

Later in the first session, the therapist asks Steve about his experience, and he discusses feeling sexually unsatisfied with Myriam, who acknowledges that her emotional state was interfering with her sex drive but that her way of leaning on him prevented him from being able to open up to her.

**THERAPIST:** What happened when she found out? I mean, how did you feel?

**STEVE:** Oh, I felt awful.

**THERAPIST:** Mm-hmm. And what was the most awful part of it?

**STEVE:** That I really hurt someone that I love and that it was very selfish behavior [*Therapist:* Mm-hmm], and I put no thought into what I was doing [*Therapist:* Mm-hmm] and that, uh, you know, and, just irresponsible. I felt like I had behaved irresponsibility and that, you know, I should have told Myriam that I wasn't happy with our sexual relationship [*Therapist:* Mm-hmm] instead of just having sex with someone else.

**THERAPIST:** Okay, can you say a bit more about that? What was happening?

**STEVE:** Well, uh, I think, for most couples, the male tends to want to have more sex than the female [*Therapist:* Uh-huh], and I know it was something we used to discuss.

**MYRIAM:** But at the time, I was going through a lot, and to be honest, I've been in therapy myself for a long time. [*Therapist:* Yes.] (Chuckles) I look back, and I was, you know, my sex drive was, was affected by all this. There was a lot going on in my life at the time, so I was, I felt like I was sort of in the midst of it all and trying to work through it all. Then the other thing that sort of comes out of that was that I used to really lean on him, you know, emotionally and confide in him, and he didn't feel that he could do the same.

## DEFINING THE COUPLE'S NEGATIVE INTERACTIONAL CYCLE

During the middle phase of therapy, the focus is on de-escalating and restructuring the couple's cycle. Specifically, the therapist works at identifying the origins of Myriam's anxiety and fear of not being able to count on Steve that drives her tendency to "overfunction" and Steve's fear of disapproval and the shame he feels when he perceives he has fallen short of expectations that lead him to avoid tasks asked of him. This identity-based cycle has consequences on their functioning in the domain of attachment: The more that Myriam feels overwhelmed by the numerous responsibilities she must manage, the more resentful she feels toward Steve and the more distant (and sexually uninterested) she becomes. Given Steve's experiences as the fifth sibling in a family of six children, Myriam's distance leaves him feeling unloved, which he manages by expressing anger toward her (in the form of criticism). This cycle also works in the opposite direction: The more anger Steve expresses to Myriam and the more he pressures her to have sex, the more overwhelmed and angry she feels because it seems like he is imposing more demands on her. In the following excerpt taken from the third session, the therapist aims to make the link between how each partner's experiences in their respective families of origin shape their current functioning in their interactive cycle.

**THERAPIST:** So, from what I observed, and you may or may not agree when I say that, Steve, you're angry! [*Steve:* Mm-hmm.] It seems to me that some of the anger is because Myriam is disappointing or frustrating you, but it's also about how you handle being neglected or feeling rejected by her. You see, I think each of you bring something into the relationship, a vulnerability or a sensitivity, and that will eventually get activated. It doesn't matter who's sat in that chair as your wife, eventually you would start to feel how you feel [*Steve:* Mm-hmm.], and similarly, you [Myriam] would start to feel how you feel. [*Myriam:* Mm-hmm.] So, can you relate that to your childhood, Steve? What did you bring to this relationship? What would you say is your main vulnerability?

**STEVE:** (Clears throat) It seems to me we're trying to talk about family dysfunctions. Is that what you're trying to bring up?

**THERAPIST:** Well, not dysfunction per se.

**STEVE:** Like that my mother ignored me because I was the second youngest of six and [*Therapist:* Yeah] that no one paid attention to me? Or is that what you want me to tell you, or what?

**THERAPIST:** Yeah, I mean, is that, is that true? Did you feel that?

**STEVE:** Sure, at times, probably, yeah. [*Therapist:* Yeah.] Other times less so. But I always felt loved. [*Therapist:* Yes, yes.] I'm actually more aware of the pressure I felt for me to do well and to excel.

**THERAPIST:** And that came from who?

**STEVE:** My father, who would want me to excel and stuff. [*Therapist:* Yeah, yeah.] Even when I phone him now, whenever I phone him, it's like he wants a report on my accomplishments at work, right? There's that and, ah, certainly as a child you're competing for attention, so I really wanted to do well.

**THERAPIST:** Mm-hmm. And you, Myriam? What was it like growing up for you?

**MYRIAM:** Um, where to start? Um, my parents didn't like each other very much, and there was a lot of conflict in our house. I felt very much on my own from a very young age. Like, um, emotionally, financially, um, like I knew that if I wanted to make something out of my life, I'd have to do it myself. [*Therapist:* I see, yeah.] So, um, I was, ah—

**THERAPIST:** I see, right, right. And how did it mark you?

**MYRIAM:** Um, how did it mark me? Um, in some ways I'm still, um, feeling like sometimes I'm just really tired of having to be the responsible one. I just (sighs) really wish at times I could depend on somebody else (sniffles).

**THERAPIST:** Mm-hmm, and so then that carries in here.

**MYRIAM:** And I don't feel like I can really depend on him very much (sniffles).

**THERAPIST:** And wh- depend on him for what?

**MYRIAM:** Um, (sighs) um, emotionally being there for me for the functioning of the house mostly and planning events and vacations. Um, I'm just really, (sighs) I have control issues where I have to have things done a certain way [*Therapist:* Right, right, right], and I'll say, "Can you relieve me of some of this burden? Could you do some of this for me?" [*Therapist:* Uh-huh], and then he's just like, "Oh, I forgot." [*Therapist:* Uh-huh.] So, I don't feel like we share the load. I think he should know how important it is for me that he does it but then, to him, it's just like, "I forgot. So, what's the big deal?"

**THERAPIST:** So, you end up feeling unloved.

**MYRIAM:** Yes!

**THERAPIST:** Whereas for him it's a practical thing.

**MYRIAM:** Right.

**STEVE:** Well, I think she, yeah, okay, she burdens herself. Myriam burdens herself [*Therapist:* Mm-hmm] mentally, and [*Therapist:* Right] so she feels because she's, let's say, worried about something [*Therapist:* Right], and I don't worry about it, [*Therapist:* Mm-hmm] that she carries the burden.

At this point in the session, Steve becomes defensive and insists he has made important changes recently. The therapist validates his efforts and reframes their conflict in light of their negative interactional cycle. He also invites them to reflect on what they need from the other, which brings to light Myriam's difficulty trusting Steve and, furthermore, the anger she feels toward him for his lack of support and the pressure to be more sexually available.

**THERAPIST:** Right, right, right. So, these are differences, and this happens in all of us, in all couples [*Myriam:* Mm-hmm], and somehow it's the difficulty in handling the difference that can become problematic, right? So, I mean you were a sort of a self-sufficient child [*Myriam:* Mm-hmm], like you were unsupported [*Myriam:* Yes], so you had to be self-sufficient, so in a way you bring that self, that anxiety and feeling like everything has to be done, but you feel burdened [*Myriam:* Right], and you want support. You also have a more organized and anxious nature, so you want to get things done in a particular way, and he doesn't function that way. [*Myriam:* Right.] The issue is how does he end up appreciating you and supporting you, and how do you end up appreciating his way of being rather than having it became a kind of blaming game. You're both involved in blaming each other [*Myriam:* Mm-hmm], and then you both feel unfairly treated, resentful and withdraw [*Myriam:* Mm-hmm], and then it sort of exacerbates because it keeps going round and round, right? [*Myriam:* Mm-hmm.] And you end up feeling angry at him for not supporting you [*Myriam:* Mm-hmm], but you also feel more anxious and afraid that it's not going to work out. So, now what is your deepest need from each other? What is it that you want from him that would touch this place inside that hurts, this feeling of unsupportiveness or feeling of anxiety?

**MYRIAM:** Um, I guess, feeling [*Therapist:* Yeah] that he's going to stick around.

**THERAPIST:** So, it is the fear of his abandonment [*Myriam:* Mm-hmm], right? That he's going to leave. (Steve shifts in his chair and exhales deeply.) And, Steve, what did you hear her say?

**STEVE:** She wants a feeling of long term commitment.

**THERAPIST:** Right, and when you hear her say it, how does it touch you inside? I mean what do you feel? Do you get angry or—

**STEVE:** It's, um, I guess my feeling is how on a continual basis am I going to convince her that I'm going to go the long term—you know what I mean? Just like [*Myriam:* I thin-.] is there something like tomorrow to the light turns on [*laughing*].

**MYRIAM:** No, but it's—

**STEVE:** And you're finally convinced I'm staying here!

**THERAPIST:** Right, or is it something like every day I have to prove myself [*Steve:* Yeah] that I'm going to stay?

**STEVE:** Yes, that's my thinking. Like how am I going to, like what can I do so that she feels comfortable in the relationship.

**THERAPIST:** Right, and is it motivated by "what can I do?" or more motivated by the feeling that "nothing will ever satisfy you"?

**STEVE:** No, it's more like "what can I do."

**THERAPIST:** Okay, will you tell her?

**STEVE:** Yeah, um, well, what can I do? [*Therapist:* Yeah.] Like what can I do to get that, for you to have that feeling?

**THERAPIST:** How do you feel when he says that?

**MYRIAM:** Well, I sort of feel like he's in a bit of a no-win situation at this point because part of it is, I think, ultimately, um, I just don't know if I'm going to be able to trust him [*Therapist:* Yeah] again.

**THERAPIST:** I want you to tell all this to him: "I don't know if I can trust you."

**MYRIAM:** I don't know if I'm going to be able to trust you, um, the same way ever again.

**THERAPIST:** I want you to respond to that. Tell her what you feel when she says that. What do you feel?

**STEVE:** (Exhales loudly) Well, I feel acceptance. I mean, I can understand why you wouldn't, wouldn't have the same level of trust, and it will need time.

## SCAFFOLDING FORGIVENESS WORK BY DE-ESCALATING THE COUPLE'S CYCLE

At this moment, there is a brief pause and the therapist, hearing Steve's regret, attempts to facilitate an apology and move the forgiveness process forward. Myriam, however, is not receptive to Steve's apology and reveals that part of her reluctance in accepting his apology stems from her difficulty trusting Steve, given the importance he places on sex. Myriam eventually states that she feels angry, and the therapist works with her so that she can express her anger to Steve directly rather than avoid it (due to her fear of abandonment and messages from past therapists about the damaging potential of anger). This piece of therapeutic work is paramount for the couple because it helps them to de-escalate their attack–defend cycle and is a preliminary step to the forgiveness work.

**THERAPIST:** And can you apologize? Have you apologized?

**STEVE:** Yes, I have.

**THERAPIST:** Can you tell her about that? I mean do you feel regretful?

**STEVE:** Definitely, I feel, definitely, I feel regret. I wish that we had worked out our problems before that, before I did what I did, and I had communicated better to you how I felt and my fears and concerns about our relationship.

**THERAPIST:** What happened?

**STEVE:** I didn't do a very good job communicating to you.

**THERAPIST:** What happens when he says this to you? Just what happens as you hear it?

**MYRIAM:** Um, I believe him. [*Therapist:* Yeah.] Um (sighs), what do I feel? (Sighs. Long pause) Hm, I can't, I can't think of how I'm feeling now.

**THERAPIST:** Mm-hmm, mm-hmm. Yes, it's complicated, I'm sure.

**MYRIAM:** Very complicated, yeah. I mean, I'm (exhales) I guess, just almost a little, it, I, feel that it's important that he, I don't know, like it, I feel that he is sorry, um, I guess (sighs) I just sort of feel that I, I feel that he's got issues of his own, and I'm not going to dea- I, I still don't think I'm going to be able to make him happy no matter what I do. I feel a bit of that, so I feel that even though, you know, he's, he's expressing that he's sorry and that, you know, that he's very insightful about what he should have done [*Therapist:* Yes] around his behavior, um, I still sometimes wonder if it's, it still, it still may happen again. I don't know, I just, like part of me thinks that, you know, if he felt he wasn't going to get caught, it still might happen again. I still feel that way.

**THERAPIST:** Mm-hmm, and what do you feel he wants, that he would do? I mean is he, what is he looking for, do you feel?

**MYRIAM:** Um, (long pause) I think a part, I think there is a big part of him that, or the way that he, I think, he receives love [*Therapist:* Yes] or feels it [*Therapist:* Yes] is by sex [*Therapist:* Yes, yes] and only sex [*Therapist:* Right, right, right], and it's just, you know, it's just something that I just don't, with everything that is going on with us, (moving in chair) um, I just don't feel that I am able to be available to him as often as he needs. I think that is ultimately what it is.

**THERAPIST:** Right, right, right. So, I want you to tell him this, especially with everything that is going on. I want you to name what everything is.

**MYRIAM:** It's, um, how busy our lives are? How complicated our lives are. Um, I'm living with you, feeling mistrustful, and feeling a lot of anger and conflict.

**THERAPIST:** S-so, with, when you say anger, it's your anger or his?

**MYRIAM:** More his anger [*Therapist:* Okay] towards me [*Therapist:* Right] that I'm not making him happy, I'm not giving him what he needs.

**THERAPIST:** Right, so tell him, "Your anger kind of leads me to not be sexually available."

**MYRIAM:** Yeah! Like I just, I—

**THERAPIST:** It's important that he understands that and that you own that: "It's hard for me to be open sexually and available when I'm feeling the anger and conflict."

**MYRIAM:** Uh-huh, and I think a lot times that I sort of feel like, yeah, I feel like—

**THERAPIST:** Right, I understand that it's the stress.

**MYRIAM:** You know, I think that there's been times th-that I feel like if he would support me more maybe in sharing the worrying. (Laughs) [*Therapist:* Yeah, yeah.] So, maybe I'm sort of saying if he's, if he'd only be somebody he isn't! (Laughs) Right? [*Therapist:* Mm-hmm.] I would feel better.

Here Myriam begins to articulate her anger about feeling unsupported by Steve and the sense of injustice that comes with feeling that she carries the responsibility of running the household and ensuring the well-being of the family. Steve becomes defensive, and the therapist confronts him about his "good boy" reaction and the anger he feels toward her that he expresses through criticism.

**THERAPIST:** Let me try to stop you. I, I understand there's a lot of stress, right? It's like you're saying, "But I need you to worry."

**MYRIAM:** Right, I just feel like I need you to care like I do. You know, I feel like [*Therapist:* Yes], like I'm carrying it all on my own. [*Therapist:* Yeah.] Because ultimately I'm the one who stays home if, if our son gets sick, or if, if something goes wrong, I'm the one who stays home. I'm the one who has to give up my job. I'm the one who has to give up my security. He's the one going to work, and I find that very difficult. (Sniffles)

**THERAPIST:** What happens with all of this, right? I mean this is a lot of the anger.

**STEVE:** I don't understand why she just said that. [*Therapist:* Uh-huh.] If something happens, usually if something happens, we discuss who's going to stay home.

**MYRIAM:** (Exhales) No, I mean if he has a cold, and he's throwing up, I mean, you know whe—

**THERAPIST:** Stop, stop. I'm sorry. It must be difficult for you when she gets this (Myriam exhales) upset, right? She's upset, and she's angry.

**STEVE:** Uh-huh [*Therapist:* Yeah], yeah, it's difficult.

**THERAPIST:** So, then you begin to, I mean what you did was you began to sort of defend yourself at a factual level (Myriam laughs), right? [*Myriam:* Yeah.] But what do you feel? Scolded? Blamed?

**STEVE:** Yeah, scolded and blamed—those are good words. I mean is, you ask—she just said it herself, she wants me to be someone I'm not.

**THERAPIST:** Yeah yeah, I imagined that that's what you were stuck with.

**STEVE:** "I want him to worry like I'm worrying."

**THERAPIST:** Yeah, and I wanted to, to intervene at that point.

**STEVE:** And I'm like, well, I can't!

**THERAPIST:** Yeah, but what, I guess you can do, or what she wants is somehow find a way of giving her support for who she is [*Myriam:* Right], but you can't.

**STEVE:** I feel I do give her support [*Therapist:* Right] for, uh, I didn't hear her saying that I'm not, I don't feel like I'm giving her support as in listening and stuff [*Therapist:* Right] because I feel very supportive, especially around work issues. At the end of the day, we're sitting down for dinner, and there's something that's happened at work, and she's upset, and she's going on about this person. I am very supportive of that.

**THERAPIST:** Yeah, yeah, I understand, but there's some, but something's broken down, right? [*Steve:* Okay] between you two, right? When she feels unsupported in these matters of worry, right? [*Steve:* Yes], but you know it ends up being you, that you feel scolded and blamed. I think, (turning to Myriam) that your worry turns into a "should." [*Myriam:* Mm-hmm.] And then you (turning to Steve) actually have a good boy response in part [*Myriam:* Mm-hmm], which is "look, I've done my work," but actually inside you must feel blamed and scolded.

**STEVE:** Right, on an emotional level, I don't feel the same as Myriam. She has an emotional feeling of some incident. [*Therapist:* Right.] She wants me to mirror that, and I don't!

**THERAPIST:** Right, there's something she wants.

**STEVE:** There's something she wants emotionally.

**THERAPIST:** Right, and that's what we're going to figure out.

**STEVE:** Some sort of feedback [*Therapist:* Right] to reassure her or—

**THERAPIST:** But what ends up happening is that you get scolded and blamed, and then it leads you to—

**STEVE:** Yeah, I feel like I'm solving the problems doing practical things [*Therapist:* Right], but that's not what she wanted.

**THERAPIST:** But I think that that, you know, that the theme [*Steve:* Mm-hmm], the underlying theme and feeling that you're left with is probably anger. [*Steve:* Mm-hmm, right.] And then when you're angry, you want to look elsewhere for somebody who won't scold and blame you so much [*Steve:* Mm-hmm], especially when sex is a difficulty, you know. When you're not feeling as confirmed or loved sexually then you want to turn outwards [*Steve:* Mm-hmm], and that's what she's worried about, and somehow it seems like unless you (Myriam) can resolve the anger difficulties, it will be hard for you to trust that he won't eventually get pissed off and look elsewhere, right? [*Myriam:* Mm-hmm.] But somehow he's saying, "I try to support you, I don't worry as much as you do."

## EXPLORING EACH PARTNER'S NEEDS

Toward the end of Session 3, the therapist refocuses the discussion on exploring each partner's needs. In discussing Steve's need for increased intimacy, the therapist makes the link to his feeling of rejection or feeling unloved and his tendency to be critical with Myriam.

**THERAPIST:** So, then let me come back to you, Steve: What do you need from Myriam?

**STEVE:** More sexual intimacy.

**THERAPIST:** Mm-hmm, and if you got the sexual intimacy, do you feel you would feel that would be sufficient to—

**STEVE:** At this point in my life, that's what I would have to say. [*Therapist:* Yeah, okay.] I mean, if our sex life was great, then I think I could go (laughs) onto the next level of feeling [*Therapist:* Yeah] something [*Therapist:* Right] or whatever that is.

**THERAPIST:** Because you feel unloved by the lack of sexual—

**STEVE:** Well, I wouldn't say unloved because I feel that she loves me just, um—

**THERAPIST:** What do you feel when you don't feel that she's sexually available? Do you feel rejected?

**STEVE:** Yes.

**THERAPIST:** Uh-huh, and then wha- what's the feeling along with being rejected? That's what I meant by unloved, you know, not to say that she doesn't love you.

**STEVE:** Yeah, I feel hurt.

**THERAPIST:** Uh huh, uh huh, and then what do you do with that hurt?

**STEVE:** I bottle it up.

**THERAPIST:** How? I mean, do you just sort of feel hurt and then you kind of maybe withdraw a little?

**STEVE:** Yes.

**THERAPIST:** Yeah, and you know what I'm going to hypothesize is that that hurt feeds the criticisms that you offer somewhere [*Steve:* Mm-hmm.] You know, we can easily see the equation that links that but then some—

**STEVE:** Mm-hmm, on some level yeah, yup, yup. I'm not disagreeing with you there. It's almost like a cycle. [*Therapist:* Yeah, yeah, and you both—] So, I have to cut down on the criticisms and then other things will flow.

**THERAPIST:** Well, it's not all. [*Steve:* Mm-hmm.] It goes round and round [*Steve:* Right!], and you're both sort of trapped.

**STEVE:** Yes! It's so true.

**THERAPIST:** The issue is how do we help you really hear each other's hurt and pain and to not feel criticized [*Steve:* Yes] by it, but just hear it [*Myriam:* Mm-hmm] and begin to be able to relate to it in a different way. (Turning to Myriam) And when he says he feels hurt and rejected, what do you feel, and how do you react?

**MYRIAM:** Um, I feel, I also feel that. I feel angry, or maybe it's more like frustrated with myself. [*Therapist:* Mm-hmm.] I guess I feel bad for not able to give him what he needs. I feel bad about that on some level, and then on another level, um, I just feel angry with him that he would expect that.

**THERAPIST:** "I'm not ready yet, I'm not open enough yet, [*Myriam:* Yeah] to thoroughly be able to do that." [*Myriam:* Right.] And I think it's important that you don't feel his anger but that you just see his hurt.

**MYRIAM:** I do see his hurt.

**THERAPIST:** Right, right. You see, I don't think it's so much that you, Steve, need to learn to dissipate your anger or control your criticism. You need to also learn to show your hurt rather than anger and to also be able to stay with your hurt a little longer rather than getting angry.

## MYRIAM EXPRESSES PRIMARY ANGER

In the fifth session, in response to the therapist's request, each partner identifies what they have the most difficulty with in this process.

**THERAPIST:** So, what's the worst for each of you now?

**STEVE:** Well, the worst for me, [*Therapist:* Mm-hmm] or I think it's two things. [*Therapist:* Yeah.] One, is, ah, it's been a burden on us moving forward because I think there's so many positives in our life right now [*Therapist:* Mm-hmm], and there's so many good things in our relationship.

**THERAPIST:** So, it's kind of like a hurdle.

**STEVE:** Yes. You know if it hadn't happened, I think we'd be so much better [*Therapist:* Uh-huh] because I think both of us, you know, both know what we want, and both have the same goals and dreams [*Therapist:* Uh-huh] and aspirations and uh—

**THERAPIST:** Uh-huh, so everything else sort of fits, but there's just this kind of—

**STEVE:** Right, I think it kind of prevents us from getting really close.

**THERAPIST:** Mm-hmm, and the second thing?

**STEVE:** Yeah, and the other thing is the issue of trust, that Myriam doesn't trust me. [*Therapist:* Yeah.] And I can understand how that is, so then I feel I have to make that extra effort [*Therapist:* Right] to be totally like, you know, and make sure nothing's last minute, there's no perception [*Therapist:* Yeah, yeah] that there's anything wrong, that I'm doing anything suspicious.

**THERAPIST:** And then, that leads you to what? To feel pressured or—

**STEVE:** Because I think it would help her too if she felt 100% confident in me, right? That I think it would help our relationship. So, those are the two things that come to my mind.

**THERAPIST:** Yes, okay. And for you, Myriam, what's the worst of it?

**MYRIAM:** Well, (sighs) you know, it kind of relates to sort of the baby in some respects because, you know, I really don't want our child to be an only child, and that's really important to me, you know, and I can't separate out his mixed feelings or ambivalence about having another baby in terms of if this all hadn't happened . . . you know, is part of him still where he was 3 years ago? And he's still struggling with staying committed, to being committed to the family, staying with me, but maybe he's just not consciously aware of it.

**THERAPIST:** So, you're unsure of his commitment?

**MYRIAM:** Yes.

**THERAPIST:** Right, right. That's really the worst of it, I mean both back then and now.

Toward the end of the fifth session, sensing Myriam's blocked anger and the impasse in which the couple is stuck, the therapist asks Myriam to express what she does not forgive Steve for and asks her to tell him what she does not forgive him for and at what she is most angry. This helps Myriam connect with and express anger and hurt at having had her wish for a family severely disrupted by Steve's affair. This expression of anger, which the couple later tells the therapist had been discouraged by previous therapists, was a critical process in helping Myriam become more assertive and in breaking the impasse in which the couple was stuck.

**MYRIAM:** It was shattering of trust, but also, um, to be honest, you know, if it didn't, if we ended up separating what it meant, for my, like the practical realities of what my life would be like and what our life would be for our child, it's not what I wanted! [Expression of secondary anger of complaint.]

**THERAPIST:** So, tell him what you are most angry at.

**MYRIAM:** I'm, uh, I'm, well, I'm so angry at you for doing this before we got pregnant.

**THERAPIST:** Right, right. Somehow, there is this sense that it's when you did this—

**MYRIAM:** Yes, for me it's the timing of it all. Um, Steve, you know, you could have, we could have said, "You're unhappy with our relationship. We need to work on it, or else you're just, you're unhappy, and you're leaving." But instead (sighs), I guess what I want for my life is a good relationship with a partner, and I want a family [*Therapist:* Yeah] (sighs), and I feel at least (*sighs, crying*) if you had before we—I—got pregnant, (sighs) I would, we could have worked out and decided whether we could stay together, or at least it would have ended, and I would have had a chance with somebody else. I just feel that (crying) I'm here with you, and we're working on this, but I still, I can't believe that I, I'm in a relationship with someone I can't really depend on, I guess, and it's very hard for me. I feel angry! [*Therapist:* Right, right.] And you know, and hurt! That, you know, I'm in this place, like I'm so angry that, you know, I didn't have a chance maybe to have a life that I wanted.

**THERAPIST:** Can you tell him how furious you are?

**MYRIAM:** I am so angry. I'm furious. I'm furious that you robbed me of the choice of whether to stay married, have a child, or what to do.

**THERAPIST:** Tell him, "I don't forgive you for—"

**MYRIAM:** I haven't been able to forgive you yet [*Therapist:* Mm-hmm] for (crying) ah, (long pause) um, I guess not letting, giving me (sniffles) a choice about what I, a choice about, ah, just [*Therapist:* Mm-hmm], just choices and having a chance to have, you know, a relationship with some-, a good relationship with someone, a family and (exhales), you know, [idiosyncratic impact of the EI] the thing I get most angry about right now is all related to having another baby [*Therapist:* Yes], like I'm, I'm in a place where I don't know if I'll even feel like I'll be able to. Even if we keep working, I just, I'm so angry about that one. [*Therapist:* Right, right.] I'm furious!

It is important to note that in response to "I don't forgive you," Myriam indicated the possibility of forgiveness by replying, "I haven't been able to forgive you yet."

## ALLOWING VULNERABILITY TO SHOW

The therapist works with Steve so that he can respond to Myriam's anger at having been betrayed and to accept responsibility for the injury in a nondefensive way. This is evident in the following excerpt.

**STEVE:** Right, I know that she's angry, and I get it. She's said it before: Why didn't I say something before if I wasn't happy with the relationship and that she didn't have the chance to do it [*Therapist:* Right, right], and it was an act of irresponsibility.

**THERAPIST:** So can you tell her that "I was irresponsible"?

**STEVE:** I was irresponsible, you're absolutely right. I mean it's a huge thing bringing a child in this world. So, if I'm irresponsible in respect to that, it doesn't matter if I'm responsible for, like, a million other things, which are, like, day-to-day little things worth, you know. But, in the, you know, in the big picture, they're really inconsequential. And the responsibility that you're looking for is, ah, you know, ah, the really important things in life that I'm there for you. Not the little, you know, filling the car up with gas or something like that but the really big things, and I'm going to be there to make sure that we're all provided for as a family.

**THERAPIST:** And if you were to let your tears speak, what would they say? I mean what do you say?

**STEVE:** I'm sorry (crying). [*Therapist:* Ah-hmm.] I wish it never happened. [*Therapist:* Ah-hmm.] I wish I'd told you sooner (crying) that I wish I wasn't trying so hard to be your rock (sniffs) because it wasn't really that helpful.

**MYRIAM:** I know you are. I know.

In the previous excerpt, we also see that as Steve takes responsibility for the EI in a nondefensive way, he quickly accesses his feeling of regret at having hurt Myriam and expresses his underlying more vulnerable feelings rather than his secondary anger and complaints. The therapist is highly attentive to Steve's expressions of regret, which have occurred multiple times over the course of therapy but now are expressed in a more vulnerable manner. The therapist guides Steve to express his regret in an enactment in an emotionally vivid manner so that Myriam can see the suffering deep inside him. This facilitates the beginning of a transformative experience for the couple.

At the end of this session, Steve discusses his self-focused regret, and the therapist's reflection brings his shame to the forefront.

**STEVE:** Yeah, I feel bad. It makes me feel, remember how much I hurt Myriam.

**THERAPIST:** Mm-hmm. Can you tell her that?

**STEVE:** Yeah, when it comes up it makes me, it kind of makes me feel like a bad person because I don't feel that in some respects,

I don't feel like I did that, you know, and almost acknowledging that I did it means that I'm a bad person. I guess that's [*Therapist:* Mm-hmm], you know, I'd rather put it behind me and think it was another person, and now I'm a new person, um.

**THERAPIST:** Right, so it sort of reconfronts you.

**STEVE:** Exactly, reminds me of how much I hurt you.

**THERAPIST:** And you're saying that you feel sort of, almost shame, I think? [The therapist names Steve's underlying shame and focuses on it.]

**STEVE:** Right, it was, it's shame.

**THERAPIST:** Can you tell her "Yeah, I feel ashamed"?

**STEVE:** I feel shameful!

**THERAPIST:** Yeah, yeah.

**MYRIAM:** And I know that, and he's said that to me [*Therapist:* Right], but as hard as it is for him to maybe have those feelings [*Therapist:* Yeah, yeah], it's equally hard for me not being able to talk about how I feel.

**STEVE:** I know.

**THERAPIST:** Right, right, right, so you're saying—

**STEVE:** Yeah, these two very intense emotions I think that, uh [*Therapist:* Right, right, right], I don't want to feel the shame, and then Myriam wants to let out her feeling of, uh [*Therapist:* Yeah], of, um, hurt!

**THERAPIST:** Right, right.

## STEVE'S SHAME AND HEARTFELT APOLOGY

At the end of this session, the therapist gives Steve and Myriam homework to consolidate the change. He directs Myriam to express three times during week what makes her most angry about the affair and for Steve to listen nondefensively to this. They begin the next session with Myriam looking a lot more relaxed and happier and discuss how previous therapists had discouraged her from expressing anger because they thought it would not be helpful and how Steve had used this as a "stick to beat her with" when she got angry. This reveals an important point about the adaptiveness of the expression of primary anger at violation and that not all anger is secondary reactive anger to underlying primary hurt.

At the end of this session, Session 6, Steve is asked to write Myriam a letter of apology at home, which he brings to the next session and reads to her in front of the therapist. Expressions of self-focused regret and shame about the EI are evident in Steve's letter, and as he reads it to Myriam. He cries, covers his face, shrinks in his chair, and can only sustain eye contact with Myriam momentarily (all of which are nonverbal indicators of shame).

The following is Steve's letter to Myriam:

> Let me start by stating how truly sorry I am for all the hurt and pain I have caused. What I did to you was absolutely wrong, and you have every right to feel how you do. I should have been honest and open in my feelings. Running away or escaping from a problem doesn't make it go away; in fact, it only makes things worse. I love you with all my heart, and I feel great shame and sorrow for the emotional hurt that I caused. I wish I could go back in time and undo those things that caused all this pain. Unfortunately, I can't. What I can do, however, is focus on right here and now, focus on us, on our great relationship and build on it so that we are both truly and deeply happy.
>
> How can I make the hurt go away? How can I bring you happiness, peace, contentment, and love? There is no magic word or potion that can do all these things. . . . The answer lies in the here and now. The answer lies in every conversation we have, every gesture I make, every feeling I share with you. . . . I want a relationship of love, trust, friendship, mutual respect, and fun and vow to make every effort to ensure we have that. . . . I want you to be happy. I want to be the person to make you happy, Myriam. I love you, and nothing gives me more pleasure than knowing that through my love for you I've made you feel love and are happy.
>
> I am 100% confident that we can build our relationship into something truly special. Over the past few weeks, I have gained incredible insight into myself and into how you think and feel. I think that with this newfound knowledge we can work together to grow our love for each other and I can return your trust in me. . . . Love, Steve.

The therapist then explores Myriam's reaction to the letter as well as Steve's experience of having written it. Myriam states that although she appreciates Steve's affirming that he loves her and his dedication to rebuilding their relationship, his affair remains a source of great suffering for her, and she needs to feel she is free to discuss all the emotions she may experience at any point in relation to the injury. The therapist begins to explore Steve's difficulties in being responsive to Myriam's pain when it reemerges, which is where the following excerpt begins. In this discussion, Steve can access his shame, and Myriam responds empathically to him while at the same time holding him accountable and acknowledging her role in the precipitating conditions that led to Steve's affair. The therapist frames Myriam's anger and pain as being linked to her fear of being hurt again. It is when the therapist asks Steve to respond to her fear that he expresses his shame in a palpable manner, to which Myriam responds with empathy and hope as she evokes an openness toward forgiving him.

**STEVE:** I understand when she brings something up it, it's, it's something that's going to be painful for me [*Therapist:* Mm-hmm] because I know in my own mind I'd rather just forget [*Therapist:* Yeah, mm-hmm] about it, wish it didn't happen because it, it, you know, brings me back to a time where I was reckless, and I was immature and all those things, right? [*Therapist:* Mm-hmm.] And, uh, I'm not proud of those things. I'm actually very ashamed of those things, and this is something I have to carry around for the rest of my life, so to be to be brought back to that point, right, uh, is very hard for me, but I understand her position.

**THERAPIST:** And how do you understand that you did betray her?

**STEVE:** Well, I still can't believe I did it because I had, you know, I always thought of myself as a very moral person, uh, [*Therapist:* Mm-hmm] and religious and, uh, and I had, you know, I carried around these values with me and (looking down) I, uh, betrayed my own values, so I betrayed myself [*Therapist:* Mm-hmm, mm-hmm] and, uh, I have to live with that.

**THERAPIST:** Right. And that's a painful thing to live with.

**STEVE:** Yeah, you know, I let myself down, and I let Myriam down. [*Therapist:* Yeah, yeah.] You know that, uh (clears throat), you know, it makes me reevaluate, you know, my value system and that if a value is a value, you don't, you can't [*Therapist:* Mm-hmm] change it. You can't say one thing and be, you know, hypocritical.

**THERAPIST:** (To Myriam) So what happens when he talks about his shame?

**MYRIAM:** I, I feel pain for him [*Therapist:* Mm-hmm] because I believe that he feels it. [*Therapist:* Mm-hmm.] It's very genuine, um, and I don't want him to feel bad at the same time. [*Therapist:* Right, right, mm-hmm.] Like I feel like [*Therapist:* Mm-hmm] (sigh) I think twice about sometimes bringing something up because I know that it's going to hurt both of us. But, um, I mean I think that, you know, to me, that's the issue. It's that when he talked about, about what he should have done was told me he wasn't happy, like to me, that ultimately is the issue. You know, he didn't [*Therapist:* Yeah], and I mean I've always since accepted that I've had a role to play in what happened. I'm not going to say, you know, oh, he's the bad guy, and I had nothing to do with it, everything was perfect [*Therapist:* Mm-hmm], but the issue is that he didn't, you know, we didn't talk about whether we were gonna work at staying together or we were gonna split up, and so he went out and meanwhile made all these permanent plans with me. [*Therapist:* Right.] That is that thing that I'm having a hard time getting over.

**THERAPIST:** Mm-hmm, and it's so frightening for you to think that this could happen again.

**MYRIAM:** Right, it is. It's really hard for me to put all of my walls down. [*Therapist:* Right.] It really is hard, um, because of what happened and, um (sniffs), I struggle with thinking I need to, if we're gonna, if we're gonna make it, but I'm just so afraid of getting hurt again.

**THERAPIST:** (To Steve) Can you let her know that you understand that?

**STEVE:** I do understand because (sniffles) my feeling is that you had the feeling of being alone your whole life (sniffles) and that you trusted me so much, (whispering) and I let you down. (Crying) I was the one person you trusted.

**THERAPIST:** So, you understand the wound? Do you understand the wound on her?

**STEVE:** (Crying) I, I just (sighs) know that if you don't get over it, you'll never have the feeling of being, like, loved or complete because I know what that feeling's like, and I have a very strong family. [*Therapist:* Mm-hmm.] Like when my brother came to visit, I hadn't seen him in a long time, but it just felt so, like, at home and at peace.

**THERAPIST:** So safe and secure.

**STEVE:** Right! And I want to make that for you [Myriam].

**THERAPIST:** Can you say that again, you want to make that for—

**STEVE:** (To Myriam) I want to make that feeling for you, [*Therapist:* Mm-hmm] so you feel at ease and at peace.

**MYRIAM:** I know you do, but I think, I know you do, but I, I think that (sighs), I think we both have to be realistic that it may never be quite the way we'll both want it. (Sniffs) I think that, I mean I'm hopeful that I'll be able to reach a place that I'll be okay, and the level of security and connection will be enough for me. Um, I feel we'll get there, but I, I just at this point, I can't imagine because I just, God, I trusted you completely and implicitly (crying), and I just don't, I just don't know if I'll ever get there ever again. It's something we're both just gonna have to both deal with and accept. [*Therapist:* Mm-hmm.] But it can, it can get better, though. Like I feel like it can get better (sighs), you know, as time goes on. It's, um (sighs), I feel that we're healing and that our relationship is healing.

It is this vulnerable expression of shame that is pivotal in transforming their bond, and that leads to a healing of the EI.

## CLOSENESS, APPRECIATION AND FORGIVENESS

During the last four sessions, the work is once again centered on restructuring the couple's negative interactional cycles and helping both Steve and Myriam express and respond to the vulnerable attachment- and identity-related emotions and needs that underlie their respective positions in the cycle. Their interactional dynamic becomes more positive; Myriam feels like Steve is finally sharing the load of the household and child care responsibilities with her, so she feels more supported and relaxed around him. Steve feels that Myriam takes a greater interest in him than ever before, that she is more prizing of him and his efforts, and so he no longer feels like he is last on her list of priorities. They reestablish a sexual relationship, and toward the end of therapy, they are discussing the possibility of having a second child, suggesting that they have reconciled. In the final session, the therapist returns to addressing the injury and discussing the couple's healing process, which is where the following excerpt begins. Both agree that the injury helped them realize that their previous way of functioning was problematic and has allowed them to finally address areas of difficulties. In the last session, despite her constructive view of the resolution process, Myriam highlights that the injury continues to be present for her even if she is beginning to forgive Steve and that this process has implied grieving and letting go of a version of Steve that she thought she knew, but that was shattered with the affair.

**THERAPIST:** So, we're going to be wrapping up briefly, and I wonder if you could say something about where you are with regards to the emotional injury that brought you here.

**STEVE:** Well, I think it's like the affair is in the past and the issues that we have, we've had since before it started [*Therapist:* Mm-hmm], and we're working on those issues to be more productive as a couple. That's my take on it.

**THERAPIST:** Right, right.

**MYRIAM:** And I think, I mean for me, that it's just sort of where it is and everything and that, you know, it was very much at the forefront for a very long time, and I think now, it's, I can't say it's in the past at all.

**THERAPIST:** Right, and you know its like forg- just using the phrase, forgiving is not forgetting. [*Myriam:* Right.] I mean, it's important to remember. It's an important thing, right?

**MYRIAM:** I mean I, I've forgiven it in some ways in that it's really much more okay. It also made me realize that there were problems in the relationship that I knew were there [*Therapist:* Yeah] that, but he didn't talk about them, and I let him not talk about them, or maybe I couldn't do anything about it [*Therapist:* Yeah, yeah, yeah], but I knew they were there. I can t pretend like they weren't there, and I can't pretend that, you know, everything was great. I often thought that, that he would leave me. He wouldn't have an affair, like I [*Therapist:* Yes, yes], I mean that was part of it, you know, initially. Like with getting to know him, I remember thinking, 'cause he really goes out of his way to help people at times, he can be very selfless at times [*Therapist:* Mm-hmm, mm-hmm], and I remember thinking, um, you know, about that he had a certain, almost a moral code that he lived by that I really admired [*Therapist:* Mm-hmm, mm-hmm] and that was completely shattered! [*Therapist:* Mm-hmm, mm-hmm.] Because if he really was, this wouldn't have happened the way it happened. [*Therapist:* Mm-hmm, mm-hmm.] So, you know, it was more, sort of really, kind of letting go of this big part of him that I really sort of very, um, almost attached to or [*Therapist:* Yes, yes, yes] he didn't, that really wasn't him, but, but also just an acknowledgment that I had certainly something to do with "it." [*Therapist:* Yes, yes, I understand that.] And, and so, and I, and I'm still there, you know. I mean there's certain things I, I feel like I'm getting beyond. Like I'm, I'm forgiving in many ways and that it's starting to go away. I don't think I'll ever trust him the same way again. [*Therapist:* Mm-hmm.] I think as time goes on I'll trust him more and more. Um, but it, it's kind of in the background, and now we really are back at what the core issues are [*Therapist:* Yes, yes], so I think in some ways this has really helped me get past just focusing on the symptom versus the problem.

## THERAPY OUTCOMES

Over the course of 11 sessions of emotion-focused therapy for couples (EFT-C), Steve and Myriam were able to resolve their EI through forgiveness. The therapist worked with the couple to restructure their negative interactional cycle and simultaneously worked on validating, exploring, and helping both partners express their underlying emotions related to the injury. Of particular importance in this aspect was helping Myriam differentiate her emotions and express her primary adaptive anger at the violation and supporting Steve so that he could validate Myriam's anger, sadness, hurt, and fear related to the injury. Steve expressed regret at various points in therapy, and the therapist helped him express responsibility in a nondefensive manner and, most important, helped him access and express his shame about the injury. Myriam responded to Steve's shame with empathy and a strong willingness to forgive him, even though she stated that rebuilding her trust in him would take time.

Restructuring the couple's negative cycle gave way to their experiencing increased closeness and a greater sense of being appreciated by the other. In the final session, Myriam states that she forgives Steve and that, in the process of resolving the injury, they arrived at treating the root of the problem rather than the symptom. For her, the affair was a manifestation of the couple's difficulties in their way of relating to each other, and in doing the therapeutic work required to restructure their cycle, she feels that the root cause has been addressed. Myriam's ratings on the Enright Forgiveness Inventory (Enright, Rique, & Coyle, 2000) increased by over 60 points over the course of therapy such that at the end of therapy she reported being highly "forgiving" as measured by this inventory. Similarly, on a 5-point single item scale asking, "To what degree have you forgiven your partner," Myriam rated herself as being at a 5, meaning "completely" forgiving. Steve's scores on these two measures were complementary, indicating that he perceived Myriam as being fully forgiving of him. These gains were maintained at the 3-month follow-up mark. The couple later contacted their therapist to inform him that they were doing well and were expecting a second child.

## CONCLUSION: REFLECTIONS ON THE THERAPEUTIC PROCESS OF STEVE AND MYRIAM

In this section, we describe our observations of the therapeutic process with Steve and Myriam to highlight that their forgiveness work happens in the context of ongoing therapy following the stages outlined by Greenberg and Goldman (2008).

Therapy with this couple begins with both partners being defensive and having difficulties validating the suffering and the needs of the other. The therapist skillfully validates each partner's secondary emotions to foster safety and trust and consistently directs each partner to attend to the vulnerable emotions underlying their defensive stance. The therapist also defines the couple's negative interactional cycles (pre- and postinjury) early in therapy and explores each partner's sensitivities (linked to their families of origin) to understand better the position they each take in the cycle. Despite Steve's initial defensiveness at the proposition that his past could be affecting the present, he does reveal, as does Myriam, his sensitivity stemming from his family of origin, which the therapist weaves into the description of their interactional dynamics. (In cases in which one or both partners are reluctant to discuss their past, the therapist is encouraged to explore this reluctance [fear], use psychoeducation to explain the link between past and present, and self-disclose their sensitivity that gets activated in intimate relationships). They also discuss their unmet needs, which the therapist again links to their cycle (i.e., Steve feels rejected and unloved by Myriam because she is not as sexually available or interested as he would like her to be). Steve's vulnerable emotions are overshadowed by his anger (i.e., constant criticisms of Myriam), which leads to Myriam distancing herself from him because she feels angry that he can dare to ask for more (when he experiences him as being unsupportive and indifferent to her sense of feeling overwhelmed in managing their family life). This negative interactional cycle gave rise to Steve looking outside the marriage to fulfill his sexual needs and thus becomes of central importance in the therapy.

Consistent with the theory of EFT-C (Greenberg & Goldman, 2008), the therapist strongly emphasizes the expression of primary, vulnerable emotions underlying each partner's positions in the cycle and works with each of them to be emotionally responsive to the emotions expressed by the other. This is transformative in that they each begin to see the other in a new light and can respond in a more validating way. The therapist has the same aim when it comes to exploring the emotions related to the injury and works with both partners to have them express primary emotion and to respond to expressed vulnerability in a responsive manner. In Myriam's case, having her express her primary anger at the injustice of not being given a choice to have the kind of life she dreamed of is a significant event in the therapy given that she had been silenced by Steve and two other therapists. Following this, the therapist works with Steve to help him take nondefensive responsibility for the injury and eventually express his regret (initially in the letter-writing homework task and then in vivo). The later part of the therapy is focused on helping the couple restructure their interactional cycle: As they begin to express more vulnerability to the each other, there is more safety and goodwill in the relationship, their attachment bond is renewed, and they both report feeling more appreciated and validated by the other. It is here that Myriam reports forgiving Steve.

Because the forgiveness work occurs in parallel to the EFT-C work aimed at restructuring the cycle, it is difficult to say whether one is a precursor to the other, but certainly, both are transformative processes. Although forgiveness is not the only way couples can "manage" an injury (some make a pact never to discuss the event again), it is in our opinion an effective way of helping couples resolve an injury and, in doing so, improve their relationship. Our nonauthoritarian approach to couple's forgiveness requires that therapists address the interactional dynamics between the partners and not rely on protocols outlining "stages" of forgiveness (e.g., empathy, remorse, apology) that push for change rather than allowing processes to unfold.

# AFTERWORD

In the preceding chapters, we elaborated on the theoretical and practical aspects of forgiveness of emotional injuries (EIs) and explained the processes involved in the therapeutic resolution of these injuries. In our experience, we have found it helpful to view forgiveness along a process-oriented continuum that ranges from a diminished need for internal avoidance and revenge all the way to a compassionate desire for the well-being of an offender. People can achieve resolution in different ways—by forgiveness, letting go, and/or holding the other accountable for wrongs done.

Throughout the book, we also provided empirical support for the effectiveness of emotion-focused therapy (EFT) for resolving EIs in both individual and couples therapy. We described the processes involved in change and reported on people's subjective reports of their experience of forgiving. One important note about the process of forgiving that emerges is that people have to deal with their anger as a necessary step along the path to resolution because unexpressed anger is a major cause of grudges. We discussed the role of the specific emotions of sadness, anger, and shame involved in resolving EIs, but we gave a special status to the emotion of anger. This is an emotion that many sectors of society and some clinical models or therapists tend to suppress. We highlighted the adaptive potential of primary assertive anger in the face of EI and contrasted it with secondary blaming anger. The EFT approach calls for

http://dx.doi.org/10.1037/0000144-010
*Forgiveness and Letting Go in Emotion-Focused Therapy,* by L. S. Greenberg and C.Woldarsky Meneses

adequate regulation and constructive use of anger—and not for its suppression. We proposed that people need, in the safety of the therapeutic situation, to express what is bothering them and express both their hurt and their constructive anger. EFT thus helps people face and deal with these feelings rather than distancing and burying them to fester unresolved.

Empirical research has found empathy to be a strong predictor of self-reported forgiveness of an offender (McCullough, 2001). We have found, however, that when people see their injurers as empathic, regretful, and even ashamed of having injured them, and when they experience compassion from the injurers for the pain the injurer caused (even sometimes in imagination), this helps to promote a more empathic stance toward the injurer. It is not the injured party's feelings of empathy toward the injurer that is causal in the forgiveness process but rather the injured person's ability to see the other, in actual interaction or imagination, as empathic, ashamed, remorseful, and compassionate. This gives therapists a new tool to focus on helping the injurer, in interaction or imaginary dialogues, express these feelings rather than defend, excuse, or apologize.

Our clinical practice has shown us that individual clients with many different types of presenting problems or diagnoses often suffer from unresolved past EIs and that many couples presenting conflicts have underlying unresolved EIs from the past. EFT interventions and processes involved in forgiveness and letting go are thus not only applicable to those clients who specifically present with EIs but also are useful for a broad range of clients. We invite readers to ponder how the practice of EFT could fit into their practice. In addition, we encourage therapists using EFT to market themselves as able to serve clients who need to forgive or resolve an EI and to make efforts to advance public understanding of the importance of forgiveness and letting go.

A variety of training and networking opportunities specific to EFT practice and research are now available internationally. Additional information is available at http://www.iseft.org. This website lists training opportunities that professionals can pursue to gain further competence and skills in the work discussed in this book.

# REFERENCES


Ahmed, E. (2001). Shame management: Regulating bullying. In E. Ahmed, N. Harris, J. Braithwaite, & V. Braithwaite (Eds.), *Shame management through reintegration* (pp. 211–314). Cambridge, England: Cambridge University Press.

Ahmed, E., & Braithwaite, V. (2004). Bullying and victimization: Cause for concern for both families and schools. *Social Psychology of Education, 7,* 35–54. http://dx.doi.org/10.1023/B:SPOE.0000010668.43236.60

Ahmed, E., & Braithwaite, V. (2006). Forgiveness, reconciliation, and shame: Three key variables in reducing school bullying. *Journal of Social Issues, 62,* 347–370. http://dx.doi.org/10.1111/j.1540-4560.2006.00454.x

Akhtar, S. (2002). Forgiveness: Origins, dynamics, psychopathology, and technical relevance. *The Psychoanalytic Quarterly, 71,* 175–212. http://dx.doi.org/10.1002/j.2167-4086.2002.tb00010.x

Akhtar, S., & Barlow, J. (2018). Forgiveness therapy for the promotion of mental well-being: A systematic review and meta-analysis. *Trauma, Violence, & Abuse, 19,* 107–122. http://dx.doi.org/10.1177/1524838016637079

American Psychiatric Association. (1994). *Diagnostic and statistical manual of mental disorders* (4th ed.). Washington, DC: Author.

Angus, L. E., & Greenberg, L. S. (2011). *Working with narrative in emotion-focused therapy: Changing stories, healing lives.* Washington, DC: American Psychological Association. http://dx.doi.org/10.1037/12325-000

Atkins, D. C., Marín, R. A., Lo, T. T. Y., Klann, N., & Hahlweg, K. (2010). Outcomes of couples with infidelity in a community-based sample of couple therapy. *Journal of Family Psychology, 24,* 212–216. http://dx.doi.org/10.1037/a0018789

Augsburger, D. (2000). *The new freedom of forgiveness.* Chicago, IL: Moody.

Auszra, L., Greenberg, L., & Herrmann, I. (2013). Client emotional productivity—Optimal client in-session emotional processing in experiential therapy. *Psychotherapy Research, 23,* 732–746. http://dx.doi.org/10.1080/10503307.2013.816882

Bakan, D. (1966). *The duality of human existence: Isolation and communion in Western man.* Boston, MA: Beacon Press.

Barber, L., Maltby, J., & Macaskill, A. (2005). Angry memories and thoughts of revenge: The relationship between forgiveness and anger rumination. *Personality and Individual Differences, 39,* 253–262. http://dx.doi.org/10.1016/j.paid.2005.01.006

Baskin, T., & Enright, R. (2004). Intervention studies on forgiveness: A meta-analysis. *Journal of Counseling & Development, 82,* 79–90. http://dx.doi.org/10.1002/j.1556-6678.2004.tb00288.x

Bass, E., & Davis, L. (1988). *The courage to heal: A guide for women survivors of child sexual abuse.* New York, NY: Perennial Library/Harper & Row.

Baumeister, R. F., Stillwell, A. M., & Heatherton, T. F. (1994). Guilt: An interpersonal approach. *Psychological Bulletin, 115,* 243–267. http://dx.doi.org/10.1037/0033-2909.115.2.243

Beck, A. T. (1976). *Cognitive therapy and the emotional disorders.* New York, NY: International Universities Press.

Berecz, J. M. (2001). All that glitters is not gold: Bad forgiveness in counseling and preaching. *Pastoral Psychology, 49,* 253–275.

Berry, J. W., & Worthington, E. L., Jr. (2001). Forgivingness, relationship quality, stress while imagining relationship events, and physical and mental health. *Journal of Counseling Psychology, 48,* 447–455. http://dx.doi.org/10.1037/0022-0167.48.4.447

Bessant, J., & Watts, R. (1995). Young people and violence: A focus on schools. In S. J. Egger & D. Chappell (Eds.), *Australian violence: Contemporary perspectives* (pp. 105–122). Canberra: Australian Institute of Criminology.

Bohart, A., & Greenberg, L (Eds.). (1997). *Empathy reconsidered: New directions in psychotherapy.* Washington, DC: American Psychological Association.

Bowlby, J. (1968). Effects on behaviour of disruption of an affectional bond. *Eugenics Society Symposia, 4,* 94–108.

Braithwaite, V., Ahmed, E., Morrison, B., & Reinhart, M. (2003). *Researching the prospects for restorative justice practice in schools: The 'Life at School Survey' 1996–9.* In L. Walgrave (Ed.), *Repositioning the restorative justice: Restorative justice, criminal justice and social context.* (pp. 169–190). Devon, England: Willan.

Brandsma, J. M. (1982). Forgiveness: A dynamic, theological and therapeutic analysis. *Pastoral Psychology, 31,* 40–50. http://dx.doi.org/10.1007/BF01744463

Burnette, J. L., Davis, D. E., Green, J. D., Worthington, E. L., Jr., & Bradfield, E. (2009). Insecure attachment and depressive symptoms: The mediating role of rumination, empathy, and forgiveness. *Personality and Individual Differences, 46,* 276–280. http://dx.doi.org/10.1016/j.paid.2008.10.016

Chagigiorgis, H., & Paivio, S. (2008). Forgiveness as an outcome in emotion-focused trauma therapy. In W. Malcolm, N. DeCourville, & K. Belicki (Eds.), *Women's reflections on the complexities of forgiveness* (pp. 121–141). New York, NY: Routledge.

Coyle, C. T., & Enright, R. D. (1997). Forgiveness intervention with postabortion men. *Journal of Consulting and Clinical Psychology, 65,* 1042–1046. http://dx.doi.org/10.1037/0022-006X.65.6.1042

Davidson, R. (2000). Affective style, mood and anxiety disorders: An affective neuroscience approach. In R. Davidson (Ed.), *Anxiety, depression and emotion* (pp. 89–108). Oxford, England: Oxford University Press. http://dx.doi.org/10.1093/acprof:oso/9780195133585.003.0005

Dean, C. J. (2011). Psychoeducation: A first step to understanding infidelity-related systemic trauma and grieving. *The Family Journal, 19,* 15–21. http://dx.doi.org/10.1177/1066480710387487

DeCourville, N., Belicki, K., & Green, M. M. (2008). Subjective experiences of forgiveness in a community sample: Implications for understanding forgiveness and its consequences. In W. Malcolm, N. DeCourville, & K. Belicki (Eds.), *Women's reflections on the complexities of forgiveness* (pp. 1–20). New York, NY: Routledge/Taylor & Francis.

Dekel, R. (2010). Couple forgiveness, self-differentiation and secondary traumatization among wives of former POWs. *Journal of Social and Personal Relationships, 27,* 924–937. http://dx.doi.org/10.1177/0265407510377216

Derogatis, L. R. (1992). *SCL–90–R: Administration, scoring and procedures manual–II for the revised version and other instruments of the psychopathology rating scale series.* Townson, MD: Clinical Psychometric Research.

Downie, R. S. (1965). Forgiveness. *Philosophical Quarterly, 15,* 128–134. http://dx.doi.org/10.2307/2218212

Elder, G. (1998). The life course as developmental theory. *Child Development, 1,* 1–12. http://dx.doi.org/10.2307/1132065

Elliott, R., Watson, J. C., Goldman, R. N., & Greenberg, L. S. (2004). *Learning emotion-focused therapy: The process-experiential approach to change.* Washington, DC: American Psychological Association. http://dx.doi.org/10.1037/10725-000

Enright, R. D. (2001). *Forgiveness is a choice: A step-by-step process for resolving anger and restoring hope.* Washington, DC: American Psychological Association.

Enright, R. D., & Coyle, C. T. (1998). Researching the process model of forgiveness within psychological interventions. In E. L. Worthington Jr. (Ed.), *Dimensions of forgiveness: Psychological research and theological perspectives* (pp. 139–161). Philadelphia, PA: Templeton Foundation Press.

Enright, R. D., & Fitzgibbons, R. P. (2000). *Helping clients forgive: An empirical guide for resolving anger and restoring hope.* Washington, DC: American Psychological Association. http://dx.doi.org/10.1037/10381-000

Enright, R. D., & Fitzgibbons, R. P. (2015). *Forgiveness therapy: An empirical guide for resolving anger and restoring hope.* Washington, DC: American Psychological Association. http://dx.doi.org/10.1037/14526-005

Enright, R. D., Gassin, E., & Wu, C. (1992). Forgiveness: A developmental view. *Journal of Moral Education, 21,* 99–114. http://dx.doi.org/10.1080/0305724920210202

Enright, R. D., Rique, J., & Coyle, C. T. (2000). *The Enright Forgiveness Inventory (EFI) user's manual.* Madison, WI: The International Forgiveness Institute.

Fergus, K. D., & Reid, D. W. (2001). The couple's mutual identity and reflexivity: A systemic-constructivist approach to the integration of persons and systems.

*Journal of Psychotherapy Integration, 11*, 385–410. http://dx.doi.org/10.1023/A:1016658301629

Fincham, F. D., Beach, S. R., & Davila, J. (2004). Forgiveness and conflict resolution in marriage. *Journal of Family Psychology, 18*, 72–81. http://dx.doi.org/10.1037/0893-3200.18.1.72

Fincham, F. D., Paleari, F. G., & Regalia, C. (2002). Forgiveness in marriage: The roles of relationship quality, attributions, and emotions. *Family Relations, 9*, 27–37.

Fitzgibbons, R. P. (1986). The cognitive and emotive uses of forgiveness in the treatment of anger. *Psychotherapy: Theory, Research, Practice, Training, 23*, 629–633. http://dx.doi.org/10.1037/h0085667

Foa, E. B., & Jaycox, L. H. (1999). Cognitive-behavioural theory and treatment of posttraumatic stress disorder. In D. Spiegel (Ed.), *Efficacy and cost-effectiveness of psychotherapy* (pp. 23–61). Washington, DC: American Psychiatric Press.

Forgiveness. (2011). In *Concise Oxford English dictionary* (8th ed.). Oxford, England: Oxford University Press.

Freedman, S. R., & Enright, R. D. (1996). Forgiveness as an intervention goal with incest survivors. *Journal of Consulting and Clinical Psychology, 64*, 983–992. http://dx.doi.org/10.1037/0022-006X.64.5.983

Frijda, N. H. (1986). *The emotions*. Cambridge, England: Cambridge University Press.

Glass, S. P. (2002). Couple therapy after the trauma of infidelity. In A. S. Gurman & N. S. Jacobson (Eds.), *Clinical handbook of couple therapy* (3rd ed., pp. 488–507). New York, NY: Guilford Press.

Goldman, R. N., & Greenberg, L. (2013). Working with identity and self-soothing in emotion-focused therapy for couples. *Family Process, 52*, 62–82. http://dx.doi.org/10.1111/famp.12021

Goldman, R. N., & Greenberg, L. S. (2015). *Case formulation in emotion-focused therapy: Co-creating clinical maps for change*. Washington, DC: American Psychological Association. http://dx.doi.org/10.1037/14523-000

Gordon, K. C., & Baucom, D. H. (1998). Understanding betrayals in marriage: A synthesized model of forgiveness. *Family Process, 37*, 425–449. http://dx.doi.org/10.1111/j.1545-5300.1998.00425.x

Gordon, K. C., & Baucom, D. H. (1999). A multitheoretical intervention or promoting recovery from extramarital affairs. *Clinical Psychology: Science and Practice, 6*, 382–399. http://dx.doi.org/10.1093/clipsy.6.4.382

Gordon, K. C., Baucom, D. H., & Snyder, D. K. (2004). An integrative intervention for promoting recovery from extramarital affairs. *Journal of Marital and Family Therapy, 30*, 213–231. http://dx.doi.org/10.1111/j.1752-0606.2004.tb01235.x

Gordon, K. C., Baucom, D. H., & Snyder, D. K. (2008). Optimal strategies in couple therapy: Treating couples dealing with the trauma of infidelity. *Journal of Contemporary Psychotherapy, 38*, 151–160. http://dx.doi.org/10.1007/s10879-008-9085-1

Gottman, J. M. (1994). *What predicts divorce? The relationship between marital processes and marital outcomes*. Hillsdale, NJ: Erlbaum.

Gottman, J. M. (2011). *The science of trust: Emotional attunement for couples*. New York, NY: Norton.

Govier, T. (2002). *Forgiveness and revenge*. New York, NY: Routledge.

Greenberg, L., & Pascual-Leone, J. (1995). A dialectical constructivist approach to experiential change. In R. Neimeyer & M. Mahoney (Eds.), *Constructivism in psychotherapy* (pp. 169–191). Washington, DC: American Psychological Association. http://dx.doi.org/10.1037/10170-008

Greenberg, L., Warwar, S., & Malcolm, W. (2010). Emotion-focused couples therapy and the facilitation of forgiveness. *Journal of Marital and Family Therapy, 36,* 28–42. http://dx.doi.org/10.1111/j.1752-0606.2009.00185.x

Greenberg, L. S. (1984). Task analysis: The general approach. In L. N. Rice & L. S. Greenberg (Eds.), *Patterns of change: Intensive analysis of psychotherapeutic process*. New York, NY: Guilford Press.

Greenberg, L. S. (1986). Change process research. *Journal of Consulting and Clinical Psychology, 54,* 4–9. http://dx.doi.org/10.1037/0022-006X.54.1.4

Greenberg, L. S. (1992). Task analysis: Identifying components of intrapersonal conflict resolutions. In S. Toukmanian & D. Rennie (Eds.), *Psychotherapy process research* (pp. 21–44). Thousand Oaks, CA: Sage.

Greenberg, L. S. (2002). *Emotion-focused therapy: Coaching clients to work through their feelings*. Washington, DC: American Psychological Association. http://dx.doi.org/10.1037/10447-000

Greenberg, L. S. (2006). Emotion-focused therapy: A synopsis. *Journal of Contemporary Psychotherapy, 36,* 87–93. http://dx.doi.org/10.1007/s10879-006-9011-3

Greenberg, L. S. (2007). A guide to conducting a task analysis of psychoherapeutic change. *Psychotherapy Research, 17,* 15–30. http://dx.doi.org/10.1080/10503300600720390

Greenberg, L. S. (2010). *Emotion-focused therapy*. Washington, DC: American Psychological Association.

Greenberg, L. S. (2015). *Emotion-focused therapy: Coaching clients to work through their feelings* (2nd ed.). Washington, DC: American Psychological Association. http://dx.doi.org/10.1037/14692-000

Greenberg, L. S., Ford, C. L., Alden, L. S., & Johnson, S. M. (1993). In-session change in emotionally focused therapy. *Journal of Consulting and Clinical Psychology, 61,* 78–84. http://dx.doi.org/10.1037/0022-006X.61.1.78

Greenberg, L. S., & Goldman, R. N. (2008). *Emotion-focused couples therapy: The dynamics of emotion, love, and power*. Washington, DC: American Psychological Association. http://dx.doi.org/10.1037/11750-000

Greenberg, L. S., James, P. S., & Conry, R. F. (1988). Perceived change process in emotionally focused couples therapy. *Journal of Family Psychology, 2,* 5–23. http://dx.doi.org/10.1037/h0080484

Greenberg, L. S., & Johnson, S. M. (1988). *Emotionally focused therapy for couples*. New York, NY: Guilford Press.

Greenberg, L. S., & Malcolm, W. (2002). Resolving unfinished business: Relating process to outcome. *Journal of Consulting and Clinical Psychology, 70,* 406–416. http://dx.doi.org/10.1037/0022-006X.70.2.406

Greenberg, L. S., & Paivio, S. C. (1997). *Working with emotions in psychotherapy*. New York, NY: Guilford Press.

Greenberg, L. S., Rice, L. N., & Elliott, R. K. (1993). *Facilitating emotional change: The moment-by-moment process*. New York, NY: Guilford Press.

Greenberg, L. S., & Ruchanski-Rosenberg, R. (2002). Therapist's experience of empathy. In J. C. Watson, R. N. Goldman, & M. S. Warner (Eds.), *Client-centered and experiential psychotherapy in the 21st century: Advances in theory, research and practice* (pp. 204–220). Herefordshire, England: PCCS Books.

Greenberg, L. S., & Safran, J. D. (1987). *Emotion in psychotherapy: Affect, cognition, and the process of change*. New York, NY: Guilford Press.

Greenberg, L. S., & van Balen, R. (1998). Theory of experience centered therapy. In L. S. Greenberg, J. C. Watson, & G. Lietaer (Eds.), *Handbook of experiential psychotherapy: Foundations and differential treatment* (pp. 28–57). New York, NY: Guilford Press.

Greenberg, L. S., Warwar, S. H., & Malcolm, W. M. (2008). Differential effects of emotion-focused therapy and psychoeducation in facilitating forgiveness and letting go of emotional injuries. *Journal of Counseling Psychology, 55*, 185–196. http://dx.doi.org/10.1037/0022-0167.55.2.185

Greenberg, L. S., & Watson, J. C. (2006). *Emotion-focused therapy for depression*. Washington, DC: American Psychological Association. http://dx.doi.org/10.1037/11286-000

Haaken, J. (2002). The good, the bad, and the ugly: Psychoanalytic and cultural perspectives on forgiveness. In S. Lamb & J. G. Murphy (Eds.), *Before forgiving: Cautionary views of forgiveness in psychotherapy* (pp. 172–191). New York, NY: Oxford University Press.

Harris, A., & Thoresen, C. E. (2005). Forgiveness, unforgiveness, health, and disease. In E. L. Worthington & Jr (Eds.), *Handbook of forgiveness* (pp. 321–333). New York, NY: Routledge.

Harris, A. H. S., & Thoresen, C. E. (2006). Extending the influence of positive psychology interventions into health care settings: Lessons from self-efficacy and forgiveness. *The Journal of Positive Psychology, 1*, 27–36. http://dx.doi.org/10.1080/17439760500380930

Hegel, G. (1965). *Philosophy of right*. Oxford, England: Clarendon. (Original work published 1821)

Hill, E. W. (2010). Discovering forgiveness through empathy: Implications for couple and family therapy. *Journal of Family Therapy, 32*, 169–185. http://dx.doi.org/10.1111/j.1467-6427.2010.00492.x

Holeman, V. (2004). *Reconcilable differences: Hope and healing for troubled marriages*. Downers Grove, IL: Intervarsity Press.

Hope, D. (1987). The healing paradox of forgiveness. *Psychotherapy: Theory, Research, Practice, Training, 24*, 240–244. http://dx.doi.org/10.1037/h0085710

Horowitz, M., Rosenbaum, R., & Wilner, N. (1988). Role relationship dilemmas: A potential new process variable. *Psychotherapy: Theory, Research, Practice, Training, 25*, 241–248. http://dx.doi.org/10.1037/h0085338

Huang, S. T. T., & Enright, R. D. (2000). Forgiveness and anger-related emotions in Taiwan: Implications for therapy. *Psychotherapy: Theory, Research, Practice, Training, 37*, 71–79. http://dx.doi.org/10.1037/h0087831

Human Development Study Group. (1991). Five points on the construct of forgiveness within psychotherapy. *Psychotherapy: Theory, Research, Practice, Training, 28*, 493–496. http://dx.doi.org/10.1037/0033-3204.28.3.493

Iwakabe, S., Rogan, K., & Stalikas, A. (2000). The relationship between client emotional expressions, therapist interventions, and the working alliance:

An exploration of eight emotional expression events. *Journal of Psychotherapy Integration, 10,* 375–401. http://dx.doi.org/10.1023/A: 1009479100305

Izard, C. E. (1991). *The psychology of emotions.* New York, NY: Plenum Press. http://dx.doi.org/10.1007/978-1-4899-0615-1

Johnson, S. M. (1996). *The practice of emotionally focused marital therapy: Creating connection.* New York, NY: Brunner/Mazel.

Johnson, S. M. (2004). *The practice of emotionally focused marital therapy: Creating connections* (2nd ed.). New York, NY: Brunner/Mazel.

Johnson, S. M., & Greenberg, L. S. (1985). Differential effects of experiential and problem-solving interventions in resolving marital conflict. *Journal of Consulting and Clinical Psychology, 53,* 175–184. http://dx.doi.org/10.1037/0022-006X.53.2.175

Johnson, S. M., & Greenberg, L. S. (1988). Relating process to outcome in marital therapy. *Journal of Marital and Family Therapy, 14,* 175–183. http://dx.doi.org/10.1111/j.1752-0606.1988.tb00733.x

Johnson, S. M., Makinen, J. A., & Millikin, J. W. (2001). Attachment injuries in couple relationships: A new perspective on impasses in couples therapy. *Journal of Marital and Family Therapy, 27,* 145–155. http://dx.doi.org/10.1111/j.1752-0606.2001.tb01152.x

Kant, I. (1963). *Lecture on ethics.* New York, NY: Harper & Row. (Original work published 1931)

Kaplan, B. H. (1992). Social health and the forgiving heart: The type B story. *Journal of Behavioral Medicine, 15,* 3–14. http://dx.doi.org/10.1007/BF00848374

Karen, R. (2001). *The forgiving self: The road from resentment to connection.* New York, NY: Doubleday.

Kircanski, K., Lieberman, M. D., & Craske, M. G. (2012). Feelings into words: Contributions of language to exposure therapy. *Psychological Science, 23,* 1086–1091. http://dx.doi.org/10.1177/0956797612443830

Krause, N., & Hayward, R. D. (2013). Religious involvement and feelings of connectedness with others among older Americans. *Archive for the Psychology of Religion, 35,* 259–282. http://dx.doi.org/10.1163/15736121-12341266

Lane, R. D., Ryan, L., Nadel, L., & Greenberg, L. (2014). Memory reconsolidation, emotional arousal, and the process of change in psychotherapy: New insights from brain science. *Behavioral and Brain Sciences, 38,* e1. http://dx.doi.org/10.1017/S0140525X14000041

Lawler, K. A., Younger, J. W., Piferi, R. L., Jobe, R. L., Edmondson, K. A., & Jones, W. H. (2005). The unique effects of forgiveness on health: An exploration of pathways. *Journal of Behavioral Medicine, 28,* 157–167. http://dx.doi.org/10.1007/s10865-005-3665-2

Lawler-Row, K. A., Hyatt-Edwards, L., Wuensch, K. L., & Karremans, J. C. (2011). Forgiveness and health: The role of attachment [Special issue]. *Mind–Body Connections in Personal Relationships, 18,* 170–183. http://dx.doi.org/10.1111/j.1475-6811.2010.01327.x

Lawler-Row, K. A., Karremans, J. C., Scott, C., Edlis-Matityahou, M., & Edwards, L. (2008). Forgiveness, physiological reactivity and health: The role of anger. *International Journal of Psychophysiology, 68,* 51–58. http://dx.doi.org/10.1016/j.ijpsycho.2008.01.001

LeDoux, J. (2012). Rethinking the emotional brain. *Neuron, 73,* 653–676. http://dx.doi.org/10.1016/j.neuron.2012.02.004

LeDoux, J. E. (1996). *The emotional brain: The mysterious underpinnings of emotional life.* New York, NY: Simon & Schuster

LeDoux, J. E. (2015). Feelings: What are they & how does the brain make them? *Daedalus, 144,* 96–111. http://dx.doi.org/10.1162/DAED_a_00319

Lichtenfeld, S., Buechner, V. L., Maier, M. A., & Fernández-Capo, M. (2015). Forgive and forget: Differences between decisional and emotional forgiveness. *PLOS ONE.* 10(5). http://dx.doi.org/10.1371/journal.pone.0125561

Lieberman, M. D., Eisenberg, N. I., Crocket, M. J., Tom, S. M., Pfeifer, J. H., & Way, B. M. (2007). Putting feelings into words: Affect labeling disrupts amygdala activity in response to affective stimuli. *Psychological Science, 18,* 421–428. http://dx.doi.org/10.1111/j.1467-9280.2007.01916.x

Luskin, F. (2007). Forgive for love: The missing ingredient for a healthy and lasting relationship. San Francisco, CA: HarperOne/HarperCollins.

Makinen, J. A. (2004). *Resolving attachment injuries in couples: Relating process to outcome* (Unpublished doctoral dissertation). University of Ottawa, Ottawa, Ontario, Canada.

Makinen, J. A., & Johnson, S. M. (2006). Resolving attachment injuries in couples using emotionally focused therapy: Steps toward forgiveness and reconciliation. *Journal of Consulting and Clinical Psychology, 74,* 1055–1064. http://dx.doi.org/10.1037/0022-006X.74.6.1055

Malcolm, W., Warwar, S., & Greenberg, L. (2005). Facilitating forgiveness in individual therapy as an approach to resolving interpersonal injuries. In E. L. Worthington Jr. (Ed.), *Handbook of forgiveness* (pp. 379–391). New York, NY: Routledge.

Mansfield, C. D., Pasupathi, M., & McLean, K. C. (2015). Is narrating growth in stories of personal transgressions associated with increased well-being, self-compassion, and forgiveness of others? *Journal of Research in Personality, 58,* 69–83. http://dx.doi.org/10.1016/j.jrp.2015.05.008

Mayer, J. D., & Salovey, P. (1997). What is emotional intelligence? In P. Salovey & D. J. Sluyter (Eds.), *Emotional development and emotional intelligence: Educational implications* (pp. 3–34). New York, NY: HarperCollins.

McCullough, M. E. (1997). Marital forgiveness. *Marriage and Family: A Christian Journal, 1,* 77–93.

McCullough, M. E. (2001). Forgiveness: Who does it and how do they do it? *Current Directions in Psychological Science, 10,* 194–197. http://dx.doi.org/10.1111/1467-8721.00147

McCullough, M. E., Pargament, K. I., & Thoresen, C. E. (2000). The psychology of forgiveness: History, conceptual issues, and overview. In M. E. McCullough, K. I. Pargament, & C. E. Thoresen (Eds.), *Forgiveness: Theory, research, and practice* (pp. 1–14). New York, NY: Guilford Press.

McCullough, M. E., Rachal, K. C., Sandage, S. J., & Worthington, E. L., Jr. (1997, August). *A sustainable future for the psychology of forgiveness.* Paper presented at the meeting of the American Psychological Association. Chicago, IL.

McCullough, M. E., Rachal, K. C., Sandage, S. J., Worthington, E. L., Jr., Brown, W. S., & Hight, T. L. (1998). Interpersonal forgiveness in close relationships:

II. Theoretical elaboration and measurement. *Journal of Personality and Social Psychology, 75,* 1586–1603. http://dx.doi.org/10.1037/0022-3514.75.6.1586

McCullough, M. E., & Witvliet, C. V. (2002). The psychology of forgiveness. In C. R. Snyder & S. J. Lopez (Eds.), *Handbook of positive psychology* (pp. 446–458). New York, NY: Oxford University Press.

McCullough, M. E., & Worthington, E. L., Jr. (1994a). Encouraging clients to forgive people who have hurt them: Review, Critique, and research prospectus. *Journal of Psychology and Theology, 22,* 3–20. http://dx.doi.org/10.1177/009164719402200101

McCullough, M. E., & Worthington, E. L., Jr. (1994b). Models of interpersonal forgiveness and their applications to counseling: Review and critique. *Counseling and Values, 39,* 2–14. http://dx.doi.org/10.1002/j.2161-007X.1994.tb01003.x

McCullough, M. E., & Worthington, E. L., Jr. (1995). Promoting forgiveness: A comparison of two brief psychoeducational group interventions with a waiting-list control. *Counseling and Values, 40,* 55–68. http://dx.doi.org/10.1002/j.2161-007X.1995.tb00387.x

McCullough, M. E., Worthington, E. L., Jr., & Rachal, K. C. (1997). Interpersonal forgiving in close relationships. *Journal of Personality and Social Psychology, 73,* 321–336. http://dx.doi.org/10.1037/0022-3514.73.2.321

McKinnon, J. M., & Greenberg, L. S. (2013). Revealing underlying vulnerable emotion in couple therapy: Impact on session and final outcome. *Journal of Family Therapy, 35,* 303–319. http://dx.doi.org/10.1111/1467-6427.12015

McKinnon, J. M., & Greenberg, L. S. (2017). Vulnerable emotional expression in emotion focused couples therapy: Relating interactional processes to outcome. *Journal of Marital and Family Therapy, 43,* 198–212. http://dx.doi.org/10.1111/jmft.12229

Menahem, S., & Love, M. (2013). Forgiveness in psychotherapy: The key to healing. *Journal of Clinical Psychology, 69,* 10–21. http://dx.doi.org/10.1002/jclp.22018

Miller, A., Worthington, E., Jr., & McDaniel, M. (2008). Gender and forgiveness: A meta-analytic review and research agenda. *Journal of Social and Clinical Psychology, 8,* 843–876. http://dx.doi.org/10.1521/jscp.2008.27.8.843

Millikin J. W (2000). *Resolving attachment injuries in couples using emotionally focused therapy: A process study* (Unpublished doctoral dissertation). Virginia Polytechnic Institute and State University, Blacksburg, VA.

Murphy, J. G. (1999). Shame creeps through and feels like retribution. *Law and Philosophy, 18,* 327–344.

Naaman, S., Pappas, J. D., Makinen, J., Zuccarini, D., & Johnson, S. (2005). Treating attachment injured couples with emotionally focused therapy: A case study approach. *Psychiatry: Interpersonal & Biological Processes, 68,* 55–77. http://dx.doi.org/10.1521/psyc.68.1.55.64183

Nadel, L., Hupbach, A., Gomez, R., & Newman-Smith, K. (2012). Memory formation, consolidation and transformation. *Neuroscience and Biobehavioral Reviews, 36,* 1640–1645. http://dx.doi.org/10.1016/j.neubiorev.2012.03.001

Negash, S., Cui, M., Fincham, F. D., & Pasley, K. (2014). Extradyadic involvement and relationship dissolution in heterosexual women university students. *Archives of Sexual Behavior, 43,* 531–539. http://dx.doi.org/10.1007/s10508-013-0213-y

Newberry, P. (2004). The three dimensions of forgiveness. *Philosophy in the Contemporary World, 11*, 73–79. http://dx.doi.org/10.5840/pcw200411223

Norlock, K. (2008). *Forgiveness from a feminist perspective*. Lanham, MD: Lexington Books.

Nussbaum, M. (2016). *Anger and forgiveness: Resentment, generosity, justice*. Oxford, England: Oxford University Press.

Oatley, K., & Jenkins, J. (1992). Human emotions: Function and dysfunction. *Annual Review of Psychology, 43*, 55–85. http://dx.doi.org/10.1146/annurev.ps.43.020192.000415

Olson, J. R., Marshall, J. P., Goddard, H. W., & Schramm, D. G. (2015). Shared religious beliefs, prayer, and forgiveness as predictors of marital satisfaction. *Family Relations, 64*, 519–533. http://dx.doi.org/10.1111/fare.12129

Orcutt, H. K. (2006). The prospective relationship of interpersonal forgiveness and psychological distress symptoms among college women. *Journal of Counseling Psychology, 53*, 350–361. http://dx.doi.org/10.1037/0022-0167.53.3.350

Ortman, D. (2005). Post infidelity stress disorder. *Journal of Psychosocial Nursing and Mental Health Services, 43*(10), 46–54.

Paivio, S. C., & Greenberg, L. S. (1995). Resolving "unfinished business": Efficacy of experiential therapy using empty-chair dialogue. *Journal of Consulting and Clinical Psychology, 63*, 419–425. http://dx.doi.org/10.1037/0022-006X.63.3.419

Paivio, S. C., & Pascual-Leone, A. (2010). *Emotion-focused therapy for complex trauma: An integrative approach*. Washington, DC: American Psychological Association. http://dx.doi.org/10.1037/12077-000

Paleari, G. F., Regalia, C., & Fincham, F. D. (2005). Marital quality, forgiveness, empathy, and rumination: A longitudinal study. *Personality and Social Psychology Bulletin, 31*, 368–378. http://dx.doi.org/10.1177/0146167204271597

Paleari, F. G., Regalia, C., & Fincham, F. D. (2009). Measuring offence-specific forgiveness in marriage: The Marital Offence-Specific Forgiveness Scale (MOFS). *Psychological Assessment, 21*, 194–209. http://dx.doi.org/10.1037/a0016068

Panksepp, J., & Biven, L. (2012). *The archaeology of mind: Neuroevolutionary origins of human emotions*. New York, NY: Norton.

Pargament, K., Magyar, G., Benore, E., & Mahoney, A. (2005). Sacrilege: A study of sacred loss and desecration and their implications for health and well-being in a community sample. *Journal for the Scientific Study of Religion, 44*, 59–78. http://dx.doi.org/10.1111/j.1468-5906.2005.00265.x

Pattison, M. (1965). On the failure to forgive or be forgiven. *American Journal of Psychotherapy, 19*, 106–115. http://dx.doi.org/10.1176/appi.psychotherapy.1965.19.1.106

Pennebaker, J. W (Ed.). (1995). *Emotion, disclosure, and health*. Washington, DC: American Psychological Association. http://dx.doi.org/10.1037/10182-000

Perel, E. (2017). *The state of affairs: Rethinking infidelity*. New York, NY: HarperCollins.

Perls, F., Hefferline, R., & Goodman, P. (1951). *Gestalt therapy*. New York, NY: Delta.

Pettigrove, G. (2004). Unapologetic forgiveness. *American Philosophical Quarterly, 3*, 187–204. http://dx.doi.org/10.1093/acprof:oso/9780199646555.003.0006

Pingleton, J. P. (1989). The role and function of forgiveness in the psychotherapeutic process. *Journal of Psychology and Theology, 17*, 27–35. http://dx.doi.org/10.1177/009164718901700106

Randall, G. K., & Bishop, A. J. (2013). Direct and indirect effects of religiosity on valuation of life through forgiveness and social provisions among older incarcerated males. *The Gerontologist, 53*, 51–59. http://dx.doi.org/10.1093/geront/gns070

Rice, L. N., & Greenberg , L. S. (Eds.). (1984). *Patterns of change: Intensive analysis of psychotherapeutic process*. New York, NY: Guilford Press.

Rice, L. N., & Kerr, G. P. (1986). *Measures of client and therapist vocal quality*. New York, NY: Guilford Press.

Rogers, C. R. (1959). *A theory of therapy, personality, and interpersonal relationships: As developed in the client-centered framework* (Vol. 3). New York, NY: McGraw-Hill.

Rowe, J. O., Halling, S., Davies, E., Leifer, M., Powers, D., & Van Bronkhorst, J. (1989). The psychology of forgiving another: A dialogal research approach. In R. S. Valle & S. Halling (Eds.), *Existential-phenomenological perspective in psychology: Exploring the breadth of human experience* (pp. 233–244). New York, NY: Plenum Press.

Sandage, S., & Worthington, E., Jr. (2010). Comparison of two group interventions to promote forgiveness: Empathy as a mediator of change. *Journal of Mental Health Counseling, 32*, 35–57. http://dx.doi.org/10.17744/mehc.32.1.274536n518571683

Scuka, R. F. (2015). A clinician's guide to helping couples heal from the trauma of infidelity. *Journal of Couple & Relationship Therapy, 14*, 141–168. http://dx.doi.org/10.1080/15332691.2014.953653

Sells, J. N., & Hargrave, T. D. (1998). Forgiveness: A review of the theoretical and empirical literature. *Journal of Family Therapy, 20*, 21–36. http://dx.doi.org/10.1111/1467-6427.00066

Shapland, J. (2016). Forgiveness and restorative justice: Is it necessary? Is it helpful? *Oxford Journal of Law and Religion, 5*, 94–112. http://dx.doi.org/10.1093/ojlr/rwv038

Sharma, R. (2007). *A task analytic examination of dominance in emotion-focused couples therapy* (Unpublished masters' thesis). York University, Toronto, Ontario, Canada.

Sharma, R. (2013). *Women's experience of forgiving and not forgiving: A grounded theory analysis* (Unpublished doctoral dissertation). York University, Toronto, Ontario, Canada.

Shults, F., & Sandage, S. (2003). *The faces of forgiveness: Searching for wholeness and salvation*. Ada, MI: Baker Academic.

Solomon, Z., Dekel, R., & Zerach, G. (2009). Posttraumatic stress disorder and marital adjustment: The mediating role of forgiveness. *Family Process, 48*, 546–558. http://dx.doi.org/10.1111/j.1545-5300.2009.01301.x

Spring, J. A. (1996). *After the affair: Healing the pain and rebuilding trust when a partner has been unfaithful*. New York, NY: HarperCollins.

Sroufe, L. A. (1996). *Emotional development: The organization of emotional life in the early years*. New York, NY: Cambridge University Press. http://dx.doi.org/10.1017/CBO9780511527661

Stern, D. N. (1985). *The interpersonal world of the infant: A view from psychoanalysis and developmental psychology*. London, England: Karnac Books.

Tabak, B. A., & McCullough, M. E. (2011). Perceived transgressor agreeableness decreases cortisol response and increases forgiveness following recent interpersonal transgressions. *Biological Psychology, 87,* 386–392. http://dx.doi.org/10.1016/j.biopsycho.2011.05.001

Thoresen, C. E., Harris, A. H. S., & Luskin, F. (2000). Forgiveness and health: An unanswered question. In M. E. McCullough, K. I. Pargament, & C. E. Thoresen (Eds.), *Forgiveness: Theory, research, and practice* (pp. 254–280). New York, NY: Guilford Press.

Tomkins, S. (1963). *Affect imagery consciousness: Vol II. The negative affects*. New York, NY: Springer.

Toussaint, L., Marschall, J., & Williams, D. (2012). Prospective associations between religiousness/spirituality and depression and mediating effects of forgiveness in a nationally representative sample of United States adults. *Depression Research and Treatment, 2012,* 1–10. http://dx.doi.org/10.1155/2012/267820

Toussaint, L., Owen, A., & Cheadle, A. (2012). Forgive to live: Forgiveness, health, and longevity. *Journal of Behavioral Medicine, 35,* 375–386. http://dx.doi.org/10.1007/s10865-011-9362-4

Toussaint, L., & Webb, J. R. (2005). Gender differences in the relationship between empathy and forgiveness. *The Journal of Social Psychology, 145,* 673–685. http://dx.doi.org/10.3200/SOCP.145.6.673-686

Traue, H., & Pennebaker, J. (1993). *Emotion, inhibition, and health*. Boston, MA: Hogrefe & Huber.

Unforgiveness. (n.d.). In *Merriam-Webster's online dictionary*. Retrieved from https://www.merriam-webster.com/dictionary/unforgiveness

Vaillant, G. (2000). Adaptive mental mechanisms: Their role in a positive psychology. *American Psychologist, 55,* 89–98. http://dx.doi.org/10.1037/0003-066X.55.1.89

Wade, N. G., Hoyt, W. T., Kidwell, J. E. M., & Worthington, E. L., Jr. (2014). Efficacy of psychotherapeutic interventions to promote forgiveness: A meta-analysis. *Journal of Consulting and Clinical Psychology, 82,* 154–170. http://dx.doi.org/10.1037/a0035268

Wade, N. G., & Worthington, E. L., Jr. (2005). In search of a common cure: A content analysis of interventions to promote forgiveness. *Psychotherapy: Theory, Research, Practice, Training, 42,* 160–177.

Walker, M. (2006). *Moral repair: Reconstructing moral relations after wrongdoing*. Cambridge, England: Cambridge University Press. http://dx.doi.org/10.1017/CBO9780511618024

Wangh, S. (2005). Revenge and forgiveness in Laramie, Wyoming. *Psychoanalytic Dialogues, 15,* 1–16. http://dx.doi.org/10.1080/10481881509348811

Webb, J. R., Hirsch, J. K., & Toussaint, L. (2015). Forgiveness as a positive psychotherapy for addiction and suicide: Theory, research, and practice. *Spirituality in Clinical Practice, 2,* 48–60. http://dx.doi.org/10.1037/scp0000054

Webb, J. R., Phillips, D., Bumgarner, D., & Conway-Williams, E. (2013). Forgiveness, mindfulness, and health. *Mindfulness, 4,* 235–245. http://dx.doi.org/10.1007/s12671-012-0119-0

Weinberg, M., Gil, S., & Gilbar, O. (2014). Forgiveness, coping, and terrorism: Do tendency to forgive and coping strategies associate with the level of posttraumatic symptoms of injured victims of terror attacks? *Journal of Clinical Psychology, 70,* 693–703. http://dx.doi.org/10.1002/jclp.22056

Weiner, B., Graham, S., Peter, O., & Zmuidinas, M. (1991). Public confessions and forgiveness. *Journal of Personality, 59,* 281–312. http://dx.doi.org/10.1111/j.1467-6494.1991.tb00777.x

Weisenthal, S. (1969). *The sunflower: On the possibilities and limits of forgiveness.* New York, NY: Schocken Books.

Wenzel, M., & Okimoto, T. G. (2010). How acts of forgiveness restore a sense of justice: Addressing status/power and value concerns raised by transgressions. *European Journal of Social Psychology, 40,* 401–417.

Weschler, L. (1998). *A miracle, a universe: Settling accounts with torturers.* Chicago, IL: University of Chicago Press.

Whelton, W. J. (2004). Emotional processing in psychotherapy: Evidence across therapeutic modalities. *Clinical Psychology & Psychotherapy, 11,* 58–71. http://dx.doi.org/10.1002/cpp.392

Wiesel, E. (1982). *Night.* New York, NY: Bantam Books.

Winch, G. (2014). *Emotional first aid: Healing rejection, guilt, failure, and other everyday hurts.* New York, NY: Avery.

Witvliet, C. V. O., Ludwig, T. E., & Vander Laan, K. L. (2001). Granting forgiveness or harboring grudges: Implications for emotion, physiology, and health. *Psychological Science, 12,* 117–123. http://dx.doi.org/10.1111/1467-9280.00320

Witvliet, C. V. O., Worthington, E. L., Root, L. M., Sato, A. F., Ludwig, T. E., & Exline, J. J. (2008). Retributive justice, restorative justice, and forgiveness: An experimental psychophysiology analysis. *Journal of Experimental Social Psychology, 44,* 10–25. http://dx.doi.org/10.1016/j.jesp.2007.01.009

Woldarsky Meneses, C. (2006). *A task analysis of forgiveness in emotion-focused couple therapy* (Unpublished master's thesis). York University, Toronto, Ontario, Canada.

Woldarsky Meneses, C. (2011). *Interpersonal forgiveness in emotion-focused couples therapy: Relating process to outcome* (Unpublished doctoral dissertation). York University, Toronto, Ontario, Canada.

Woldarsky Meneses, C., & Greenberg, L. S. (2011). The construction of a model of the process of couples' forgiveness in emotion-focused therapy for couples. *Journal of Marital and Family Therapy, 37,* 491–502. http://dx.doi.org/10.1111/j.1752-0606.2011.00234.x

Woldarsky Meneses, C., & Greenberg, L. S. (2014). Interpersonal forgiveness in emotion-focused couples' therapy: Relating process to outcome. *Journal of Marital and Family Therapy, 40,* 49–67. http://dx.doi.org/10.1111/j.1752-0606.2012.00330.x

Woldarsky Meneses, C., & Greenberg, L. S. (2015). Forgiveness: A route to healing emotional injuries and building resiliency. In K. Skerrett & K. Fergus (Eds.), *Couple resilience* (pp. 179–196). Dordrecht, Netherlands: Springer.

Worthington, E. L., Jr. (1998a). An empathy–humility–commitment model of forgiveness applied within family dyads. *Journal of Family Therapy, 20,* 57–74. http://dx.doi.org/10.1111/1467-6427.00068

Worthington, E. L., Jr. (1998b). Empirical research in forgiveness: Looking backward, looking forward. In E. L. Worthington Jr. (Ed.), *Dimensions of forgiveness* (pp. 321–339). Philadelphia, PA: Templeton Foundation Press.

Worthington, E. L., Jr. (2001). *Five steps to forgiveness: The art and science of forgiving*. New York, NY: Crown.

Worthington, E. L., Jr. (2006). *Forgiveness and reconciliation: Theory and application*. New York, NY: Routledge.

Worthington, E. L., Jr., & Sandage, S. J. (2016). Forgiveness in couples and family therapy. In E. L. Worthington, Jr., & S. J. Sandage (Eds.), *Forgiveness and spirituality in psychotherapy: A relational approach* (pp. 223–245). Washington, DC: American Psychological Association. http://dx.doi.org/10.1037/14712-011

Worthington, E. L., Jr., & Scherer, M. (2004). Forgiveness is an emotion-focused coping strategy that can reduce health risks and promote health resilience: Theory, review, and hypotheses. *Psychology & Health, 19*, 385–405. http://dx.doi.org/10.1080/0887044042000196674

Worthington, E. L., Jr., & Sotoohi, G. (2010). Physiological assessment of forgiveness, grudges, and revenge: Theories, research methods, and implications. *International Journal of Psychology Research, 5*, 291–316.

Worthington, E. L., Jr, Witvliet., V. O, C., Pietrini, P., & Miller, A. J. (2007). Forgiveness, health, and well-being: A review of evidence for emotional versus decisional forgiveness, dispositional forgiveness, and reduced unforgiveness. *Journal of Behavioral Medicine, 30*, 291–302. http://dx.doi.org/10.1007/s10865-007-9105-8

Zauszniewski, J. A., McDonald, P. E., Krafcik, K., Chung, C., Dobratz, M. C., & Downe-Wamboldt, B. (2002). Acceptance, cognitions, and resourcefulness in women with diabetes. *Western Journal of Nursing Research, 24*, 728–750. http://dx.doi.org/10.1177/019394502762476951

Zeichmeister, J. S., & Romero, C. (2002). Victim and offender accounts of interpersonal conflict: Autobiographical narratives of forgiveness and unforgiveness. *Journal of Social and Clinical Psychology, 82*, 675–686.

# INDEX

# ABOUT THE AUTHORS

**Leslie S. Greenberg, PhD,** is Distinguished Research Professor Emeritus of Psychology at York University in Toronto. He has authored key texts on emotion-focused psychotherapy, from its inception in the 1980s through today. He has received the Senior Distinguished Research Career Award of the Society for Psychotherapy Research as well as the Carl Rogers Award and the Award for Distinguished Professional Contributions to Applied Research of the American Psychological Association. He conducts a private practice for individuals and couples and provides training on emotion-focused approaches. Visit http://www.emotionfocusedclinic.org for information on training.

**Catalina Woldarsky Meneses, PhD,** is a psychotherapist who works with individuals and couples in private practice. She is also an adjunct professor at Webster University's Graduate Counselling Program, Geneva campus. She completed her doctorate in clinical psychology at York University, under the guidance and mentorship of Leslie S. Greenberg. She is involved in supervising and training therapists learning emotion-focused therapy in North America and Europe and is one of the founding members and current vice president of the Swiss Society for Emotion-Focused Therapy. Dr. Woldarsky Meneses was born in Chile, grew up and studied in Canada, and now lives in Switzerland with her family.